Saint Bonaventure's

DISPUTED QUESTIONS ON THE MYSTERY OF THE TRINITY

An Introduction and Translation

WORKS OF ST. BONAVENTURE

Edited by
†GEORGE MARCIL, O.F.M.

SAINT BONAVENTURE'S

DISPUTED QUESTIONS ON THE MYSTERY OF THE TRINITY

Introduction and Translation
by
ZACHERY HAYES, O.F.M., D. TH.

The Franciscan Institute
St. Bonaventure University
St. Bonaventure, New York 14778
2000

All rights reserved.
Copyright © 1979 The Franciscan Institute
Reprinted 2000

No part of this book may be reproduced or transmitted in any form or by any means, electronic or mechanical including photocopying, recording, or any information storage and retrieval system, without permission in writing from the publisher:

The Franciscan Institute
St. Bonaventure University
St. Bonaventure, New York 14778

Library of Congress
Catalog Card Number 79—50321

ISBN: 1-57659-045-3

Printed and bound in the United States of America by
BookMasters, Inc.
Ashland, Ohio

TABLE OF CONTENTS

EDITOR'S FOREWORD 7

TRANSLATOR'S FOREWORD 9

INTRODUCTION 11

CHAPTER ONE: HISTORICAL ORIENTATION 13
- I. The Trinitarian Perspectives of St. Augustine and Richard of St. Victor 13
- II. The Trinitarian Works of Bonaventure . . . 24
- III. The Disputed Questions on the Trinity . . . 26

CHAPTER TWO: BONAVENTURE'S TRINITARIAN THEOLOGY IN GENERAL 30
- I. The Trinity in the Bonaventurean System . . 30
- II. The Point of Departure 32
- III. The Constitution of Personhood 37
- IV. The Father 41
- V. The Son 43
  The titles of the second person
  The Son as center
- VI. The Holy Spirit 54
  The titles of the third person
- VII. Missions and Appropriations 62

CHAPTER THREE: TRINITARIAN THEMES IN THE DISPUTED QUESTIONS 67
- I. The Foundations 69
- II. Unity and Trinity 80
- III. Simplicity and Trinity 84
- IV. Infinity and Trinity 87
- V. Eternity and Trinity 91
- VI. Immutability and Trinity 93
- VII. Necessity and Trinity 97
- VIII. Primacy and Trinity 100

**THE TEXT OF ST. BONAVENTURE IN TRANSLA-
TION** 105

QUESTION I: Concerning the certitude with which the
existence of God is known, and concerning the faith by
which the trinity of the same God is believed . . . 107
    Article I - Article II (p. 122)

QUESTION II: Whether a trinity of persons can exist
with unity of nature 138
    Article I - Article II (p. 147)

QUESTION III: Whether the trinity can exist together
with the highest simplicity 159
    Article I - Article II (p. 171)

QUESTION IV: Whether the trinity exists together with
the highest infinity 184
    Article I - Article II (p. 194)

QUESTION V: Whether the trinity of persons can exist
together with highest eternity 203
    Article I - Article II (p. 214)

QUESTION VI: Whether the trinity can exist together
with supreme immutability 224
    Article I - Article II (p. 237)

QUESTION VII: Whether the trinity can exist together
with necessity 246
    Article I - Article II (p. 253)

QUESTION VIII: Whether the trinity can exist together
with supreme primacy 260

EDITOR'S FOREWORD

With the printing of this volume the Franciscan Institute continues a series of Bonaventurean translations begun decades ago by Fr. Philotheus Boehner. Volume I was printed in 1940 and reissued in 1955; it was a translation and study of St. Bonaventure's *De Reductione Artium ad Theologiam*. Volume II, printed in 1956, was a study and translation of the *Itinerarium Mentis in Deum*.

It was desirable to make the present volume as much as possible like the first two works. But due to a number of factors, including the rise of printing costs and the declining use of Latin by young students, it was deemed better not to print the original Latin text with the facing translation. An interested scholar will usually find the Latin text accessible in the Quaracchi edition's volume V, pp. 45-115.

The Franciscan Institute is proud to add this volume to the Englished WORKS OF SAINT BONAVENTURE. It is also grateful to Fr. Zachary Hayes, O.F.M. for having prepared the translation and the scholarly introduction. The *Disputed Questions on the Mystery of the Trinity* deserves to be better known.

GEORGE MARCIL, O.F.M.

The Franciscan Institute
St. Bonaventure University
December 20, 1978

TRANSLATOR'S FOREWORD

The purpose of the present translation is to make available to an English-speaking audience a text of trinitarian theology which is unique in the history of Christian thought. The distinctiveness of the text lies in the fact that it carries out an analysis of the interrelationship between philosophical metaphysics and trinitarian doctrine with an explicitness and thoroughness seldom if ever found elsewhere.

A quick glance at the text reveals the fact that it is a highly specialized treatise which makes no pretense of presenting the basic trinitarian issues. For this reason, the text published without an adequate introduction would be useable only for those who are already thoroughly familiar with the trinitarian thought of the Seraphic Doctor and have some awareness of its place in the history of theology. Since English readings in this area are virtually non-existent, it was felt necessary to include a rather lengthy introduction.

After locating Bonaventure's thought historically, we have presented a detailed statement of his approach to the major trinitarian questions. Because of the nature of this material, these two chapters have been heavily documented. The third chapter is an essay-introduction to the content of the *Questions on the Trinity* presented in this volume. Since the first of the questions deals with genuine foundational issues, it was felt advisable to treat this with considerable completeness with a fully documented text that works out the relation between the materials treated here and the other writings of Bonaventure. Beginning with the second question, the nature of the materials seemed to exclude the necessity of such an approach. Since there is no other place in his works where Bonaventure carries out the project which he here undertakes, it was felt advisable to limit the introductory remarks to an analysis of the *Questions* themselves. The relation between the introduction and the *Questions* from here to the end seems too self-evident to warrant any further documentation.

It is our hope that the inclusion of such an introduction, lengthy as it is, will serve to make the publication of this translation all the more serviceable to the reader.

ZACHARY HAYES, O.F.M.

Catholic Theological Union
Chicago, Illinois
December 21, 1977

INTRODUCTION

CHAPTER ONE

HISTORICAL ORIENTATION

I. THE TRINITARIAN PERSPECTIVES OF ST. AUGUSTINE AND RICHARD OF ST. VICTOR

To the great theologians of the Patristic and Scholastic ages, the mystery of the trinity was seen as foundational to the Christian faith. It seemed impossible to say what Christians felt obliged to affirm concerning the person and destiny of Jesus Christ without in some way expanding the concept of God mediated by the Old Testament in *Exodus* 3, 14. Neither was it possible to accept at face-value the Platonic or the Aristotelian versions of metaphysics, for both seemed incapable of providing an adequate framework in which to express and speculate on the matter of God's self-communication to the world for the world's salvation in the person of Jesus Christ. The trinitarian dogma has emerged in the Christian world as a function of Christology, dealing first with the theological understanding of the Word and later with the question of the Holy Spirit. Moving from the basis of the dogma, theological reflection has — over the centuries — developed a form of metaphysical reflection on the nature of the first Principle of reality which differs profoundly from anything which the heritage of Greek philosophy could offer. In its full flowering in the Scholastic period, trinitarian thought was not only a religious dogma but a highly developed metaphysical doctrine which held pride of place in the great theologians of the thirteenth century.

There are two figures in the history of Western thought who must be considered in approaching the trinitarian style of Bonaventure; namely, Augustine and Richard of St. Victor. Already in the fifth century, Augustine had seen his task to lie in the pursuit of a deeper understanding of faith. As worked out in reference to the dogma of the trinity, this program would clearly reflect philosophical structures of a neo-Platonic inspiration as well as a profoundly moving psychological analysis of the experiences of the human spirit.[1] It was clear to the Bishop of Hippo that Scripture required faith in the trinity. While earlier theologians had sought to shed light on the dogma by making use of analogies drawn from the realm of physical nature, Augustine sensed that the inadequacy of such images was all too obvious. He was familiar also with certain emanationist forms of neo-Platonism, forms which assumed, at times, triadic structures, as in the case of Plotinus.[2] But none of these, as they stood, were adequate to carry out what Augustine felt was necessary.

"Unless you believe, you will not understand."[3] Faith can enlighten and purify reason. One must love God and desire Him in order to enter more deeply into some understanding of that which one loves. Such a view could help the theologian grow in understanding even while avoiding the excesses of rationalism which Augustine saw in Sabellianism and Arianism. In his own attempts to develop trinitarian speculation, Augustine would employ the philosophical tools available to him so as to move beyond the limitations of the earlier physical analogies and to develop a more apt understanding of relation, thereby making it possible to conceive of one God in three persons without introducing division or inequality into the Godhead.

The broader lines of Augustine's notion of the human person as an image of God are deeply rooted in Plotinian emanationism. That which is said to emanate is the image of that from which it flows. An image, therefore, is that which flows from another; but its existence as an image is brought to its fullness in as far as it turns back to its source. It is precisely in the turning back to its source that it is constituted as an image in the full sense. The image can then project itself into yet another as its image; and thus a series of emanations arises.[4] Augustine's general understanding of the created world reflects this emanationist structure, though in a cor-

---

[1] M. Schmaus, *Die Psychologische Trinitätslehre des hl. Augustinus. Münsterische Beiträge zur Theologie*, Heft 11 (Münster, 1927, 1967) p. 1-10. Also, in the 1967 reprint, the *Nachwort*, p. III-XXI; A. Schindler, *Wort und Analogie in Augustins Trinitätslehre. Hermeneutische Untersuchungen zur Theologie*, 4, Ed. Ebeling, Fuchs, Mezger (Tübingen, 1965) p. 196-228.
[2] J. M. Rist, *Plotinus, The Road to Reality* (Cambridge, 1967, 1977) p. 21-52, 66-83 of 1977 edition; J. Hirschberger, *Geschichte der Philosophie. Altertum und Mittelalter*, Vol. I (Herder, 1961⁵) p. 303-307; I. Brady, *A History of Ancient Philosophy* (Bruce, 1959) p. 180-186; F. Copleston, *A History of Philosophy*, Vol. 1, prt. 2 (Newman, 1946) p. 463-475.
[3] *Is.* 7, 9. This text in the Old Latin version inspired Christians early in Western history to the program of faith seeking understanding.
[4] J. E. Sullivan, *The Image of God. The Doctrine of St. Augustine and Its Influence* (Priory Press, 1963) p. 3-25; M. Schmaus, op. cit., p. 195-200.

rected form. He recognizes in the world a hierarchy of participations, of weaker and stronger resemblances. To exist as an image of God will mean, for Augustine, to exist in the tension between the going-forth and the return, and thus to be characterized by a deep and abiding tendency of the soul to God who is always present to the soul as both source and goal.

If the human person is constituted as an image of God, it should be possible — by probing into the deep recesses of human experience — to derive some clues as to the nature of the ultimate source and goal of the image. Thus, the latter books of the *De trinitate* (Bk. 9-15) are devoted to the elaboration of triadic structures in the human person which provide more adequate analogies for speaking of the triune nature of God. The triads *mens-notitia-amor* and *memoria-intelligentia-voluntas* were to have a profound effect on centuries of trinitarian speculation in the West, lending to it a strongly psychological tone.

This understanding of the human person as an image of God together with the development of the doctrine of relation set the stage for centuries of theological work. Yet it was not the only style of trinitarian thought to develop in the West, for out of the Victorine school of the twelfth century was to come an approach which differed markedly from that of Augustine. The difference is all the more significant in view of the fact that the Victorines clearly knew the work of Augustine.[5] Yet, the influence of the great African was not so great as to obliterate other possibilities. It is above all in Richard of St. Victor that we discern a new and original style of trinitarian reflection. While aware of the heritage of Augustine, Richard's primary orientation seems to be not through the analysis of human cognitional experience, but through an analysis of the nature of love.[6] He thus chose an element which was marginal in Augustine and placed it in the center of his own thought.

After showing through an analysis of certain attributes of God that there can be but one God from whom all creatures proceed,[7]

---

[5] Hugh of St. Victor, *Summa Sententiarum*, tr. I, c. 6 (PL 176, 51) and *De Sacramentis* I, 3, c. 20 (PL 176, 225); c. 21 (PL 176, 225); c. 25 (PL 176, 227); c. 26 (PL 176, 227-228) clearly indicate an awareness of the Augustinian heritage.

[6] E. Gössman, "Die Methode der Trinitätslehre in der Summa Halensis," in: *Münchener Theol. Zeitschrift* 6 (1955) p. 256: "Der methodische Neuansatz Richards von St. Viktor ist der Grund, weshalb im Mittelalter die Trinitätslehre unter Beibehaltung der dogmatischen Definitionen aus der Väterzeit eine eigenständige Fruchtbarkeit erreicht hat." Gössman argues that the major difference between Augustine and Richard lies in the fact that the former takes his primary analogies from the individual human soul whereas the latter draws his from the love relation between several human persons (p. 256-7).

[7] *De Trinitate* I c. 14 — II, c. 8 (PL 196, 898-905).

Richard states that the God who is *substantialiter unus*[8] is the highest good and consequently is goodness itself.[9] The first two books lead to the conclusion that God is the fullness and perfection of all goodness. But of all things that are good, nothing is better or more perfect than charity.[10] Charity is the supreme content of the good. Thus two important themes are brought into conjunction: the concept of God as perfect goodness, and the New Testament concept of altruistic love which is seen as the highest form of goodness. The line of Richard's development begins to emerge clearly. However we approach the mystery of God, He is to be seen as the fullness of all perfections. But, "where the fullness of divinity is found, there is the fullness of goodness, and consequently the fullness of charity."[11]

Charity, which is the supreme form of the good, becomes the basis for showing the necessity of a plurality of persons in the Godhead. Since charity necessarily involves a relation to another,[12] there can be no charity where there is no plurality. Charity must be in proportion to the good that is loved. A creature, as a limited good, cannot be the object of the highest love of God; for such love would be inordinate and would conflict with divine wisdom. Since God alone is supreme goodness, He alone is supremely lovable. Hence, God cannot show supreme love to anyone who lacks divinity. The fullness of divinity cannot exist without the fullness of goodness. And the fullness of goodness cannot exist without the fullness of charity; nor can the fullness of charity exist in God without some sort of plurality in God Himself; for the supreme charity which must be found in God must be directed to God Himself if it is not to be inordinate.[13] Hence, it is the nature of charity, which is the highest form of the good, that necessarily requires a plurality in God; and this plurality Richard locates at the level of person.

A further analysis of the communication of love leads to the conclusion that such a communication must involve no less than three persons. If there were only one person in God, then a perfect self-communication would not be possible at all; for no creature could sustain such a communication. So, there must be at least two persons

---

[8] *De Trin.* I, c. 16 (PL 196, 898).
[9] *De Trin.* II, c. 16 (PL 196, 910).
[10] *De Trin.* III, c. 2 (PL 196, 916).
[11] *De Trin.* V, c. 7 (PL 196, 954). Richard bases his view on a well-known passage of Gregory (*In Evangelia Hom.*, 17 [76, 1139]).
[12] *De Trin.* III, c. 2 (PL 196, 916): "Oportet itaque ut amor in alterum tendat, ut charitas esse queat."
[13] *De Trin.* III, c. 2 (PL 196, 917).

in God; there must be a perfectly lovable other. But if there were only two, then there could only be their love for one another; and this would not be the fullness of love. For if love by nature involves a relation to another, the highest perfection of love demands that each of the two persons in love share that love with yet another. Hence, Richard argues that there must be in God not only a *dilectum* but a *condilectum* as well.[14] *Condilectio* is found where a third is loved by two in harmony.[15]

This style of reflection leads to an understanding of God in terms of modalities of love. There are three such modalities in God: *amor gratuitus*, *amor debitus*, and *amor ex utroque permixtus*, which describe the three persons of the trinity.[16] The first is found in the Father in as far as He is love who freely gives without having received. The third is found in the Holy Spirit in as far as He returns love to those from whom He has received the free gift of love. The second corresponds to the Son who both receives the free gift of the Father's love, and together with the Father confers the gift of free love on the Spirit. Chapters 17-19 of the fifth book make an extended application of this analysis of the modalities of love, and chapter 20 makes use of the analysis to show why a fourth person is impossible.

Here the groundwork is laid for a style quite different from the Augustinian psychological theory; yet it also may be seen as rooted in an analysis of psychological experience, though it seems to be located above all in those areas which we would designate as interpersonal and moral. It is a theology which would never achieve a position of equal influence, but which would play a significant role in the thought of the early Franciscan school and to some degree in the work of St. Bonaventure, though the elements which the Seraphic Doctor employs are transformed into a framework which draws its inspiration from quite different sources.

In the late nineteenth century, De Regnon produced a study of the history of trinitarian thought[17] which argued eloquently for the presence of different traditions in Western trinitarianism, pointing out the existence of fundamental differences between Aquinas and Bonaventure, tracing Bonaventure's roots through the *Summa fratris Alexandri* proximately to Richard of St. Victor and remotely to Pseudo-Dionysius. By way of contrast, the lineage of Aquinas

---

[14] *De Trin.* III, c. 14 (PL 196, 924-5).
[15] *De Trin.* III, c. 19 (PL 196, 927).
[16] *De Trin.* V, c. 16 (PL 196, 961).
[17] Th. De Regnon, *Etudes de théologie positive sur la sainte Trinité*, 3 vols. (Paris, 1892-98).

was seen to be rooted in Augustine. The two major lines of development which De Regnon traces are: 1) Dionysius - Richard of St. Victor - William of Auvergne - William of Auxerre - Alexander - Bonaventure; and 2) Augustine - Anselm - Lombard - Albert - Aquinas. The fundamental differences between the two he traces to the dynamism of neo-Platonic thought in the first line and the static character of Aristotelian thought in the second.[18]

De Regnon's thesis was to set the tone for many studies of Medieval thought, influencing even the Quaracchi-editors of the *Summa fratris Alexandri*. Stohr's extended study of Bonaventure[19] focuses primarily on the historical sources and the scientific dimensions of Bonaventure's work. While criticizing many particular points of De Regnon's study, Stohr accepts the main line of the argument and interprets Bonaventure accordingly. Despite the extensive influence of Augustine elsewhere in Bonaventure's writings — so writes Stohr — hardly a trace of the African's influence can be found at the roots of Bonaventure's trinitarian theology while the influence of Richard and Pseudo-Dionysius is everywhere apparent.[20] Stohr agrees with De Regnon's assessment of the Dionysian character of Richard's thought,[21] but he differs in his understanding of the *Summa* both as regards its own theology and as regards its influence on Bonaventure.

Standing within the same basic framework are the studies of Schmaus, Imle-Kaup, Villalmonte, and Szabo.[22] With minor variations, the basic argument of De Regnon lived on and influenced subsequent historical studies to a significant degree. Of fundamental importance in this thesis is the question of the sources of Bonaventure's theology, particularly Richard of St. Victor and Alexander of Hales, for the way in which one understands these two in relation

---

[18] Op. cit., vol. 2, p. 448 ff.
[19] A. Stohr, *Die Trinitätslehre des hl. Bonaventura: Eine systematische Darstellung und historische Würdigung. I Teil, Die wissenschaftliche Trinitätslehre* (Münster, 1923).
[20] Op. cit., p. 34.
[21] Op. cit., p. 78. Stohr speaks with approval of De Regnon's analysis of two theories in Richard; the first a metaphysical theory of the good; the second, a psychological theory of love.
[22] M. Schmaus, *Der Liber Propugnatorius des Thomas Anglicus und die Lehrunterschiede zwischen Thomas von Aquin und Duns Scotus. II Teil, Die Trinitarischen Lehrdifferenzen* (Münster, 1930); F. Imle - J. Kaup, *Die Theologie des hl. Bonaventura. Darstellung seiner dogmatischen Lehren* (Werl, 1931); A. de Villalmonte, "Influjo de los Padres griegos en la doctrina trinitaria de San Buenaventura," in: *XIII Semana Española de Teologia*, 14-19 Sept. 1953 (Madrid, 1954) p. 553-557; T. Szabo, *De ss. Trinitate in Creaturis Refulgente Doctrina S. Bonaventurae* (Rome, 1959).

to Bonaventure as well as in the inspiration of their own thought will significantly influence one's historical assessment of Bonaventure.

In a more recent study, Olegario Gonzalez[23] takes up the question in a fresh way in the light of new materials concerning Richard of St. Victor.[24] So significantly have the results of studies in that area changed the terrain that Gonzalez does not hesitate to speak of a "Copernican revolution."[25] The earlier position tended to present Richard as a deserter from the camp of Augustine who drank deeply from Greek streams and thus developed a style that was truly competitive to the Augustinian tradition. More recent studies have shown Richard to be far more Latin than would have been allowed in the older interpretation.[26] Recognizing the importance of the concept of love in the Victorine's work, Gonzalez writes: "Lo que in Ricardo es una intuición explicativa de toda la obra, es una nota marginal en Agustin."[27] While the older theory placed great weight on the Dionysian influence in Richard, the more recent studies indicate two significant facts which oppose that view: 1) the concept of the good in Richard finds a more likely explanation in Anselm's "being than which no greater can be conceived;"[28] and 2) the dominant idea in Richard's thought is not the idea of the good but

---

[23] O. Gonzalez, *Misterio Trinitario y existencia humana: estudio historico teologico en torno a san Buenaventura* (Madrid, 1966).
[24] Richard of St. Victor, *De Trinitate. Texte critique avec introduction, notes et tables*, publié par J. Ribaillier, en *Textes philosophiques du Moyen Age* 6 (Paris, 1959); G. Salet, *La Trinité. Text Latin, introduction, traduction et notes de G. Salet;* en *Sources Chrétiennes* 63 (Paris, 1959); G. Dumeige, *Richard de Saint Victor et l'idée chrétienne de l'amour* (Paris, 1952).
[25] Op. cit., p. 337: "...tenemos que confesar que la investigación de los últimos quince años ha realizado un giro copernicano."
[26] Op. cit., p. 337-8: "Ricardo es uno puro latino, un agustiniano, que su teologiá ha surgido bajo la fascinación de Agustin; y que, si no exclusivamente, sí fundamentalmente es agustiniano."
[27] Op. cit., p. 338. Also, Ribaillier (op. cit., p. 136-7) suggests an Augustinian inspiration for the notion of *caritas ordinata*, which plays a significant role in Richard's argument. Cf. Augustine, *De Doctrina Christiana*, I, 27 (PL 34, 29-30).
[28] Gonzalez, op. cit., 345. One need simply add to the Anselmian concept the idea that goodness is a perfection which must therefore be found in such a being. In his critical edition of the Victorine text, Ribaillier (op. cit., p. 123-126) suggests only Latin sources, including Anselm and Boethius, as the inspiration for Richard's chapters on the good (III, c. 16-19). Cf. also Ribaillier, op. cit., p. 18-19 on patristic sources represented in Richard's *De Trinitate*. Ribaillier indicates that the definition of charity is inspired by Gregory the Great while the concept of ordered love is drawn from Augustine, and the notion of beatitude is inspired by Boethius. Cf. also Salet, op. cit., p. 10-13.

the psychological analysis of love.[29] Dumeige concludes that there is scarcely a trace of the Dionysian concept in the whole of Richard's work on the trinity.[30] This is not to deny that there is a neo-Platonic influence in Richard. Ribaillier sees such an influence reflected in Richard's frequent use of ternary groups, the over-all double movement of his dialectic, and in the concept of harmonious beauty.[31] Yet at the core of the Victorine argument for a plurality of divine persons lies not the Dionysian concept of the good, but the analysis of charity. Neither does this deny the existence of an alternative system of trinitarian theology in the Middle Ages contrasting with that developed by Aquinas out of largely Augustinian sources. But if there is such an alternate trinitarianism living largely from Dionysian neo-Platonism, this would not be traced to Richard as has been done repeatedly. While his trinitarian thought is different from that of Augustine, the difference does not lie in the fact that one is Latin and the other Greek; for it seems that Richard's trinitarian thought can be accounted for on the basis of Latin sources, including Augustine himself.

This shift in Victorine studies unavoidably raises many new questions about Bonaventure, for it has long been assumed that he was deeply influenced by Richard, and that he imbibed a Dionysian inspiration from the great Victorine. If such an inspiration is lacking in Richard, it is — nonetheless — present in Bonaventure. But from what sources is it derived ? And what is the precise nature of the tie between Richard and Bonaventure if the latter is fundamentally Dionysian while the former is not ? These questions raise the further question of Alexander of Hales both in relation to Richard and Dionysius on the one hand, and to Bonaventure on the other.

In view of the still unresolved question of the *Summa fratris Alexandri*, it is necessary to distinguish between the *Summa*, which

---

[29] The structure of Richard's argument appears clearly in *De Trinitate* III, c. 2 (PL 196, 926-7). A comparison with Bonaventure's *Itinerarium* 6, 1-2 (V, 310-311) shows a dramatic contrast at least between these two works. To what extent the *Itinerarium* is characteristic of Bonaventure's work as a whole will be examined later. It is, indeed, the concept of charity which plays the decisive role in Richard's view, not a supposedly Dionysian metaphysic of the good. Cf. also Salet, op. cit., p. 477-480.

[30] *Dictionnaire de Spiritualité*, art. *Denys*, col. 327: "Son grand ouvrage sur la Trinité ne porte pas trace des conceptions dionysiennes." Gonzalez also concludes that while Richard is an original thinker, the source of his thought is not Greek but Latin; Dionysius has no influence on his trinitarian speculation, nor was Plotinus known to him. If one is to speak of a Greek-Dionysian movement, it must be placed after Richard, op. cit., p. 363.

[31] Op. cit., p. 24-27.

is a compilation,[32] and those works which may be ascribed to Alexander with certainty, such as the *Quaestiones disputatae* and the *Glossa* on the *Sentences* of Lombard.[33] The trinitarian doctrine of the *Quaestiones* reveals abundant references to Augustine's *De trinitate*. While citations of Richard of St. Victor are scarce,[34] his definition of person is known. Citations of Pseudo-Dionysius are frequent. While the texts cited reveal a knowledge of the concepts of fontality, fecundity, and goodness, the ideas are not developed as they will be later by Bonaventure.

In contrast with the *Quaestiones*, the *Glossa* in its treatment of the same matters cites Richard with great frequency. Among the texts quoted are those which are especially characteristic of Richard,[35] and which will play a very important role in Bonaventure. We find also significant citations of Pseudo-Dionysius on the nature of God as the supreme good, as well as a Dionysian description of love as a circle: "Amor ostenditur sicut quidam aeternus circulus, per optimum, ex optimo, in optimo et in optimum..."[36] Such language will be found later in Bonaventure where it will express a view that has become fully personalized by the Seraphic Doctor. Thus, in his certainly authentic writings, Alexander both knows and uses Pseudo-Dionysius and Richard of St. Victor, though the characteristic insights of neither are developed to a significant extent.

---

[32] *Summa Theologica, Tome IV* (Quaracchi, 1948). Section II, LIX-LXXXI; V. Doucet, "A New Source of the 'Summa Fratris Alexandri'" in: *Franciscan Studies* 6 (1946) p. 403-417; V. Doucet, "The History of the Problem of the Authenticity of the Summa," in: *Franciscan Studies* 7 (1947) p. 26-41; 274-312. Esp. Doucet's carefully worded conclusions on p. 310-312. To a great extent, the first three books were compiled before Alexander's death. These books are clearly compilations which draw from the writings of John of Rupella and Alexander among others. As to the more precise clarification of the origin of these books, the problem has yet to be solved. The first three books reflect a strong influence of Alexander which may by clarified by the fact that he was one of the compilers, and that his works were an important source and were used extensively.

[33] *Quaestiones Disputatae 'antequam esset Frater.' Bibliotheca Franciscana Scholastica Medii Aevi*, XIX-XXI (Quaracchi, 1960); *Glossa super IV Libros Sententiarum. Bibliotheca Franciscana Scholastica Medii Aevi*, XII-XV (Quaracchi, 1952-57).

[34] Of the few references to Richard's work, two are mistakenly attributed to Augustine and one to Hugh of St. Victor.

[35] *Glossa*, I, d. 3, p. 74 cites a text which gives the characteristic argument of Richard for the plurality of persons in God. The argument moves from the fullest goodness to the fullest charity to the plurality of persons. Cf. Richard, *De Trinitate*, III, c. 2 (PL 196, 916 ff.). Also d. 18, p. 182 cites Richard on the three modes of love (PL 196, 978); d. 19, p. 195 cites the argument for supreme charity in God from the highest felicity (PL 196, 928).

[36] *Glossa*, I, d. 17, p. 173.

While the *Summa* in its entirety is not the personal work of Alexander, yet he is certainly a major influence behind the work of the compilers. The *Summa* manifests Aristotelian, Platonic, Dionysian, Augustinian, and Victorine influences. The only Greek sources to which it refers are Pseudo-Dionysius and John Damascene.[37] Two factors which will later assume the most fundamental role in Bonaventure's development of trinitarian theology stand out as significant already in the *Summa*: 1) the predominant role of the Dionysian concept of *bonum diffusivum sui* in arguing for the existence of the trinity; 2) the Aristotelian principle affirming two perfect modes of procession, i.e. by nature and by will.[38] The Dionysian concept of the self-diffusive good plays a leading role, though it is joined with elements drawn from Anselm and Richard.[39] Together with John Damascene, Pseudo-Dionysius is the most frequently cited source, and in this regard the *Summa* seems to go beyond Alexander's authentic writings.

We may, therefore, conclude that Bonaventure became familiar with both Pseudo-Dionysius and Richard through Alexander as well as through the developments in the early school of the friars after the death of Alexander in 1245. To what degree Bonaventure's contact with these two sources may have been the ordinary contact which would have been a self-evident part of his education at Paris at that time remains unclear. As we will see, the Dionysian tradition will assume a unique importance in Bonaventure's trinitarian thought, and the Victorine insights will be exploited in a distinctively personal way. Despite the obvious historical and literary relations between Bonaventure and the *Summa*, it is indisputable that the Seraphic Doctor's trinitarian theology transcends that of the *Summa* in unity

---

[37] De Regnon's statement (op. cit., II, p. 355) that the *Summa* appealed to all the Greek Fathers appears as an exaggeration in the light of this. Cf. also *Summa* IV, sec. II, § 2, cap. 1, V, p. LXXXIX.
[38] *Summa Theol.* I, prol., sec. II, § 1, p. XVIII-XXXV; cf. E. Gössmann, "Die Methode der Trinitätslehre..." p. 253-262. The *Summa* makes use of the Dionysian concept of the self-diffusive good to derive the persons in the trinity and to explain the incarnation, but it is used only in a modified sense in the area of creation theology, probably because of the danger of pantheism (p. 255-6). Cf. also. E. Gössmann, *Metaphysik und Heilsgeschichte. Eine theologische Untersuchung der Summa Halensis* (München, 1964) p. 363-370.
[39] Dionysian, Anselmian, and Victorine overtones are present in the *Summa's* description of the highest diffusion: "Summa autem diffusio est qua maior excogitari non potest; maior autem diffusio cogitari non potest quam illa quae est secundum substantiam et maxime secundum totam; ergo summum bonum necessario se diffundit secundum substantiam totam... (*Summa*, I, n. 295, p. 414). Though Richard is cited several times in this question, no reference is made to his concept of charity in explaining the generation of the Son.

and coherence of thought. It clearly bears the mark of a single, keen mind that has appropriated the tradition in a personal way. Bonaventure expresses his respect for Alexander explicitly on several occasions[40] and his intention of following the opinions of the early school.[41] His references to Alexander are best seen as pointing to Alexander himself rather than to the *Summa*, though Bonaventure's writings frequently show entire sections that parallel the *Summa* at times only in general structure, but at other times even down to particular arguments. The Dionysian concept of the good, already present in Alexander[42] and in the *Summa*,[43] becomes dominant in a very personal way in Bonaventure; thus his trinitarian thought is deeply conditioned by the Areopagite, certainly through indirect contact, and possibly by direct contact as well.[44]

The *Summa* already had transformed Victorine materials in the light of the metaphysics of the good. Even more so is this the case with Bonaventure whose fundamental arguments for the trinity are clearly different from those of Richard. Yet, there are many ties with Richard that become apparent especially in Bonaventure's terminology. While for Richard the principle argument for the plurality of persons is drawn from the analysis of love, in the theology of Bonaventure the same argument is integrated into a metaphysics

---

[40] *Prael. ad* II *Sent.* (II, 1); II *Sent.* d. 23, a. 2, q. 3, ad 7 (II, 547); *Epis. de Tribus Quaestionibus* n. 11 (VIII, 335).
[41] *Hex.* 11, 4 (V, 381).
[42] *Glossa*, I, d. 3, p. 71; d. 8, p. 100.
[43] Cf. *Summa Theol.* I, prol., sec. II, § 2, p. XXXV-XXXVIII. "Etenim Alexander a schola S. Victoris repetit principium fundamentale, non solum suarum inquisitionum circa mysterium SS. Trinitatis, ut iam recte observaverat cl. de Régnon, S.I., sed etiam totius sui systematis generalis, scilicet conceptionem extaticam summi boni sive amoris." Also, *Summa* I, n. 64, ad 4, p. 96 and ad 5, p. 96. The idea of the good is basic in the derivation of the plurality of persons. The good is to be understood not only in the absolute sense, but also in as far as it is in the person of the Father, who is "principium totius divinitatis" (n. 297, ad 10, p. 427; and ad 23, p. 429). The argument from *caritas* is also in the *Summa*. Perfect charity tends to another because "nunquam potest esse solitaria" (n. 324, ad 4, p. 440). The communication of the good can take place in only two ways: *per modum naturae* and *per modum voluntatis* (n. 319, sol. p. 469).
[44] Both the *Summa* and Bonaventure cite the translation of John Sarracenus whose work, together with that of Thomas of Vercelli, opened Western theology to the influence of the Areopagite. To trace the influence of Dionysius on Bonaventure would require a separate study. On the one hand, there seem to be no cogent textual reasons to assume an influence beyond that which would have normally been expected in the Schools of that time. On the other hand, the fact that a number of crucial Dionysian concepts assume an exceptional importance as early as the *Sentence Commentary* suggests that it must remain an open question whether Bonaventure may have had a close personal acquaintance with the works of the Areopagite. Cf. J. Ratzinger, *The Theology of History in St. Bonaventure*, tr. Z. Hayes (Chicago, 1971) p. 86-94.

based expressly on the concept of the good. Thus, the terminology itself, though it sounds Victorine, frequently takes on a new meaning as it is conditioned by the dynamics of fecundity which played no role in Richard.[45]

In attempting to assess Bonaventure's work in relation to its sources, Gonzalez concludes that there is indeed a style of trinitarian thought in the thirteenth century that differs fundamentally from that of Thomas; its creator and systematizer, however, is not Richard but Bonaventure.[46] Its fundamental inspiration is to be sought in the religious experience of St. Francis and in philosophical elements drawn from Pseudo-Dionysius and Aristotle as these had been transmitted to Bonaventure by Alexander and by the developments of the early school of friars at Paris. Other elements, including the Augustinian and the Victorine trinitarian traditions, are transformed within the framework which was built upon these primary sources. Thus Bonaventure's trinitarian view of reality, while it draws from many and disparate sources, appears as a highly personal synthesis. In this sense, we can continue to speak of two styles, as De Regnon had argued, but our understanding of the author and the sources of the one has been drastically revised.

II. THE TRINITARIAN WORKS OF BONAVENTURE

The materials presented in the *Disputed Questions on the Trinity* in no way represent a full treatment of trinitarian theology. On the contrary, they are limited in scope and presuppose the work which the Seraphic Doctor had already done in his *Sentence Commentary*. It is in the latter work that he treats scientifically the major problems of both the metaphysical and logical orders. His doctrine on the divine processions, relations, persons, properties, notions, appropriations, and the questions of logic and language are all found there in the fullest treatment he was ever to give them. None of these materials are repeated in the *Disputed Questions*, though the treatment found in the latter is clearly shaped by the *Commentary*.

Written after both the *Sentence Commentary* and the *Disputed*

---

[45] Gonzalez, op. cit., p. 363. Gonzalez sees Richard's influence on Bonaventure as minimal in the basic trinitarian arguments though Bonaventure does share Richard's confidence in reason.

[46] Op. cit., p. 363: "El creador-sistematizador de la doctrina trinitaria, que correrá paralela a la tomista repartiéndose el siglo XIII, no es Ricardo, sine San Buenaventura.

Questions, the *Breviloquium* may be dated about 1257,[47] which would place it at the end of Bonaventure's university career or at the beginning of his work as Minister General. Conceived as a sort of summary for students of theology, it is a most valuable source for Bonaventure's own synthesis. While some development over the *Sentence Commentary* may be noted in the treatment of Christology, the presentation of trinitarian materials seems to be but a concise statement of major positions worked out in the *Commentary*, here presented in almost skeletal form and devoid of all arguments.

The *Itinerarium*, which dates from 1259, is a work written without the pressure of the demands and expectations of the university discipline. It is written in a more personal style and reveals with greater clarity the characteristic concerns of the Seraphic Doctor, who was already General of the Order at the time he wrote this remarkable text. It becomes immediately clear to what extent trinitarianism pervades his entire vision of reality. The sixth chapter provides a specifically trinitarian reflection in which we see to what extent Bonaventure's thought was influenced by the Dionysian concept of the good. Traditional materials stemming from Augustine are transformed under the power of that concept, while materials from Richard of St. Victor will provide a complementary line of argument as needed to fill out some of the inadequacies of the neo-Platonic tradition. Thus this work, brief as it is, and rich with insights into the work of Bonaventure as a whole, is equally significant for what it reveals of his trinitarian style and its relation to his predecessors.

Nowhere is the trinitarian vision of reality more persistent than in the *Collations on the Hexaemeron*, the final work of Bonaventure.[48] Here more than anywhere his thought appears in a dense and many-layered style of theology. His vision appears like a tightly drawn circle. Regardless of where one takes hold of it, it reaches out to the trinity and Christology, to creation and man, to metaphysics and epistemology. Behind the bewildering complexity of symbolism and historical-theological speculation, one feels the presence of a mind that has a penetrating insight into the fundamental structures of reality that pervades all that is said. Woven within a text that is trinitarian throughout are particular sections more expressly trinitarian in tone, such as *Collation X*, 4. 16. 17, and *Collation XI*.

---

[47] For questions of chronology, cf. J. Bougerol, *Introduction to the Works of Bonaventure* tr. J. de Vinck (Paterson, 1963) p. 171-182; J. F. Quinn, "Chronology of St. Bonaventure," in: *Franciscan Studies* 32 (1972) p. 168-186.

[48] Dated to 1273, the work was left incomplete by his elevation to the Cardinalate and his subsequent activity at the Council of Lyons.

Beyond these major works, trinitarian motifs appear universally in Bonaventure's spiritual and mystical writings as well as in his sermons, two of which expressly reproduce the conclusions of his scientific work.[49] While the sermons and ascetical writings may be taken as an indication of the close relation between scientific theology and spirituality, they offer no fundamentally new insights into the major trinitarian questions.

III. THE DISPUTED QUESTIONS ON THE TRINITY

Thus, the *Disputed Questions on the Trinity* stand in the context of a rich body of literature treating the same theological concerns, all of which can shed light on the concerns of the *Questions*. As the title indicates, this work follows the form of the Scholastic disputation.[50] The set of questions on the trinity is one of three sets published in the fifth volume of the Quaracchi edition; it is judged both from internal and from external evidence to be an authentic work of Bonaventure. The work is commonly dated between 1253 and 1257, which places it later than the *Sentence Commentary* and shortly before Bonaventure's departure from the university. The state of the manuscript tradition indicates that the latter part of the work, beginning with the middle of the response of question six, article two, is found in only one manuscript. This might legitimately raise the question as to whether the work was left unfinished by Bonaventure and completed from notes by someone else.[51] If this is the case, the question then arises as to what might have lead Bonaventure to break off his work at this point. Could it have been his appointment as General of the Order? If so, this would allow for a dating from late 1256 to early 1257, since Bonaventure's appointment occurred in February of 1257. The question cannot be decided definitely without more work on the chronology of Bonaventure during this period of his life.

---

[49] *Sermo I: De Triplici Testimonio Sanctissimae Trinitatis* (V, 535-538); *Sermo de Trinitate* (IX, 351-357).

[50] Of the two types of Scholastic disputes, the ordinary and the quodlibetal, these conform more closely to the former. Quodlibetal questions reflect a more wide-ranging style while the ordinary questions are restricted in scope. Bonaventure has left no questions in the quodlibetal form.

[51] The Quaracchi editors (V, VI) say: "It is certain that even the final questions are genuine" since the text refers expressly to the preceding questions (e.g. Q. 7, a. 1, ad 8 [V, 109]). Though the material may be genuinely Bonaventurean, this does not exclude the possibility that the latter questions in their present form may be the work of another hand.

Even though they contain authentic Bonaventurean materials of great significance, the *Disputed Questions* have been generally neglected over the centuries. The Quaracchi editors describe the *Questions on the Trinity* as a work that stands "inter praestantissima eiusdem opera;"[52] and which is carried out in a style that is "modo prorsus singulari."[53] A close reading of the text shows that this is scarcely an exaggeration. Simply in terms of its general structure, the *Questions on the Trinity* stand out in the history of trinitarian literature. Rarely if ever has the relation between the philosophical doctrine of being and the trinitarian dogma of faith been worked out with such elaborate care, the result being that the major categories of the traditional philosophy of being are subjected to a new interpretation in the context of faith. In its very structure as well as in its content this work is illustrative of the most basic characteristics of Bonaventure's theological style, revealing fundamental tendencies in his style of argumentation as well as the characteristic Bonaventurean concept of God.

The *Questions* offer a powerful picture of a mind well trained in the art of logic in a theologian who is all too often viewed only as a mystical theologian. The all-pervasive argument is that of the Bonaventurean *reduction* whereby the mind attempts to trace reality to its ultimate source and goal. Reduction can be seen at two levels. The first, and perhaps the most obvious, is the level of logical analysis and argument; here reduction is realized in the cognitive order. Reduction at this level, however, is intimately related to an ontological reduction, which is the real return of creatures to God through grace. "Therefore it follows that eternal life consists in this alone, that the rational spirit, which emanates from the most blessed trinity and is a likeness of the trinity, should return after the manner of a certain intelligible circle — through memory, intelligence and will — to the most blessed trinity by God-conforming glory."[54] The concept of reduction at both levels reveals the neo-Platonic structure of emanation and return which is so basic to Bonaventure's vision of reality, and is frequently symbolized by the circle. God Himself is an intelligible circle;[55] all created beings flow from this source to move in a circle to their goal. Especially

---

[52] (V, prol. III).
[53] Ibid.
[54] *Qq. Dd. de Trin.* q. 8, ad 7 (V, 115).
[55] I *Sent.* d. 37, p. 1, a. 1, q. 1, ad 3 (I, 639); *De Reduc.* 7 (V, 322); *Brevil.* 5, 1 (V, 253); *Hex.* 1, 18.19.20 (V, 332-333). Cf. also, Z. Hayes, *What Manner of Man ? Sermons on Christ by St. Bonaventure. Translated with an Introduction and Commentary* (Chicago, 1974) p. 91, n. 45.

in human beings is that circular movement most clearly realized as the spiritual powers of the finite spirit move into ever greater conformity to the knowledge, the will, and the governing power of God.

At the cognitive level, reduction means — among other things — that all imperfect forms of being must be reduced to more perfect forms logically since they are grounded ontologically in the more perfect. One cannot recognize a limit as a limit unless one is somehow beyond the limit; hence, one cannot know a limited good as limited except through reduction to an unlimited good in the same order. The over-all structure of the *Questions* is a clear reflection of this conviction.

Within that over-all framework, some more specific concerns of Bonaventure's thought are obvious. Bonaventure views theology as a practical science whose basic purpose is to help human beings achieve their ultimate goal in life. Since that goal is not speculation for its own sake but loving union with God, rational argument, though important, has an ancillary role. There is in Bonaventure a tendency to prefer opinions which seem more religious even though other opinions are logically possible. His concern is expressed pointedly in the axiom that we are to think of God "altissime et piissime,"[56] a principle whose influence is extensive both in the arguments and in the language of the *Questions*. The constant flow of the arguments of the reduction is to that which is highest in any particular category, while the language itself reflects the axiom in its frequent use of superlative forms.

Bonaventure's guarded optimism in the power of reason is reflected in his appeal to necessary reasons, where he is under the influence of Anselm and Richard of St. Victor. That there should be necessary reasons in trinitarian theology is not surprising in the context of Bonaventure's metaphysical and epistemological convictions. If God is what He is necessarily, then there must be necessary reasons for what He is. The question would then be whether such reasons are accessible to the human mind, and if so, under what conditions. What sources of light must come together to enable us to see the reasons and to see them precisely as necessary? If God is necessary being, then there should be a necessary relation between the unity of His essence and the trinity of persons. If the necessary attributes of being accessible to reason are necessary attributes of God, then there ought to be some rational connection between these attributes and the mystery of the trinity. This mode of argumentation

---

[56] *Brevil.* 1, 2 (V, 211).

does not pretend to offer philosophical demonstrations for the trinity itself, for it operates within the framework of faith. Its purpose is to make faith intelligible, and through the contact between faith and reason to bring reason to its fuller possibilities. Thus in carrying out his reduction, Bonaventure finds it possible to encounter God in every category of being, not only as God but as trinity also.[57]

---

[57] Salet, op. cit., p. 465-467; Ribaillier, op. cit., p. 89; A. de Villalmonte, "El argumento de 'razones necessarias' en San Buenaventura," in: *Estudios Franciscanos* 53 (1952) p. 5-44.

CHAPTER TWO

BONAVENTURE'S TRINITARIAN THEOLOGY IN GENERAL

"The created world is like a book which reflects, represents, and describes the creative trinity..." Brevil. 2, 12 (V, 230).

I. THE TRINITY IN THE BONAVENTUREAN SYSTEM

One cannot read the works of Bonaventure for long without sensing that the mystery of the trinity pervades the whole of his vision of reality. It is a fundamental structural component of his thought both in its broader vision and in its smaller units, and even conditions the choice of language and phraseology.

As a convincingly articulated wisdom-theology, Bonaventure's thought is concerned not with knowledge for its own sake, but with saving knowledge. "Now this is everlasting life, that they may know You, the only true God, and him whom You have sent, Jesus Christ."[1] To know God in a saving way is to know Him as He truly is; and He most truly is in the way He has revealed Himself to be in the New Testament, above all in the person of Jesus Christ. Therefore a truly saving knowledge of God is to be found at the level of trinitarian theology. The first principle sought by philosophy is identical, in the final analysis, with the trinitarian God of the New Testament revelation. If all finite reality emanates from the first principle, this can be understood in a fuller sense only when we perceive that the limited emanation of the created world is grounded in the prior and perfect emanations of goodness in the first principle itself.

Hence, the entire theological endeavor of Bonaventure is inspired by the contemplation of the trinity. If the trinity is source of all, then it should not be surprising that it would leave its stamp upon the world. Indeed, for Bonaventure this is the case at every level. As the objectification of the Absolute Spirit, the world as a whole

---

[1] *Jn.* 17, 3.

is a symbol of the trinity. The world is like a book which reflects its trinitarian author at three levels; that of the vestige, that of the image, and that of the similitude. Every creature is a vestige representing the trinity in a distant and unclear way; but the image, found only in intellectual creatures, reflects the trinity in a closer and more distinct way. The similitude is that most intense reflection which is found in the rational spirit that is conformed to God through grace. These three levels are like the steps of a ladder by which the human mind is designed to ascend gradually to the supreme principle who is God.[2] The world emanates from the trinitarian exemplar and reflects the trinitarian order at various levels and degrees.

In Bonaventure's thought, the trinity and Christology are inseparably intertwined. It is the mystery of Christ that leads us to the trinity; and the trinitarian concept of God is developed as a function of Christology. At one level, the whole of the trinity is seen as the exemplar of the world while at another level, the mystery of exemplarity is concentrated in the second person; for the divine Word is the total expression of all that the divine love is in itself and can be in relation to the finite. The entire triune structure of God, including the procession of the Spirit is focused in the Word in an exemplary way.[3] In as far as the Word is the expression of the entire inner-trinitarian life of God, that which is created as an expression of God bears a relation not only to the trinity as such, but to the Word in particular.

The human person, created as an image of God, reflects its creative source in two ways. The spiritual soul reflects the one spiritual nature of God, while the spiritual powers of memory, intelligence, and will reflect the mystery of source, origin, and order characteristic of the trinitarian life of God. There is here a limited reflection of the unity and trinity of God. That which Bonaventure designates as an image of God is, in a sense, an open possibility which must be brought to actualization. By reflecting either on itself or on things above itself, the image becomes an express image. The fullest historical realization of this is found in the gift of grace whereby the human person is transformed to true God-likeness and the soul becomes a similitude of the trinity. The world of created reality which comes forth from a trinitarian source is here approaching its God-appointed end in the mystery of grace which finds its completion in

---

[2] *Brevil.* 2, 12 (V, 230). For an excellent study of Bonaventure's theology of creation, cf. M. Wiegels, *Die Logik der Spontaneität. Zum Gedanken der Schöpfung bei Bonaventura* (Freiburg-München, 1969).
[3] *Hex.* 3, 7 (V, 344); *Hex.* 9, 2 (V, 373).

glory, where the most perfect conformity between the created trinity and the creative trinity is realized. Again the mystery of the trinity is intertwined with the mystery of Christ. Created as the finite image of God, the human person is given the task of shaping human life personally in the likeness of the perfect Image, and thus of moving from image to similitude. To the degree that this is accomplished, the human person is personally moulded into the mystery of the Image who is the Son, and thus enters into the Son's relation to the Father and the Spirit. By becoming Christ-like, the human person is conformed to the trinity.

It is clear that Bonaventure's theology is trinitarian in a way that is profoundly different from that of his contemporary, Aquinas. His is a view that may be seen as a consistent economic trinitarianism for which the world and its history is a vast symbol of the trinitarian God who communicates Himself in being, in grace, and in consummation.

II. THE POINT OF DEPARTURE

"No one is good but only God." Lk 18, 19.

While it is clear that Bonaventure never gives an extended treatment of the nature of God independently of the doctrine of the trinity,[4] yet it would be deceptive to say that he begins his trinitarian theology from a consideration of the individual persons as such. The problem from which he begins in each of his major treatments is the problem of how we are to conceive of the movement from the unique and unified nature of God to the existence of three persons.

The early Franciscan school appears to have been deeply concerned with the theological implications of the religious experience of St. Francis who, because of his experience of Christ, came to emphasize the nature of God as a good and loving Father. The *Summa* of the early friars gives considerable emphasis to God under this image and makes extensive use of the Dionysian metaphysics of the self-diffusive good to elaborate this religious ex-

---

[4] In none of his works is there a tract corresponding to the familiar *De Deo Uno*. The *Sentence Commentary*, after one brief question on the one-ness of God, proceeds directly to the question of the plurality of persons (I *Sent.* d. 2, a.u., q. 1-2 [I, 51-53]). The *Breviloquium* follows the same pattern (*Brevil.* 1, 2 [V, 210]). We look elsewhere in vain for such a treatment. The development of the attributes of the divine nature is presented within the framework of the trinitarian question.

perience at the theological level. Through the influence of Alexander of Hales and other early friar theologians, this was to become a significant factor in Bonaventure's personal synthesis.

The emphasis on the nature of God as primal goodness is seen by Bonaventure to correspond to the New Testament revelation of the divine name: "No one is good but only God."[5] As *being* seems to be the proper name of God in the Old Testament and corresponds to the concerns of philosophy, *goodness* is the proper name of God in the New Testament and will lead eventually to trinitarian theology.[6] Thus a clear point of contact can be seen between the religious experience of Francis and the writings of Scripture on the one hand, and between the experience of Francis and the theology of the early friars, including Bonaventure, on the other hand. But elsewhere in the New Testament we read that "God is love."[7] This designation of God would also play a leading role in the history of Christian thought, and would enter into the structure of Bonaventure's trinitarianism, though without explicit citations from the New Testament.

Both the idea of the good and the concept of love are fundamental in Bonaventure's attempt to show the derivation of the persons in the trinity, and his arguments reveal how he has employed both the neo-Platonic thought of Pseudo-Dionysius as well as the theological insights of Richard of St. Victor in a way that is distinctively his own. In the Dionysian view, goodness is the preeminent attribute of God; it is the very definition of the superessential Godhead and the deepest basis for God's creative activity. Since God is good, and since the good is by nature self-diffusive, it follows that God is necessarily self-communicative. This tradition is taken up by Bonaventure and is used to argue for the necessary self-communication of the divine nature. It provides the metaphysical basis for understanding the first emanation within God as a natural emanation which flows necessarily from the dynamism of the divine nature. But, for Bonaventure, this is not sufficient for trinitarian theology since it specifies neither the mode nor the number of divine emanations.

To fill up the incompleteness of the Dionysian model, Bonaventure reaches to Richard's reflections on love. Richard himself had seen love as the supreme form of the good and had employed the former rather than the latter in working out his understanding of the trinity. For Bonaventure, this approach — while not adequate

---

[5] *Lk.* 18, 19; also, *Mt.* 19, 17.
[6] *Itin.* 5, 2 (V, 308); and 6, 2 (V, 310).
[7] 1 *Jn.* 4, 8.16.

3 St. Bonaventure, Disputed Questions

in itself — can be used in conjunction with the Dionysian metaphysics to supplement the understanding of the trinity. This model offers the possibility of moving beyond the necessary, natural emanation to an understanding of the dynamism of the will from which proceeds a free self-communication; this provides the basis for understanding the procession of the Spirit as an emanation *per modum liberalitatis;* or *per modum amoris.* While the first approach emphasizes the necessary diffusiveness of a fecund nature, the second highlights the communication of liberality from a fecund will. While the nature is the primary principle in the generation of the Son (*natura est principium concomitante voluntate*),[8] the will is a real principle in the spiration of the Spirit (*voluntas est principium concomitante natura*).[9] Since it is the fecundity of the nature and the will from which the emanations flow, and since the intellect precisely as intellect is not fecund, Bonaventure always uses the term *per modum naturae* to designate the first procession.[10] The Augustinian tradition of an intellectual emanation is thus subsumed within this dominant framework.

While both the argument from the good and the argument from love lead to the affirmation of a plurality of persons in God, the analysis of love provides further clues for limiting the number of persons to three. In the general argument of the *Sentence Commentary* for the plurality of persons,[11] the concepts of goodness and love are subsumed under the notion of beatitude. By way of contrast, in answering the question of why there are only three persons, the notion of beatitude again stands in the first place; but in the analysis of beatitude, the concept of goodness is omitted, and only the notions of *germanitas* and *caritas* are employed.[12] Here the understanding of charity as perfect love which is both liberal and shared[13] is employed to show that there must be both *dilectio* and *condilectio;* hence there can be no less than three persons. The argument from love appears here as a necessary argument, while later the three modes of love

---

[8] I *Sent.* d. 6, a.u., q. 2, resp. (I, 128).

[9] Ibid.

[10] Bonaventure uses the terms *per modum naturae* and *per modum voluntatis* to designate the two trinitarian emanations. The terms are inspired by Aristotle's principle that there exist only two perfect modes of production; namely, natural and free. I *Sent.* d. 2, a.u., q. 4, fund. 2 (I, 56) cites Aristotle, *Lib. II Phys.* text. 49 (c. 5); cf. also, *Brevil.* 1, 3 (V, 211).

[11] I *Sent.* d. 2, a.u., q. 2, fund. 1 (I, 53).

[12] I *Sent.* d. 2, a.u., q. 4, fund. 1 (I, 56).

[13] Ibid. *Amor liberalis* is seen as a love which "tendit in alterum." The *amor communis* is described as one which "vult illum diligi ab altero et diligere alterum." Cf. also the *response* (I, 57) where the first argument of necessity follows the same line of thought.

formulated by Richard of St. Victor appear as the first argument from congruity.[14] Bonaventure's argument is constructed around two poles which reflect both the Dionysian and the Victorine concern. Neither of these poles can be reduced to the other since each provides only a limited vision of the mystery of God. The same bipolar argumentation appears again in the *Itinerarium*,[15] but with a certain priority given to the Dionysian pole. In his final work, which we may see as his mature thought on the matter, the two poles are in fact presented as two parallel arguments,[16] thus confirming the view that there is a basic distinction between the argument from the good and the argument from love.

The argument from simplicity, which appears in the *Sentence Commentary*[17] is a variation of the argument from goodness. Simplicity is understood to mean indivision, lack of composition, lack of constitutive parts, and lack of immanent actions really distinct from the essence.[18] As such, it is a pure perfection and must be posited in God, who is the highest perfection. The expansive power of the good which is concentrated in the one, simple divine essence raises unity to multiplicity without multiplying the essence. It is precisely because of His supreme simplicity that God is supremely communicable.[19] If God is most simple, He is most communicative and productive in proportion to His being. Therefore, simplicity includes a plurality of persons.

The argument from perfection appears in different forms in the *Sentence Commentary*[20] and in the *Hexaemeron*.[21] Perfection is understood broadly as the ability to communicate or to produce another like oneself; it refers to productive power. In the *Commentary* this is taken primarily in the sense of a dynamic power, while in the *Hexaemeron*, it has more of an aesthetic quality reflecting a state of being in God, including origin, order, and lack of division.[22]

All these arguments flow together into the notion of primacy which lies at the heart of Bonaventure's doctrine of God. It is a concept which is involved in some way in the resolution of all the major trinitarian questions: 1) the movement from unity of nature

---

[14] I *Sent.* d. 2, a.u., q. 4, resp. (I, 57).
[15] *Itin.* 6, 2 (V, 310-311).
[16] *Hex.* 11, 11 & 12 (V, 381-382).
[17] I *Sent.* d. 2, a.u., q. 2, fund. 3 (I, 53). It is found also in *Qq. Dd.* q. 3, a. 1, resp. (V, 70).
[18] I *Sent.* d. 8, q. 2, a.u., q. 1, ad 1-4 (I, 166).
[19] I *Sent.* d. 8, p. 2, q. 1, ad 1 (I, 166); d. 2, q. 2, resp. (I, 54).
[20] I *Sent.* d. 2, a. 2, fund. 2 (I, 53).
[21] *Hex.* 11, 6 ff. (V, 381).
[22] The elements of this argument will be treated further below.

to trinity of persons;[23] 2) the procession of the Spirit from the Father and the Son;[24] 3) the impossibility of more than three persons;[25] and 4) the personal constitution of the Father.[26] Employing the philosophical principle that a being is cause of others because it is first, Bonaventure states that the more a being is prior, the more it is the fecund source of others.[27] This may be understood in a broad sense to speak of the divine essence with respect to the world, at which level it corresponds to the doctrine of creation. The divine nature is the rich fountain from which flows the entire created universe.[28] But Bonaventure pushes beyond this to argue that the concept of primacy may be traced into the depths of the divine nature itself where it may be seen as the characteristic of the first divine person. As the divine nature is absolutely prior with respect to all other essences, and thus is *a se* in the fullest sense of the word, so the Father, as that person who is *non ab alio*, is first with respect to the other persons. Hence, there is in God one in whom resides the fullness of divine fecundity with respect to the persons.[29] But since whatever God is in Himself He is in act, it follows that the divine fecundity with respect to God Himself must be in act, and hence there must be a plurality of persons in God.

The survey of the full range of Bonaventure's arguments reveals that his primary concern is to uncover an intelligible connection between the one divine essence and the trinity of persons. The concepts of goodness, primacy, love, perfection, and simplicity do this, each from a particular perspective. Underlying all the arguments is a rich and dynamic image of the divine reality. God is the infinitely rich and fecund mystery whose eternal being is a dynamic ecstasy of goodness and love. The divine nature is not a static, monadic being, but is to be conceived more as a unifying power which, in the unity of the divine fecundity, produces a plurality without multiplying the nature. The trinity of persons is the fruit of the most perfect unity which, while subsisting in a multiplicity of persons, is yet not multiplied in itself.[30]

---

[23] I *Sent.* d. 2, a.u., q. 2, fund. 4 (I, 53).
[24] I *Sent.* d. 11, a.u., q. 2, resp. (I, 215).
[25] I *Sent.* d. 2, a.u., q. 4, resp. (I, 57).
[26] I *Sent.* d. 27, p. 1, a.u., q. 2, resp., and ad 3 (I, 469-470).
[27] Aristotle, I *Poster.* c. 2; *Liber de Causis*, prop. 1 and 17; Bonav., I *Sent.* d. 2, a.u., q. 2, fund. 4 (I, 53).
[28] I *Sent.* Prooemium (I, 1-6).
[29] This concept of the first person as *plenitudo fontalis* is called the *antiqua opinio* (I *Sent.* d. 2, a.u., q. 2, resp. [I, 54]).
[30] *Hex.* 11, 8 (V, 381); *Qq. Dd.* q. 2, a. 2, fund. 6 (V, 64).

III. THE CONSTITUTION OF PERSONHOOD

It is on the basis of the emanations that one is lead to speak of relations in God, and eventually of persons. But, in what sense is the term *person* applicable to God? Augustine had found difficulty in using such a word, fearing it would do violence to the unity of the divine nature. Because of the nature of the problem, theologians over the centuries have attempted to find more serviceable definitions of person and a clearer articulation of the way in which we might conceive of the constitution of the persons in the trinity.

The Boethian definition conceived of a person as "an individual substance of a rational nature."[31] This definition would have an extensive influence in Western theology despite the obvious difficulties contained in it. If it were applied without qualification to God in a trinitarian framework, it would seem to lead to a form of tritheism. Thus, while the definition is widely accepted by theologians, it is generally accepted only with considerable criticism, as is clearly the case with Aquinas.[32] Richard of St. Victor formulated a definition which seems to avoid some of the problems inherent in the Boethian definition. The Boethian *individual substance* is replaced by the notions of *incommunicable* and *singular existence*. Recognizing the impossibility of defining the infinite yet recognizing the need of saying something, Richard defines a divine person as an *incommunicable existence of the divine nature*.[33] Theologians following the Augustinian inspiration will tend to see the divine persons as constituted by relations, while Richard will see them as distinguished *per originem*.[34]

After some etymological reflections on the Latin word *persona* and the Greek word *prosopon*,[35] Bonaventure expresses a distinct preference for the Victorine definition in speaking of God, seeing it as a correction of the Boethian definition.[36] But if person refers precisely to that which distinguishes the three, is it possible to use the term commonly of all three? The term certainly expresses incommunicability, and in this sense it points to the lack of com-

---

[31] *Liber de Persona et Duabus Naturis* 3, 1-5 (PL 64, 1343).
[32] *S. Th.* I, q. 29, a. 1-4.
[33] *De Trin.* IV, c. 18 (PL 196, 941); IV, c. 21 (PL 196, 944-945); IV, c. 22 (PL 196, 945). Richard argues that the Boethian definition applies only to created persons; the term *individua substantia* is at the center of his critique. His own definition is presented with a clear recognition of its inadequacy. "Non inconvenienter fortassis dicere poterimus, quod persona divina sit divinae naturae incommunicabilis existentia."
[34] *De Trin.* IV, c. 15 (PL 196,939).
[35] I *Sent.* d. 23, a. 1, q. 1, resp. (I, 405).
[36] I *Sent.* d. 25, a. 1, q. 2, ad 4 (I, 441).

monness.³⁷ But Bonaventure attempts to establish a level of commonness distinct from that of the essence, yet sufficient to enable him to say that the predication implies more than an *ens rationis*. He argues that though it is true that the term *person* signifies incommunicability and therefore implies a lack of commonness, yet this incommunicability is a positive quality more than a privation. More specifically, it implies a similarity of relationship to the essence. Therefore, person is more than a mere *ens rationis* since it refers to something real in God. Because of the similarity of relation between each person and the divine nature, the term may be used analogously of all three,³⁸ just as it may be predicated analogously of God and of creatures.³⁹

While in God all exists with absolute simultaneity, theology as reflective thought which seeks to understand the inter-relationship between the various predications made about God is intimately tied to the human experience of temporal relations. As the theologian seeks to understand the logical relations involved, those things which are really simultaneous appear in temporal language which creates the impression of prior and posterior in God. Therefore, it is inevitable that the question of the constitution of the person should arise. Generally, theologians following the Augustinian tradition tend to identify person with relation in such a way that relation is the constitutive principle of person. This is clearly the case with Aquinas, for whom relation has a dominant role to play. Bonaventure also sees the persons as subsistent relations,⁴⁰ though this insight never assumes the centrality which it has for Aquinas. Though Bonaventure's position is not fully clear, he seems to favor the origins or processions over the relations as constitutive of the persons. In this regard, he reflects the view of Richard, for whom the persons are distinguished *per originem*.⁴¹ The question of the constitution of the persons is particularly problematic in the case of the first person. If the persons are constituted by relations, and if relation arises from procession, must not the first procession logically presuppose a person who actively generates? But if so, then the first person is prior to the relation by which He is said to be constituted. Bonaventure's approach to this problem reveals both the centrality of the concept of primacy and his inclination to see the persons as constituted *per originem*. He understands the

---
³⁷ I *Sent.* d. 25, a. 2, q. 1, resp. (I, 442-443).
³⁸ Ibid.
³⁹ I *Sent.* d. 25, a. 2, q. 2, resp. (I, 444-445).
⁴⁰ Cf. Stohr, op. cit., p. 120-122.
⁴¹ *De Trin.* IV, c. 13 ff.; V *per totum* (PL 196, 938 ff.); also, Stohr, op. cit., p. 114-120.

innascibility of the first person to have both a negative and a positive meaning. Precisely in as far as He is not from any other, He is the fruitful source of all others. Therefore, logically prior to His full and actual paternity which is the active relation to the Son that constitutes Him as Father in the full sense, He is Father already in an inchoative sense in as far as His personal property of being fecund source of all others has a logical priority to any actual emanations.[42]

Relations, Properties, Notions

Relations in the trinity are based on the two emanations. They are active generation, by which the Father generates the Son; passive generation, which is the Son's relation to the Father; active spiration, by which the Father and the Son together breathe forth the Spirit; and passive spiration, which is the Spirit's relation to the Father and the Son.[43] Intimately related to these are the concepts of property and notion, which Bonaventure uses in both a broad and in a narrow sense. In the broad sense, they are virtually synonymous and are used interchangeably. Hence, we find such combibinations as: *proprietas relativa; notio, scil. personalis proprietas*, etc.

The term *notion* is used to designate the relations in as far as they provide the basis for making known something about the three persons, the term *notion* being derived from the Latin verb *innotescere*. Since all four of the relations can be seen in this way, there are at least four notions. But since the Father is distinguished by innascibility, which is not formally identical with paternity, we can conclude that there are five notions in all: innascibility, paternity, filiation, active spiration, and passive spiration.[44] As they relate to our knowledge about God, the notions make possible a knowledge not of the essential divine attributes but of the personal qualities of the three persons.

In this sense, they are related to what theology calls the personal properties. Yet something that is common to several persons cannot

---

[42] *Brevil.* 1, 3 (V, 212). This is treated more fully below in the discussion of the person of the Father. Stohr (op. cit., p. 123) sees this as an inconsistency in Bonaventure's thought and attributes it to the Seraphic Doctor's unwillingness to place the concept of paternity higher than that of primacy. It is possible to see this in another way, for it can be interpreted as the most fundamental instance of the dialectical structure of Bonaventure's thought. The dialectical structure of the coincidence of opposites is grounded in the very mystery of the Father. On the coincidence of opposites, cf. E. Cousins, "The Coincidence of Opposites in the Christology of St. Bonaventure," in: *Franciscan Studies* 28 (1968) VI, p. 27-46.
[43] *Brevil.* 1, 3 (V, 212).
[44] Ibid.

be seen as a personal property in the strict sense. Therefore, active spiration, which is common to the Father and the Son, is not a property. This would leave four properties, as the *Sentence Commentary* indicates.[45] On the other hand, the *Breviloquium* speaks of three properties indicated by the names: Father, Son, Holy Spirit.[46] Thus, even though innascibility is proper to the Father, He is more clearly known in a positive and fuller sense through paternity; that is, through the actual generation of the Son. For this reason, paternity stands parallel to Sonship and to passive spiration as the most characteristic properties.

Since the personal properties are more than mere logical concepts, and are really distinct among themselves and yet not totally identical in all respects with the divine persons, there are three modes of predication concerning God: the essential mode, the personal mode, and the notional mode. The essential mode of predication is that by which we speak of God in terms of His divine nature and its essential attributes; the personal mode is that whereby we speak of God in terms of properties that truly distinguish the persons from one another; the notional mode, while distinguishing the persons, is broader than the personal mode since it involves predications that express relations among the persons. A brief example may help to clarify these three modes of predication. It is commonly said in Christian theology that God is love. Bonaventure distinguishes three ways in which love is predicated of God in a trinitarian context. As an essential predication, it designates that love which pertains to the very nature of God and which is predicated of all three persons. As a personal predication, it designates that person who is love that is produced from perfect liberality. As a notional predication, it refers to the concord of will between the Father and Son whereby they breathe the Spirit from perfect liberality.[47] Viewed in another way, essential predications speak of the divine nature in response to the question *quid;* personal predications speak of a determinate person in response to the question *quis;* notional predications refer to the persons in an indeterminate way in response to the question *qui*. It would be a violation of logic to cross the lines between these three modes of predication and would lead to confusion.

---

[45] I *Sent*. d. 26, a.u., q. 1, resp. (I, 452); and, q. 4, fund. 2, and resp. (I, 460).
[46] *Brevil.*, loc. cit.
[47] I *Sent*. d. 10, a. 2, q. 1, resp. (I, 210); *Brevil*. 1-4 (V, 212); I *Sent*. d. 32, a. 1, q. 1, fund. 1 and resp. (I, 557-558). Also, W. Principe, "St. Bonaventure's Theology of the Holy Spirit as Love between Father and Son," in: *Cord* 24 (1974) 7, p. 235-256, esp. p. 245-246; and "St. Bonaventure's Theology of the Holy Spirit with Reference to the Expression 'Pater et Filius diligunt se Spiritu Sancto,' " in: *Bonaventura IV* (Grottaferrata, 1973-4) p. 243-269.

IV. THE FATHER

"It is proper to the Father to be innascible or unbegotten; to be the principle that proceeds from no other principle; to be Father as such." Brevil. 1, 3 (V, 212).

Characteristic of Bonaventure's doctrine of the trinity is the peculiar emphasis given to the first person whose personal property is expressed in the title *Father*. Here it becomes more apparent how the concept of primacy is applied to the inner-divine life. The basis of the emanation of the created world is found in the two inner-divine emanations from which arise the Son and the Spirit; but the basis of the inner-divine emanations lies in the innascibility of the Father in whom the fontal fullness of the Godhead is focused in a unique way. Thus, the Father receives an emphasis that would be foreign to the thought of either Augustine or Aquinas, and is similar to the theology of the classical Greek Fathers. It is here that we find the pivotal point of Bonaventure's entire metaphysics of *exitus* and *reditus*, for it is the Father who is source and goal of all created reality; in Him is found ultimately the *status* in which the entire creative process finds its fulfillment.[48]

To speak of the Father as innascible or unbegotten seems at first glance to be a purely negative way of defining the property of the first person; and so it had appeared to Aquinas. But in Bonaventure's view, innascibility is not a mere negation; for it involves both a negative and a positive aspect. Negatively, it affirms a lack of origin. But to exist as one who has no origin is to be first in an absolute sense, and to exist as first is the highest of all perfections.[49] Here again we encounter Bonaventure's concept of primacy. That person in God who is first is the fontal fullness; precisely as the person who is innascible, He is the richest source of all the immanent processions and the external productions.[50]

If from revelation we know that God eternally generates a Son, then we know also that God as Father is the mystery of absolute

---

[48] I *Sent.* d. 2, a.u., q. 2, ad 4 (I, 54). "In personis divinis est una persona, a qua sunt aliae et ad quam, et in illa est status originis, quia illa a nullo; et haec est persona patris."

[49] I *Sent.* d. 27, p. 1, a.u., q. 2, ad 3 (I, 470). "...innascibilitas est privatio quae secundum rem est perfecta positio. Innascibilis enim dicitur Pater, quia non est ab alio; et non esse ab alio est esse primum, et primitas est nobilis positio... Unde quia primum, ideo principium... ratio primitatis in aliquo genere est ratio principiandi... Pater principium totius divinitatis, quia a nullo."

[50] I *Sent.* d. 27, p. 1, a.un., q. 2, ad 3 (I, 470) and *Brevil.* 1, 3 (V, 212). That we are here dealing with a particular concern of Bonaventure is reflected not only in the content but also in the length of the treatment given to the question in the *Sentence Commentary.*

origin and is therefore innascible, since there is nothing prior to Him.[51] It appears, then, that we come to know the Father by the relation of origin. But if generation is the act of a person who begets, is that person constituted as person by the act of generation ? Or is that person constituted in his personal property prior to the act of generation ?[52] For Bonaventure, the act of generation is logically prior to paternity,[53] though in reality paternity and generation are identical.[54] Viewed from the negative perspective (innascibility), the Father can be said to be constituted in His personal property prior to the act of generation, though this negative dimension is not adequate for a full understanding of the Father. Corresponding to the bipolar concept of the first person described above, we must go beyond the negative to the complementary positive which would lead to the conclusion that the Father is constituted as Father in the full sense in the act of generation: "Ideo Pater, quia generat."[55] The constitution of the Father, therefore, is understood in a less full and in a fuller sense corresponding to the negative pole of innascibility and the positive pole of fecundity and primacy. This is the ultimate extension of the principle: "Principium quia primum." Because the Father is innascible, He is absolutely first; and because He is absolutely first, He is the fecund source of others. Because He is innascible, He is known as Father, but He is Father in the fullest sense in the act of generation. The philosophical principle drawn from the *Liber de causis* has been fully exploited to single out the Father as dynamic source whose fecundity finds its first expression in the two inner-divine emanations.[56]

Paternity, then, is the notion that best designates the first person in His personal property; since it designates Him in a positive sense

---

[51] This bipolar concept of the Father may be seen as underlying much of the dialectical style of Bonaventure's thought. It is seen by E. Cousins as the real basis for the thought pattern described as the coincidence of opposites, and which Cousins traces throughout Bonaventure's system. In this instance, innascibility and fecundity are mutually complementary opposites which cannot be formally reduced to one or the other; the Father is generative power precisely because He is unbegotten. Cf. Cousins, ibid.

[52] I *Sent.* d. 27, p. 1, a.un., q. 2 (I, 468) where the question is raised: "...utrum hypostasis Patris sive Pater ideo generat, quia Pater est, vel ideo sit pater, quia generat." Bonaventure's position favors the latter: "Pater, quia generat."

[53] Loc cit., p. 469: "...prius est generare quam esse patrem secundum ordinem intelligendi."

[54] I *Sent.* d. 27, p. 1, a.un., q. 1 (I, 468): "...omnino sunt eadem proprietas secundum rem." However, they signify in different ways at the logical level.

[55] I *Sent.* d. 27, p. 1, a.un., q. 2, resp. (I, 469).

[56] I *Sent.* d. 27, p. 1, a.u., q. 2, ad 3 (I, 471): "...primitas in prima persona est ratio producendi alias; et quia innascibilis dicit primitatem, hinc est quod dicit fontalem plenitudinem respectu productionis personalis."

and in terms of His relation to the Son, which is proper to the Father alone. Even though innascibility or primacy lies at the root of the personal character of the Father, it is in paternity that He finds the fullness of His personal reality.[57] While innascibility is logically prior, paternity is that which distinguishes the Father fully from the other persons.[58]

Other notions that pertain to the Father are spirator and principle. Spirator designates Him, together with the Son, as the source of the Spirit while principle designates Him as the point of origin for the immanent processions and as ultimate source of all creation. Thus, He is principle in a two-fold sense; namely, principle precisely as point of origin for another when no causal relationship is involved; and principle as cause with respect to created reality.

In this understanding of the proper characteristic of the Father, we see the ultimate basis of Bonaventure's metaphysical system whereby all comes forth from the Father and returns to the Father.[59] Not only does the gift of existence flow from the Father, but the gifts of knowledge and grace as well, coming to us from the loving Father who loves us with the same act of love by which he loves the Son and the Spirit. The religious development of the human person is nothing other than the entrance of the created spirit into that life-giving and beatifying movement of all reality from the Father and to the Father; and in this is rooted the spiritual journey of humankind.[60]

V. THE SON

> *"Sacred Scripture says that God has an offspring whom He loves supremely, a Word coequal with Him 'whom He has begotten in eternity and in whom He has disposed all things.'"* Brevil. 1, 2 (V, 211).

As we have seen above, God is by His very nature a mystery a self-diffusive good. It is, therefore, the emanations from that primal goodness, focused most radically in the Father, that give rise to the two other divine persons. The emanations, consequently, are modes

---

[57] I *Sent.* d. 29, dub. (I, 517); d. 28, q. 3, resp. (I, 501). "Proprietas personalis Patris est paternitas, non innascibilitas."

[58] I *Sent.* d. 28, dub. 1 (I, 504). "Distinctio... quasi inchoatur in innascibilitate... consummatur in paternitate."

[59] *Hex.* 1, 17 (V, 332): "Per primariam veritatem omnes redire debent, ut, sicut Filius dixit: Exivi a Patre et veni in mundum; iterum relinquo mundum et vado ad Patrem; sic dicat quilibet: Domine, exivi a te summo, venio ad te summum et per te summum."

[60] *Qq. Dd.* q. 8, ad 7 (V, 115).

of production immanent to the life of God. To clarify more exactly the meaning of these productive emanations, Bonaventure reaches to the philosophy of Aristotle. There are three types of emanations, writes the Philosopher, fortuitous, natural, and voluntary.[61] But since Bonaventure could see nothing fortuitous in God, he considers only the latter two and concludes that there are only two perfect modes of emanation which are found in God who is the supremely communicative good. Thus are derived the two terms *per modum naturae* and *per modum voluntatis* to designate the two inner-divine emanations.[62]

Since generation is a mode of communicating reality from one being to another, and since God is supremely communicative and the source of all coummnication, generation ought to be present in Him in some way.[63] In searching for an analogue to clarify the meaning of generation in God, Bonaventure chooses that sort of generation by which one organic, living being emerges from another.[64] The superiority of this type of production lies in the fact that here is found the most complete likeness between the producer and that which he produces. If we were to remove any type of imperfection from this example, it could serve as an analogy for speaking of God. We must say, for example, that in God the one who is produced is not separated from the producer and has no need to grow, but is produced totally in his full perfection. Nor is the one produced formed from a part of the divine substance. Rather, the one who produces communicates totally the substance of divinity to the one produced.[65] When all imperfections are thus removed from the example, it is possible to say that God, as Father, generates a Son by communicating the whole of His substance to His offspring. The Son proceeds from the Father *substantialiter et originaliter*,[66] in the sense that He has His source in the Father.

When generation is conceived in this way, the result is the existence of a total, personal similitude. Such likeness pertains to the essence of the concept of generation. Thus, while the analogy of generation provides the basis for designating the term of the ge-

---

[61] *Metaph.* 6, t. 22 (Bekker 1032, a 12-13).
[62] I *Sent.* d. 2, a.u., q. 4, fund. 2 (I, 56); *Brevil.* 1, 3 (V, 211).
[63] I *Sent.* d. 9, a.u., q. 1, resp. (I, 181).
[64] Ibid. Other types of production which he rejects as less adequate are: 1) the manner of production whereby a ring produces an image in wax; 2) the production found in the inorganic realm, as a fire can be produced from wood (sic generatur elementum ab elemento). These seem far less adequate than the type of production found at the level of living beings.
[65] I *Sent.* d. 5, a. 1, q. 2, resp. (I, 115).
[66] Ibid.

nerative act as *Son*, the element of perfect likeness leads to the use of the terms *Word* and *Image*.[67]

As we have indicated above, Bonaventure's understanding of the generation of the Son is ultimately rooted in the Dionysian metaphysics of the good. This implies a certain type of necessity which is expressed in the term: emanation *per modum naturae;* for at this level, God is conceived in terms of a necessary self-communication which arises by reason of His very nature as the good. The term *natural emanation* expresses an understanding of generation different from that of Augustine and Aquinas, both of whom prefer to speak of this as an emanation by way of the intellect. Bonaventure also sees the intellect to be involved. But his guiding light is the concept of primal, fecund goodness. The intellect precisely as intellect is not fecund; it is so only in as far as it springs from the fecund nature of God. Thus, the primary principle of the Son's generation is the divine nature; the natural fecundity of the neo-Platonic tradition dominates this understanding. The Augustinian tradition is integrated within this framework. That which flows from the divine essence naturally does so as a perfect self-expression of the Father; it is the Word of the intellect.[68]

The generation of the Son cannot be conceived in this way without raising the question of necessity and the relation of such generation to the divine will. Without doubt, there is a type of necessity involved here. But how is it to be conceived? Of the many types of necessity that can be distinguished,[69] only the necessity of immutability may be applied to God. It cannot be a necessity that

---

[67] I *Sent.* d. 27, p. 2, a.u., q. 1, fund. 5 (I, 481); d. 27, p. 2, a.u., q. 3, resp. (I, 488); I *Sent.* d. 31, p. 2, a. 1, q. 2, fund. 3 (I, 541). These names for the second person will be treated more fully below.

[68] I *Sent.* d. 27, p. 2, a.u., q. 4, resp. (I, 496): "sic verbum intellectus a mente procedit per modum naturae per omnia ei simile et aequale."

[69] I *Sent.* d. 6, a.u., q. 1, resp. (I, 125 ff.); *Qq. Dd.* q. 7, a. 1 & 2 (V, 106-112). The following types of necessity are distinguished:

a) *Disconveniens*	Violence.	One is moved against his nature from outside.	
	Coaction.	One is moved against his will from outside.	
b) *Deficiens*	Indigence.	The needs internal to a nature with respect to something external to it. E.g. food and drink as needs of human beings.	
	Inevitability.	A necessity arising from some defect. E.g. death because of sin.	
c) *Conveniens*	Exigence.	Found in a principle that has a natural ordination to another. E.g. Matter has exigence for form.	
	Completion.	Also called "necessity of immutability." It is totally immanent to the nature involved.	

is imposed on Him from outside Himself; nor can it be any sort of divine need for a created being as the necessary condition for His existence as God. It can only be the inner necessity of the divine being to be always and completely self-sufficient and totally in conformity with itself.[70] Because God is totally self-sufficient and completely true to His nature as the fecund good, He can and will communicate the totality of His substance without loosing His own identity. He who is fully sufficient in His own being, precisely for that reason can be fully self-communicative without threat to Himself. In this sense, the necessity of immutability sheds further light on the generation of the Son.

Is there, then, no relation between this generation and the divine will ? Since the divine nature and the divine will are really identical, that which pertains to the nature cannot be totally unrelated to the will. Just as there is a relation between the divine intellect and generation, so there is a relation between the divine will and generation. The will can be viewed in two principal ways; either as the principal productive power, or as a will that accompanies and approves that which proceeds from the nature.[71] The will as a productive power is reserved by Bonaventure for the analysis of the procession of the Holy Spirit. As regards the generation of the Son, since this proceeds from the nature as from its primary principle, the will accompanies the act of generation as *approbans*.[72] Thus, Bonaventure can conclude that the Son is produced "ut omnino similis et per modum naturae, nihilominus ut dilectus;"[73] though He proceeds by necessity of nature, yet He proceeds as the Beloved of the Father. The creaturely categories of necessity and freedom are transcended in the dialectical unity of the necessity of immutability with the accompanying and approving will.

The Son, who proceeds from the Father as a Word, proceeds by way of exemplarity.[74] Exemplarity has a critical role to play in Bonaventure's thought both at the philosophical and at the theological levels. It is only exemplarity that can unlock the deepest meaning of created reality to the human mind, for it is only when we perceive the world in its symbolic nature as the objectification of the self-knowledge of God that we know it in its true reality. In the most basic sense, it is God in His own self-knowledge who is the exemplar of all else; but since God exists only as a trinity, exem-

---

[70] I *Sent.* d. 6, a.u., q. 1, resp. (I, 126): "Quia ipse solus est qui sibi omnino sufficit et qui secum omnino convenit."
[71] I *Sent.* d. 6, a.u., q. 2, resp. (I, 127-128).
[72] Ibid.: "...natura est primum principium, concomitante voluntate."
[73] Ibid.
[74] I *Sent.* d. 6, a.u., q. 3, fund. 1 (I, 129).

plarity refers to the entire trinity. But in a special manner, the mystery of the trinity itself is reflected in the mystery of the second person. As the full and total expression of God's primal fruitfulness, the Son is simultaneously the expression of all that God can be in relation to the finite. The question of exemplarity, therefore, is fundamental to any consideration of Bonaventure's treatment of the generation of the Son.

The question is raised first of all in the discussion of the generative act in God.[75] Here Bonaventure distinguishes two ways in which a procession of exemplarity can be understood. The first way refers to the *exemplatum* in the proper sense; that is, it refers to a being which is truly other than and distinct from the original which it resembles. Understood in this way, it is the created world that is the *exemplatum* proceeding from God as from its exemplar.[76] The second way refers to the very *ratio exemplandi*[77] that is, to the very basis in God Himself for all exemplarity. This refers to the emanation of the Son who is the Word of God's self-expression in whom God disposes all things. Quoting St. Augustine,[78] the Seraphic Doctor describes this as the divine art of all living things, whence flows the truth and beauty of all things;[79] as the representation of God, the Word is also the model of all God does and can do. Such a mode of procession can only be a natural one and stands in contrast with the emanation of creatures whose production flows from a decree of the divine will. Thus, while at one level the whole of the trinity is exemplary with respect to the world, at another level the mystery of exemplarity is concentrated in a unique way in the Son. To speak of Him as exemplar designates not a mere appropriation but a property of the second person.[80] The triune structure of God Himself is expressed in the Son.[81] The relation between Father and Son is the first and primal relation, and the basis for all other relation. So it is that, as the Word is the inner self-expression of God, the created order is the external expression of the inner Word. Whatever created reality exists possesses in its inner consti-

---

[75] I *Sent.* d. 6, a.u., q. 1-3 (I, 124-130). The question of generation in God is treated in three questions: 1) Whether the generation of the Son is necessary; 2) Whether it proceeds from the will of God; and 3) Whether it proceeds in an exemplary way. The content of the first two questions has been analyzed above.
[76] Loc. cit., q. 3, resp. (I, 129) "...sic creatura procedit a Deo tanquam exemplatum ab exemplari, et sic exemplar importat causalitatem formalem respectu exemplati."
[77] Ibid.
[78] *De trin.* VI, 10, n. 11 (PL 42, 931).
[79] I *Sent.* d. 6, a.u., q. 3, resp. (I, 130); *Brevil.* 1, 8 (V, 216); *Hex.* 1, 13 (V, 331).
[80] I *Sent.* d. 6, a.u., q. 3, ad 4 (I, 130).
[81] *Hex.* 9, 2 (V, 373); 3, 7 (V, 344).

tution a relation to the uncreated Word; and since the Word, in turn, is the expression of the inner trinitarian structure of God, that which is created as an expression of the Word bears the imprint of the trinity.

THE TITLES OF THE SECOND PERSON

"By the fact that He is Son, He is also Image, and for that very reason, He is Word." I Sent. d. 31, p. 2, a. 1, q. 2, resp. (I, 542).

Scripture speaks of the second person not only as Son, but as Image and as Word as well. Bonaventure employs each of these titles to express particular aspects of the mystery of the second person. The Son is He who is conceived from the depths of divine goodness; Image designates Him precisely as self-likeness; but Word adds over and above this that He is the *ratio exprimendi et manifestandi*.[82]

Son. It is clear from Bonaventure's approach to the major trinitarian questions that the first title to be applied to the second person is the title of Son. This title names a person precisely in as far as he is begotten by another as a distinct person who is the perfect likeness of the generative source and who is intimately related to its source by love.[83] In this description can be seen the major elements involved in Bonaventure's analysis of generation. Central to that notion of generation is the likeness between the producer and the one produced.[84] Corresponding to the natural emanation is the idea that the Son represents a likeness in the order of nature. In as far as the term of the emanation is a hypostasis, it is called also a hypostatic likeness or a personal likeness.

Although the title Son is the first designation of the second person, and is in full harmony with the general framework of the theology developed by Bonaventure, yet it has decided limitations;

---

[82] I *Sent.* d. 27, p. 2, a.u., q. 3, resp. (I, 488).
[83] I *Sent.* d. 31, q. 2, a. 1, q. 2, resp. (I, 542); *Brevil.* 1, 3 (V, 212).
[84] I *Sent.* d. 27, p. 2, a.u., q. 1, ad 4 (I, 483). It is proper to the Father alone to beget a Word. While the Son and the Spirit know themselves, they do not beget a Word from themselves because they do not possess the *fecunditas ad generandum* which is the Father's alone. It is necessary, therefore, to distinguish between the essential act of knowledge and the notional act. The first is common to all three persons; by virtue of it each knows himself and the other persons together with all created things. The second is that act by which the Father produces the Word from His fecund self-knowledge.

for it designates the Son only in terms of His relation to the Father.[85] There is much more that can and must be said about the second person, and this will appear under Bonaventure's analysis of Image and Word. But even though the range of significance for this title is limited, it has the decided advantage of emphasizing the fact that the fruit of the first divine emanation is fully and totally personal being as is the Father. The term lends itself to further interpretation through the analysis of the modalities of love. While the Father is love that is totally active and communicative, and the Spirit is love that is totally receptive, the Son is that modality of love *ab utroque permixtus;*[86] He is love as first receptive and then as responsive and communicative. From all eternity, therefore, the Son is one who is totally from the Father and totally responsive to the Father. If we recall that the relation between Father and Son is the ontological basis of all other relations, it appears that created reality should bear the stamp of Sonship in the deepest core of its being. As the Son is from the Father, so all created reality is at root the pure reception of being. As the Son responds to the Father and in His response together with the Father breathes forth the Spirit, so all created reality is destined to return to the Father.[87] We see here the basis for the metaphysical structure of *egressio — regressio* which we have already referred to in speaking of the mystery of the Father. The whole of creation is stamped by this law of Sonship — both in its over-arching structure and history as well as in particular creatures. It is above all in humanity that this ontological structure may be perceived, where we find created beings who are consciously present in time and who experience the polarity between origins and eschatology, *exitus* and *reditus,* in each present moment of their existence, the human person is called to the active, personal response of trust, love, and hope in the fulfillment of its being.

Thus, although from one perspective, the meaning of the title Son is limited in scope, from another perspective it has a remarkable theological depth which aids in clarifying more adequately the personal ground of the created world.

Image. The title Image adds yet another dimension of meaning to the understanding of the second person. In the *Breviloquium,* Bonaventure writes that this term emphasizes the degree of like-

---

[85] I *Sent.* d. 31, p. 2, a. 1, q. 2, resp. (I, 542): "Sed filius dicit solum respectum ad Patrem."
[86] I *Sent.* d. 2, a.u., q. 4, resp. (I, 57); *Itin.* 6, 2 (V, 311); III *Sent.* d. 1, a. 2, q. 3, resp. (III, 29 ff.).
[87] I *Sent.* d. 2, q. 2, ad 4 (I, 54): "In primo est status" is here applied specifically to the Father.

ness; it is *expressed* and *conformed*,⁸⁸ and may be called a true imitation. It means far more than a mere chance or superficial resemblance. While the Son does not imitate the Father in the latter's strictly personal property of *being without source*, yet the imitation goes so far as to include the reflection of the Father's character as *source of others*.⁸⁹

This is clarified in more detail in the *Sentence Commentary*. When the term Image is applied to God, it signifies not only expression but the highest expression.⁹⁰ Such an expression involves two elements: 1) that it be one expression of one being; 2) that it be an expression in every respect. That being which is supremely one will find its highest self-expression not in a multiplicity of images, but in one only, which would be the most perfect reflecting likeness. Unless such an image would reflect its source in every way possible, it would not express it in the highest degree.

The first element leads Bonaventure to conclude that only the Son is truly the Image of the Father, because only He proceeds from one person alone, while the Spirit proceeds from two persons, expressing both of them, and hence expressing neither of them in the fullest degree.⁹¹

The explanation of the second element is considerably fuller, and it is especially here that we see how the title Image has a wider range of significance than the title Son. While Son designates only the relation of the second person to the Father, Image designates the Son's relation to the Father "a quo est" as well as His relation to the Spirit "qui ex ipso est."⁹² In terms of the first relation, the Son proceeds naturally from the Father as Word and Species and as a totally expressive likeness. The second relation involves the fact that the Son is coprinciple with the Father in the spiration of the Spirit. As Image, therefore, His likeness approaches the very property of the Father Himself. Though it does not push to the level of innascibility in its negative side, it does include the reflection of the positive side; the Son, like the Father and together with the Father, is the active source of another.⁹³ Thus it becomes clear why the term Image is applied only to the Son and not to the Spirit.

---

⁸⁸ *Brevil.* 1, 3 (V, 212).
⁸⁹ Ibid.
⁹⁰ I *Sent.* d. 31, p. 2, a. 1, q. 2, resp. (I, 542); d. 3, p. 2, dub. 4 (I, 94); d. 27, p. 2, dub. 2 (I, 491).
⁹¹ Ibid.
⁹² Ibid.
⁹³ Ibid.

Word. Bonaventure frequently expresses a preference for the title *Word*, which appears to him to be the richest in meaning. In the *Sentence Commentary*, he contrasts it with the previous two titles briefly by saying that it expresses the relation of the second person both to the Father and to creation.[94] In his *Commentary on John* this is expressed far more elaborately:

> ...the term "word" expresses not only a relation to the one speaking, but to that which is expressed through the word, to the sound with which it clothes itself, and to the knowledge effected in others through the mediation of the word. And since here the Son of God is to be described not only in terms of His relation to the Father from whom He proceeds, but also in terms of His relation to the creatures which He has made, as well as to the flesh with which He was clothed and to the truth which He has given us, He is most nobly and fittingly described as the Word; for that name includes all these relations, and a more fitting name could not be found anywhere in the world.[95]

Here the second person is related not only to the Father, but to the entire mystery of creation, revelation, and incarnation. He is seen as the one through whom all the Father's self-communications take place. As the Word is the self-expression of the Father within the Godhead, the world is the external objectification of that self-utterance in that which is not God. And the humanity of Jesus is the fullest objectification of that self-utterance within the created world.

In explicating the meaning of the Word, Bonaventure draws extensively from the human experience of self-consciousness and knowledge, making full use of the elements of the cognitive process: concept, word, and vocal expression.[96] Bonaventure distinguishes a two-fold speaking. There is an inner speaking to oneself, a speaking in the spirit, which is none other than our awareness of self or of another. This inner presence of that which is known is a sort of spiritual process of conception and birth which terminates in an inner word, or the conscious knowledge of that which is known. This inner speech precedes any external speaking whereby the inner word is communicated to another spiritual being.[97] Transferring the genesis of knowledge and speech analogically from the human person

---

[94] Ibid.
[95] *Comm. in Joan.* c. I, p. 1, q. 1 (VI, 247).
[96] I *Sent.* d. 27, p. 2, a.u., q. 3, resp. (I, 487).
[97] I *Sent.* d. 27, p. 2, q. 1, resp. (I, 482).

to God,[98] Bonaventure shows again to what extent the generation of the Word is a natural generation. God is the supreme form of spiritual being, and as such, He is both perfectly simple and supremely fecund. It cannot be, therefore, that He is in any way less than the created spirit found in the human person. If self-consciousness and self-knowledge are truly perfections of spiritual being, it follows that they must be found in God in the highest degree. Such self-knowledge is called an inner word.

> "A word is nothing other than an expressed and expressive likeness conceived by the power of an intelligent spirit by which it knows itself or another."[99]

The inner Word of God, therefore, is the self-knowledge of God precisely as goodness and love, as fecund source of all that is and can be. In His inner Word, God knows not only Himself, but all the ways in which He can communicate Himself to others, including this actual world-order and all other possible worlds which will never be created. Such self-knowledge flows from the very nature of God as spiritual being that is goodness and love, and hence is to be distinguished from the speaking of the external word which is not an act of nature but one of the will. Thus, the external word which proceeds from God is not to be identified with God; it is a creature. Though it is other than God in being, yet it reflects the mystery of God since the divine trinity is the fecund exemplar of all actual and possible things.[100]

In summary, the title *Word* designates the second person precisely as the perfect imitative likeness of the Father who is the fecund source of all (= *similitudo Patris imitativa*); but precisely as such, He is simultaneously the exemplar of creation (= *similitudo rerum exempla-*

---

[98] I *Sent.* d. 27, p. 2, a.u., q. 1, resp. (I, 482); q. 2, resp. (I, 485).
[99] I *Sent.* d. 27, p. 2, a.u., q. 3, resp. (I, 488).
[100] I *Sent.* d. 27, p. 2, a.u., q. 1, resp. (I, 482). Bonaventure distinguishes between *loqui ad se* and *loqui ad alterum*. The first refers to the inner act of intellectual generation whose term is the conceived word. As it refers to God, it designates the *verbum natum et aeternum*. The second refers to the projection of our knowledge in an external form; it is the *verbum prolatum*. As applied to God, it signifies the *verbum creatum et temporale*. Therefore, there is a most intimate relation between God's inner speaking and His external speaking, and hence between the Word and the world. Indeed, the Word is the *mundus archetypus*. I *Sent.* d. 27, p. 2, q. 2, resp. (I, 485); *Hex.* 3, 4 (V, 343-344). While there is a strong line of continuity between the inner and outer word, Bonaventure's doctrine of the analogy of being excludes any Hegelian interpretation of the God-world relationship.

tiva). Thus He holds a middle place, as it were, between the Father and the world, and it is through the Word that the Father Himself is operative (= *similitudo operativa*).[101]

THE SON AS CENTER

Already in the *Sentence Commentary*, Bonaventure conceives of the second person as the center of the life of the trinity thus establishing a motif which would eventually assume far-reaching significance in his later writings. In the text just cited above, Bonaventure sees the Word to hold a middle place between the Father and the world. But as regards the inner life of God Himself, the person of the Son is placed at the very center of the divine reality.

This appears first in the derivation of the divine emanation from the analysis of love. Following the Victorine tradition, Bonaventure distinguishes a love which is totally *gratuitus* and another which is totally *debitus;* between them is a modality of love which is *ab utroque permixtus;*[102] one which gives, one which receives, and one which both receives and gives. The same type of structure appears if we view the persons in terms of the mystery of origin. There is one person who is origin alone; there is another who comes forth but is in no way origin of another; there is a third who both comes forth and is principle of another.[103] The underlying structure may be seen in the following schema:

Totally active and communicative	→	First receptive and then communicative	←	Totally passive and receptive

These conform fully to Bonaventure's understanding of the three persons and the mystery of the eternal emanations. Here also is the metaphysical basis for the Bonaventurean esthetics of order.[104] In viewing the world, he sees the beauty of its order to consist in the fact that all things have a beginning, a middle, and an end. In this

---

[101] I *Sent.* d. 27, p. 2, a.u., q. 2, resp. (I, 485): "Verbum, quod est similitudo Patris imitativa et similitudo rerum exemplativa et similitudo operativa; et ita tenet quasi medium, et dicitur Pater operari per Verbum..."
[102] I *Sent.* d. 2, a.u., q. 4, resp. (I, 57); *Itin.* 6, 2 (V, 311).
[103] Ibid.
[104] Cf. A. J. W. Hellmann, *Ordo: Untersuchung eines Grundgedankens in der Theologie Bonaventuras* (Schöningh, 1974). The whole of this study is devoted to the concept of *ordo* and its far-reaching significance in the total thought of the Seraphic Doctor. Hellmann has succeeded admirably in elaborating the metaphysical and Christological grounding of the concept.

way, they can be seen to reflect the orderly life of the triune God in whom there may be seen an analogous structure. The theme of the center would become ever more crucial in Bonaventure's thought, finding its most consistent and compact expression in the *Hexaemeron*[105] where we find it applied to all levels of the mystery of Christ. The eternal Son who is the center of the trinity, and who mediates all the divine works of creation and illumination, in becoming incarnate assumes His place as the center of the created universe and its history. Thus, theology, Christology, anthropology, creation, illumination, revelation are brought together tightly around the one universal center of meaning.

Not only does all emanate from the Father through the Word; but the return of all things back to the Father can take place only through the same Word who stands at the very center of reality. And through the whole of the divine economy, the Seraphic Doctor can see a common principle operative which reflects the universal mediatorial significance of the Word: "It is the law of the divinity that lower beings be led to the highest beings by means of beings that lie in the middle between the extremes."[106]

Together with the Father, the Son may be designated by the notion *spirator;* for both together constitute one principle of a common spiration. Since the Spirit proceeds from the Son as well as from the Father, the Son also may be called *principle;* but to distinguish Him from the Father, it is necessary to qualify this as *principle from another.* The term expresses both His relation to the Father as well as His relation to the Spirit; He is totally from the Father; and together with the Father, He is the principle from which the Spirit comes.

VI. THE HOLY SPIRIT

> "*The Holy Spirit proceeds as love; He is the Gift in whom all gifts are given.*" I Sent. d. 6, a.u., q. 3, resp. (I, 129).

It is above all in the emanation of the Holy Spirit that we discover Bonaventure's personal appropriation of the Victorine tradition. While it was possible to use the Dionysian argument from the good to arrive at a plurality springing from the dynamism of the divine nature, it was not only possible but necessary to augment this by the personal and psychological dimensions present in the Victorine analysis of love. Corresponding to the natural emanation of the Son,

---

[105] *Hex.* 1, 10-39 (V, 330-335).
[106] *Brevil.* 2, 9 (V, 226).

the full perfection of God requires that there be also a voluntary emanation proceeding from pure liberality; for God is not an impersonal good, but the primal good existing precisely as supreme personal good. But the perfect actuality of personal being is to exist as love, and love is an act of the will from which flows all liberality. If, then, God is to be conceived as a personal God, there must be in Him liberality as well.[107] For Bonaventure, this is the question of the procession of the Spirit who proceeds *per modum voluntatis;*[108] since the divine nature which is supremely fecund can do no other than produce a person, so also the divine will which is supremely liberal can do no less.[109]

The argument from love first appears in the *Sentence Commentary* as one of the arguments for a plurality in God. It appears there in a simple form: "Caritas non sit amor privatus, sed ad alterum."[110] It is used later to argue for limiting the number of persons to three since love exists in three primary modalities.[111] In treating the question of the emanation of the Spirit, it becomes necessary to give greater precision to the meaning of the term *love*.

In Bonaventure's view, love is the first of all the affections and root of all the others.[112] Love is the gift in which all other gifts are given, and without which nothing else is truly a gift. Love is the most noble of the affections because it involves true liberality and generosity.

As the term is applied to God, it is understood at three levels: 1) love as essential; 2) love as notional; and 3) love as personal.[113] Essential love designates that love which is found in all three persons by reason of their nature as God, by which they love themselves; it is divine love in the absolute sense. Notional love is that which is common to the Father and the Son; the act by which each is turned to the other in mutual love. This is the summit of love, for nothing is more delightful than mutual love; and without love, nothing else is truly enjoyable. Yet, if love is directed to another, then the mutual love of two directed to each other would become a sort of mutual narcissism if they did not mutually turn their love to a

---

[107] I *Sent.* d. 10, a. 1, q. 1, resp. (I, 195).
[108] I *Sent.* d. 6, a.u., q. 2, resp. (I, 128): "Processus per modum voluntatis concomitante natura."
[109] I *Sent.* d. 10, a. 1, q. 1, resp. (I, 195).
[110] I *Sent.* d. 2, a.u., q. 2, fund. 1 (I, 53).
[111] I *Sent.* d. 2, a.u., q. 4, resp. (I, 57).
[112] I *Sent.* d. 10, a. 1, q. 2, resp. (I, 197). Cf. also, R. Prentice, *The Psychology of Love according to St. Bonaventure* (N.Y., 1957) p. 80-81.
[113] I *Sent.* d. 10, a. 2, q. 1, resp. (I, 201).

third who could share it.[114] It is this mutual love between the Father and the Son which is called *concord*,[115] and from it proceeds the Spirit. Bonaventure clarifies this with the following example.[116] The love between a husband and wife by which they intend to live together is called social love, and may be taken as an analogue for the essential love in God. Their conjugal love by which they love each other with a view to begetting a child corresponds to the concord between the Father and the Son. If their mutual love were to bring forth only a spiritual emanation between them, that emanation — their spiritual offspring — could justifiably be called *amor*. When, in fact, such love finds its fruit in the begetting of a child, the child is called not *amor*, but *amatus;* it is not love itself, but is the loved one. Applying the analogy to the trinity, Bonaventure concludes that that which proceeds in liberality from the concord between the Father and the Son is truly and properly *amor*. He is love because He proceeds from perfect liberality; He is person because, though He is distinguished from those who produce Him, yet He cannot be distinguished from them in essence. The distinction, therefore, must be one of person.[117] It is in this sense that the Spirit is called personal love; and His procession is designated as an emanation *per modum voluntatis, concomitante natura*.[118]

This sheds light on the question of the relation of Father and Son to the Spirit. The Spirit is personal love that proceeds from the mutual love between the Father and the Son who, as one principle, breathe forth the Spirit. Fully aware of the Greek position on this question,[119] Bonaventure expounds his thesis quite fully, presenting

---

[114] I *Sent*. d. 10, a. 1, q. 1, fund. 1 (I, 194-195). "Perfectior est dilectio mutua quam reflexa, et perfectior adhuc mutua communicata quam non communicata, quia talis scilicet non communicata, videtur sapere amorem libidinosum."
[115] I *Sent*. d. 10, a. 2, q. 1, resp. (I, 201).
[116] Ibid.
[117] Ibid.
[118] I *Sent*. d. 6, a.u., q. 2, resp. (I, 128). Other terms used by Bonaventure are *procedens per mutuum amorem;* and *per modum liberalitatis*.
[119] I *Sent*. d. 11, a.u., q. 1 (I, 209-213); Stohr, op. cit., p. 56 ff. Bonaventure's response is given totally to the discussion of the Latin-Greek controversy. He sees the Greeks to be using analogies that are more material and therefore less apt than the analogies used by Latin theology. In doing so, the Greek position limits the understanding of Scripture to the temporal procession of the Spirit and thus leads to a distortion in the understanding of the doctrine. Concerning the actual profession of faith in the Greek understanding, Bonaventure's judgment is harsh, seeing the error to proceed from ignorance, pride, and stubbornness and leading to heresy and schism. Bonaventure stands in close relation to the *Summa Halensis* (I, q. 43, m. 4); none of the content of Bonaventure's position is original to him, though it is presented in a more compact and orderly way. To what degree this understanding of the Greek position is an accurate reflection of their own theology remains a disputed question.

arguments both from Scripture and from theological reasoning. The Scriptural arguments are drawn from *John* 15, 16; *John* 16, 14; and *Galatians* 4, 6; texts which indicate that the Spirit is the Spirit both of the Father and of the Son. The arguments reflect Bonaventure's economic trinitarian style clearly in as far as each is based on the factual correspondence between the mission of the Spirit in the history of grace and the eternal emanation. Accordingly, one who is sent by the Father and Son in history is the one who proceeds from the Father and Son eternally.

The first three theological arguments are drawn from titles commonly used to name the Spirit; gift, love, and bond.[120] Scripture designates the Spirit as the gift given us by the Son, and both the Greeks and the Latins agree on this. But the gift is given only by a person from whom the gift proceeds; therefore, if the historical mission corresponds to the eternal emanation, the Spirit must proceed from the Son. Since it is theologically undisputed that the Spirit proceeds from the Father, it follows that He must proceed from both the Father and the Son. It is commonly held that the Spirit proceeds as love; but love is not in the Father alone but in the Son as well. If love proceeds from the Father, it proceeds from the Son as well. A third commonly used title for the Spirit is *bond;* for He is the bond between the Father and the Son. But He would be a bond in a more perfect sense if He stood in an immediate relation to both of the other persons than if He stood in an immediate relation to one and in a mediate relation to the other. The understanding of bond may be further clarified by the argument from *germanitas*. The relation between two productive persons is more intimate if, in the act of production, they are not independent of each other, but mutually related in the productive act. Such an intimate interrelation would include a greater degree of unity between them, and consequently a greater degree of bliss. The final theological argument clearly reflects what was said earlier concerning the Son as the Image of the Father. The Son would be a more perfect Image of the Father if He reflected the Father not only in terms of His divine nature but in terms of His personal property, if that be possible without negating the identity of the Father. As Image, the Son shares in the positive dimension of the mystery of the Father, that aspect which designates the Father as fecund source of others. Thus, without sharing in the negative dimension of innascibility, the Son, like the Father and together with the Father, is the source of another to whom, with the Father, He communicates the divine nature.

---

[120] I *Sent.* d. 11, a.u., q. 1 (I, 210-211) for all the following arguments.

Throughout, Bonaventure sees the Father and Son in terms of the greatest intimacy. So great is their intimacy that the Spirit proceeds from them as from one principle in as far as they are one in the fecundity of the divine will.[121] Again the notion of primacy appears in the argument. Both the Father and the Son are logically prior to the procession of love and therefore possess the full fecundity of the divine will. Since this fruitfulness is but one and is found in both the Father and the Son, they must be seen as one unified principle of the Spirit. Corresponding to the property of the Father, in whom the fullness of primacy resides, He is prior to both emanations. The Son, on the other hand, is Himself generated but is prior to the second emanation. The Spirit proceeds from the Father and the Son not precisely in as far as they are different, but in as far as there is one fecund will in both of them.[122]

Though the Father and the Son are together involved in the act of spiration, yet a distinction must be made between them since the Father is the source of the Son. Consequently, the Son's ability to spirate is a power which He receives from the Father. This must be understood to refer strictly to priority of origin and in no way to a priority in duration or causality.[123] In this sense, it is possible to say that the Spirit proceeds from the Father *principaliter et per se*.[124] From this perspective, it is possible to say that the Spirit proceeds both mediately and immediately. He proceeds mediately in as far as He proceeds from the Son who Himself proceeds from the Father. But He proceeds immediately in as far as He proceeds from the Father, who proceeds from no other source.[125]

The emanation of the Spirit is from the most perfect act of will. Yet the liberality from which He proceeds must be clearly distinguished from the freedom by which God creates the world. The liberality by which the Spirit emanates is a necessary quality of the mystery of divine love while the freedom by which God creates involves an emanation which can in no way be qualified as necessary. As in treating the emanation of the Son, Bonaventure distinguishes that which necessarily proceeds from God as the exemplar of all reality and is therefore the very *ratio exemplandi* from that which proceeds as *exemplatum;* so also here, he distinguishes between the emanation of the Spirit as the very *ratio volendi* from the *volitum*,

---

[121] I *Sent.* d. 11, a.u., q. 2, resp. (I, 215).
[122] Ibid.
[123] I *Sent.*, d. 12, a.u., q. 1, resp. (I, 220-221).
[124] I *Sent.* d. 12, a.u., q. 2, resp. (I, 222).
[125] I *Sent.* d. 12, a.u., q. 3, resp. (I, 223).

or created reality as an actual object of the divine will.[126] Viewing the two emanations together, we can conclude that the created world is known by God in the knowledge whereby He generates the Son and is loved by Him in the love by which He spirates the Spirit. But while the inner emanations are intrinsic to His very nature as supreme goodness and love, the actual projection of the world as an external expression of His knowledge and love remains always a non-necessitated act. God does not need the world in order to exist as God, for the full and necessary self-communication of goodness and love resides in God Himself prior to any further self-communication. It is precisely this which allows the act of creation to be radically free on the part of God and which accounts for the radical contingence of the present world-order.

In the light of the above, we can now understand Bonaventure's understanding of the traditional phrase which states that the Father and the Son love each other by the Holy Spirit.[127] In no way does the Spirit exercise an active role with respect to the Father and the Son. If He is called the bond between them, this is to be understood not in an active sense as though He did something to join them, but in a passive sense; namely, in the sense that He proceeds from each of them in as far as they are actively united with each other in love (= notional love). The Spirit is the bond not because He gives something to the other persons, but because He is fully receptive. If we were to put this in the language of cause-and-effect, Bonaventure sees the Spirit as more similar to an effect than to a cause. Therefore, the ablative case found in the phrase "by the Holy Spirit" must be applied to love as notional which refers to the fecundity of the will found in only the first two persons whereby they are able to produce a third person. The Father and Son are said to be joined in the Holy Spirit, or by the Holy Spirit, not in the sense that they receive something from Him, but in the sense that there is something in them (= notional love) whereby they are the principle of the Spirit.

The two immanent emanations are distinct not only logically but in reality, since they are different both in terms of their origin and in terms of the relations which are involved.[128] Emanations exist

---

[126] I *Sent.* d. 6, a.u., q. 3, resp. (I, 129). To proceed from liberality can be taken in two ways: 1) that which proceeds is itself not liberality but something that comes from liberality. In this way, the world comes to be; 2) to proceed as the very *ratio liberalitatis*. This is to proceed as love. He who proceeds in this way is the gift in which all gifts are given. Also, I *Sent.* d. 10, a. 1, q. 1, ad 1 (I, 195) expresses the difference by using the terms *volitum* and *ratio volendi*, or *donatum* and *ratio donandi*.
[127] I *Sent.* d. 10 (I, 194 ff.) and I *Sent.* d. 32 (I, 555 ff.). The question has been studied closely by W. Principe, cf. foot-note 47 above.
[128] I *Sent.* d. 13, a.u., q. 3, resp. (I, 235).

in God because God exists as most perfect and fecund being in whom are found the two perfect modes of production; that of nature and that of will.[129] But it is not sufficient to say that there are emanations; it is necessary to show how they differ from each other. For Bonaventure, this is done most adequately in terms of the differences in the point of origin and in the relations corresponding to each. Generation is from one person, while spiration is from two. Hence, they differ in origin. The active generation of the Son in itself does not necessarily imply a third person; active spiration, on the other hand, does, since the love of the Father and Son is directed to a third without whom it would not be perfect love; hence, the Spirit proceeds as that which can be given as gift.[130] In brief, the first emanation is *per modum naturae, concomitante voluntate*, while the second is *per modum voluntatis, concomitante natura*.

THE TITLES OF THE THIRD PERSON

The names which Bonaventure favors as designations of the third person are: Love, Bond, Holy Spirit, and Gift, all of which help to express the relation of the third person to the other divine persons as well as to creation.[131]

Love. As we have seen above, the term *love* is to be understood in three ways: essential, notional, and personal.[132] The first refers to the divine essence itself, that love whereby the divine persons love themselves and all of creation. The second refers to the concord of will between the Father and the Son, or their reciprocal love from which the Spirit emanates. It is called notional to indicate that it is this love by which the second procession becomes known. As distinct from these two understandings of love, the Spirit is the hypostatic or personal love which proceeds from the perfect liberality of the divine, fecund will found in the Father and the Son. He who proceeds *per modum amoris* is Himself *Amor*.

Bond. The meaning of this title is clear from the discussion in the preceding section. It signifies that the Father and the Son are most intimately joined in the common possession of the one fecundity of will and thus, though distinct as persons, are but one principle in

---

[129] Loc. cit. (I, 236).
[130] Ibid.
[131] *Brevil.* 1, 3 (V, 212).
[132] I *Sent.* d. 10, a. 2, q. 1, resp. (I, 201).

the emanation of the Spirit. The Spirit *joins* the Father and the Son in the sense that He proceeds from the concord of their will and from their perfect liberality.[133]

Holy Spirit. While the term *spirit* can be used in various ways and can be applied both to creature and to God, it has a particular relevance with respect to the third divine person.[134] The act of breathing in our bodily life is a continuous, internal, life-giving act that arises from the warm depths within the body. It can, therefore, serve as an apt analogy for our understanding of the third person as a spiration of love. Love proceeds from the warm depths as a continuous, life-giving act; and since love is the form which human life should take, a human person is more perfect to the degree that that such love is realized. Thus, love appears as spiritual warmth, and only love is said to emanate spiritually.[135]

Thus, while at one level, the whole of the trinity is called spiritual being since it lacks all materiality, at another level, the term *spirit* has a special appropriateness in reference to the third person who proceeds as love from spiration, since in spiritual beings spiration arises only from love. And since the love that is the Spirit is most pure, perfect, and ordinate, He is called not only Spirit, but Holy Spirit.[136]

Gift. The title *Gift* is deeply rooted in the Augustinian tradition and provides the basis for a rich theology of grace. As a title, it is proper to the Spirit,[137] expressing first of all His relation to the Father and the Son as the fruit of their mutual self-giving.[138] In that is contained the fact that it is the Gift in whom all gifts are bestowed on us, but not in the sense that every gift we receive includes an unfailing communication of the Spirit Himself.[139] While it is possible that we may possess a created gift without thereby receiving the Spirit within ourselves, it is not possible that there

---

[133] I *Sent.* d. 10, a. 2, q. 2, resp. (I, 202).
[134] I *Sent.* d. 10, a. 2, q. 3, resp. (I, 204).
[135] Ibid.
[136] Ibid. In as far as the terms *holy* and *pure* have particular relevance to the will's act of love rather than to an act of nature, they are not used to designate the natural generation of the Son.
[137] I *Sent.* d. 18, a.u., q. 4, resp. (I, 328). Bonaventure distinguishes three levels of predication. 1) The whole of the trinity may be said to give itself. This is an essential predication. 2) In as far as both the Son and the Spirit are sent, they can be said to be given. This is a personal predication. 3) In the proper sense, the Holy Spirit is said to be Gift since the title expresses both His relation to the Father and the Son as well as His relation to creatures.
[138] *Brevil.* 1, 3 (V, 212). He is Gift as the one who is given through the will.
[139] I *Sent.* d. 18, a.u., q. 1, resp. (I, 323).

should exist any created gifts whatever unless there were first the eternal Gift of the Spirit who is the *ratio donandi*.

The title can be understood also in terms of causality.[140] When causality is taken simply and with no further qualifications, the three persons are not distinguished since all gifts are given by all three equally. When causality is understood together with relations among the persons particularly with respect to subauthority, the Spirit is distinguished from the Father, but not from the Son, since the Father confers all gifts through the Son and through the Spirit. When causality is seen together with subauthority and exemplarity, the proper application to the Spirit emerges; as the first gift, He is the exemplary basis of all proper and free giving.[141]

It is with the spiration of the Holy Spirit that the trinitarian circle of divine life is completed. Less than three persons would be inadequate for the divine perfection, and more than three persons would be superfluous. If there were to be more than three, there would have to be more than two perfect modes of emanation. Bonaventure rejects that possibility on the authority of Aristotle. The only other possibility would be to say that there are more than one person proceeding from each of the modes of emanation. But this would be the same as saying that the products of the divine emanations are not perfect and adequate to the divine reality in every way; and that therefore the acts of production are imperfect. This would violate the basic concept of God as most perfect and fully actual being. But if the productive act is perfect, then the product of that act is the full and adequate expression of divine reality in one person. There can be, therefore, only two perfect modes of emanation and hence only two emanating persons. Any duplication is unnecessary and superfluous.[142] The circle of divine life is closed.

VII. MISSIONS AND APPROPRIATIONS

It is in the trinitarian doctrine that conceives of God as supremely communicative being that Christian theology made a major departure from the metaphysical understanding of antiquity. While for Plato and for Aristotle, the first principle was never conceived as a creator in the strict sense of the word, it is precisely this that concerns

---

[140] Loc. cit. (I, 324).
[141] Ibid.
[142] I *Sent*. d. 10, a. 1, q. 1, ad 4 (I, 196); *Brevil*. 1, 3 (V, 211); *Qq. Dd*. q. 4, a. 2, resp. (V, 85). Also, I *Sent*. d. 2, a.u., q. 4 (I, 56 ff.) for the specific arguments which have already been discussed.

Christian theology. Because theology conceived of God as immensely rich and communicative being within Himself, it could readily move to the further, free communication of being which takes the form of the doctrine of creation, or the communication *ad extra*. Viewed in this way, the mystery of the created world appears as an external and free expression of the inner, spiritual fecundity of the divine being. For Bonaventure, as we have seen, this includes the convinction that the world reflects not only the divine nature as one, but the divine nature as trinitarian also. In its unity and in its rich diversity, the world is a symbol of that being in whom unity and multiplicity are united in a most perfect way. Though, in general terms, the whole of creation bears a relation to the trinity, there are particular points in the history of the world at which the inner divine emanations become manifest with a peculiar clarity. This is the question of the divine missions in history.

The divine missions must be understood within the broader context of the Scholastic doctrine of God's presence to the world "by essence, power, and presence."[143] Bonaventure, like his contemporaries generally, distinguishes various modes of divine presence. Of particular importance here is the distinction between God's universal presence to all of creation as its creative, sustaining, and perfecting cause, and the presence by means of indwelling which refers specifically to spiritual creatures. Indwelling designates a spiritual effect in the rational creature together with the creature's acceptance of it, the result of which is the indwelling of the trinity as a personal presence in the human person and the corresponding transformation of the human person into an ever more perfect similitude of the trinity present to it.

Such an understanding of the indwelling of God directs our attention no longer to the structure of the created world as such, but more specifically to the history of grace which, for Bonaventure, also reveals a trinitarian structure; for through this history, the mystery of the eternal emanations is made known to humankind in a particularly express way.[144] The technical term *mission* is used to

---

[143] I *Sent.* d. 37, p. 1, a. 3, q. 2, resp. (I, 648); *Brevil.* 1, 5 (V, 213-214).

[144] The relation between the trinity and the theology of history raises the question of yet another influence on Bonaventure's thought which was not treated above in the discussion of historical influences. It is the very complex and as yet unresolved question of the work of Joachim of Fiore. This issue was not mentioned above because it does not enter into the basic trinitarian issues discussed there. But our understanding of the present issue must remain fragmentary until the as yet unresolved question of the influence of Joachim on Bonaventure has been studied more thoroughly. Ratzinger has singled out a number of points in which Bonaventure seems clearly under Joachim's influence even though he rejected the Joachimite concept of the age of the Holy Spirit which

designate the salvific activity of the trinity whereby the distinction of persons is made known.

The word *mission* involves two elements: emanation and manifestation.[145] Emanation refers to the eternal procession while manifestation designates some historical effect generally perceptible to the senses and having an explicit revelatory meaning. Derived as it is from the Latin verb *mittere*, the substantive form *mission* may have either an active or a passive meaning. Its usage at this level reflects the active and passive dimensions of the eternal emanations, so that there is a positive correspondence between the emanations and the historical manifestations. Thus, we can move from the historical mission of one who is sent as Son to an awareness of the eternal procession of the Son from the Father in which the possibility of the historical mission is grounded. Similarly, when the Spirit is known as the one sent by the Father and by the Son, we can move to an awareness of the eternal emanation of the Spirit from both the Father and the Son as described above. The most proper usage of the term *mission* is seen at this level where the person producing is said to send the person produced. In a less proper though possible sense, one can say that the persons send themselves in as far as all possess the divine nature. But since the passive sense of *mission* always involves a passive emanation, it is theologically incorrect to say that either the Father or the whole of the trinity sends itself.[146]

Mission, therefore, means that an eternal emanation has a temporal effect by which it becomes known in history. In the case of the Son, the entire doctrine of the incarnation is nothing but an extended treatment of the visible mission of the Son; and the visible mission of the Spirit from the Father and the Son is seen in the sending of the Spirit on the Church in the form of a dove or in tongues of fire. In both cases, the spatial imagery of descent is used, not to say that these persons leave heaven and come down to earth in a spatial

---

stood in sharp contrast with Bonaventure's own Christo-centric vision. Cf. Ratzinger, *Theology of History*... p. 104 ff.; 117 ff.; W. Schachten, "Die Trinitätslehre Bonaventuras als Explikation der Offenbarung vom personalen Gott," in: *Franziskanische Studien* 56 (1974) 2/4, p. 191-214.

[145] I *Sent*. d. 15, p. 1, a.u., q. 3 (I, 263); *Brevil*. 1, 5 (V, 213-214).

[146] I *Sent*. d. 15, p. 1, a.u., q. 3 & q. 4 (I, 263-266). This is based on the general principle that the direct meaning of mission is the historical manifestation while its connotation is the eternal emanation. Whether in the active or passive form, the term implies some relation to a principle or source. Hence, it is used most properly when that relation is most clearly expressed. To say that the "Father sends the Son" is equivalent to saying that He manifests the emanation of the Son; to say that "the Son is sent" is equivalent to saying that in an historical effect it is made known that the Son emanates from another. Since the term *mission* always implies an emanation, it should never be applied to the Father nor to the trinity as such, for neither of these can be said to emanate.

sense, but to say that — while the emanations are eternal — the visible mission has a beginning in time.[147] The goal of the visible missions is the internal mission, or the presence of God to the created spirit. This is developed theologically in the doctrine of grace.[148]

We find in Bonaventure's understanding of mission a consistent, logical expression of economic trinitarianism. God communicates Himself in history as He is in Himself. There is, then a positive correspondence between the economy of grace and the trinitarian structure of God because of which it is possible to come to a knowledge of the distinction of the persons from the history of grace. The economy of a trinitarian history is grounded ontologically in the immanent trinitarian mystery of God Himself.

Bonaventure's understanding of appropriation reveals from yet another perspective the same perception of the trinity. Appropriation is a mode of predication whereby something which is common to all three persons is predicated of one in particular. However, as Bonaventure warns, this should not be done in a haphazard way or it will lose all significance and will ultimately confuse the entire question of the trinity.

The primary purpose of appropriation is to facilitate our awareness of the individual divine person in His personal mode of being. It can do this only if sufficient care is taken to search out and to clarify the particular relation between the essential attribute under consideration and the property of the particular person to whom it is appropriated. This basic principle can be seen clearly in the three most basic appropriations:[149]

1) *Power* is appropriated to the Father. In itself power is not a personal property but an essential attribute of the divine nature and, hence, common to the three persons. Yet, it has a particular affinity with the property of the Father as sourceless Source. Therefore it can shed some light on the property of the Father.

2) *Wisdom* is appropriated to the Son. Scriptural evidence for such an appropriation is ambiguous, since 1 *Cor.* 12, 8 ff. seems to warrant an appropriation of wisdom to the Spirit. On the other hand, the liturgical tradition seems to attribute it commonly to the Word. For Bonaventure, the appropriation will be exclusively to the Word

---

[147] *Brevil.* 1, 5 (V, 213-214).
[148] *Brevil.* 4, 1-10 (V, 241-252).
[149] I *Sent.* d. 34, a.u., q. 3, fund. 1-2; and resp. (I, 592). "Si autem loquamur quantum ad ordinem vel originem, quem connotant, sic approprientur a parte rei propter convenientiam cum propriis personarum."

since, in a preeminent sense, He is divine truth. As the Father has expressed Himself perfectly in His Word, the Word may be called the "expressed Wisdom of God." Since He contains in His personal reality the intelligibility of all things, the term *wisdom* is fittingly appropriated to Him.[150]

3) *Goodness* is appropriated to the Spirit. This is based on Bonaventure's understanding of the emanation of the Spirit by liberality; this is the self-communication of God precisely as divine charity. But the charity by which the Father and Son breathe forth the Spirit is not essentially different from the love whereby God confers on creatures the gift of existence as well as the further gift of sharing in God's own love and beatitude. If both our existence as such and our graced-existence as well are gift and goodness, is it not fitting to appropriate this to the one who is the uncreated Gift that proceeds from infinite Goodness?

These three cases indicate clearly the inner logic of appropriations as seen by Bonaventure. Beyond these, he draws up a more extensive series of appropriations which may be less clear, but still reflect the order of origin of the persons.[151]

Father	*Son*	*Spirit*
Unity	Truth	Goodness
Eternity	Beauty	Delight
Principle	Exemplar	End
Efficiency	Exemplarity	Finality
Power	Wisdom	Goodness

Such appropriations are important for Bonaventure since he is convinced that all creatures exist, are sustained, and are brought to their completion by the three-fold action of the trinity. The search for such appropriations is the fitting response of the finite spirit to the mystery of the divine self-communication to the world.

---

[150] I *Sent.* d. 27, p. 2, a.u., q. 2, resp. (I, 485).
[151] *Brevil.* 1, 6 (V, 214-215); *Sermo de Trin.* (IX, 351-357).

CHAPTER THREE

TRINITARIAN THEMES IN THE DISPUTED QUESTIONS

Bonaventure indicates his intention of establishing two foundational issues: The existence of the one God, and His existence as a trinity. The one is an issue of human reason; the other an issue of faith. In so doing, he sets up the pillars of the structure for the entire series of questions in which is worked out the relation between the nature of the one God with its necessary attributes on the one hand, and the trinitarian nature of God as known by faith on the other hand. The structure reflects Bonaventure's conviction that the God who can be known and is known in a limited way by reason is identical with the God who reveals Himself as trinitarian in the history of salvation. Since God is one, and since the world is a unified cosmos coming from God, and since there is a positive relation between human knowledge and the objects of that knowledge, it follows that there should be a positive correspondence between reason and faith; for the truth of reality is fundamentally one and grounded in one God. But since the possibilities of reason are limited, and since God is free to communicate Himself to the human race in ways other than through the structures of the created order alone, if He has communicated Himself — as He has in the history of salvation — it follows that such a self-communication, while not contradicting what is accessible to reason, may also extend the range of human knowledge in a way not predictable from reason alone. Since, for Bonaventure, this is the case, he can give full tribute to the power of reason while recognizing its limitations and demanding that the basic categories whereby reason expresses and interprets reality must be held open to expansion and possible correction in the light of faith.

It is for this reason that we frequently find a clear dialectical structure which reflects these basic convictions. An outstanding case of such dialectic is found in the fifth and sixth chapters of the *Itinerarium*, reflecting first on the attributes of God as Being, and then on the attributes of God as Good.[1] The first level is a metaphysical reflection which corresponds to the Old Testament revelation of God as "He who is;" here one sees the intimate relation between the categories of the classical metaphysics of being with the Old Testament revelation. But the history of revelation stops neither with philosophy nor with the Old Testament, but goes on to a revelation which, while it does not negate the former, yet moves beyond, revealing that God, who is Being, is Goodness and Love. Thus, what has been established in the fifth chapter must be held open to what remains to be done in the sixth chapter. It is here, in reflecting on the New Testament, that we arrive at the highest level of metaphysical reflection; a level that we may truly call theological metaphysics, since it is truly metaphysical in character, though it takes its decisive clues as to the nature of reality from a particular religious experience. The dialectical structure of these chapters clearly reflects the basic metaphysical convictions of the Seraphic Doctor. In its basic outline, it is the same structure which provides the framework for the *Disputed Questions*, a structure which is established in the first question and carried out consistently as each of the attributes under consideration (with the exception of primacy) is studied in two articles; the first dealing with how that attribute is derived by reason, and the second employing reason to show how the same attribute finds its fullest meaning in a God who is trinitarian. The basic philosophical concepts are given a fuller content in this confrontation with faith which — for Bonaventure — is the final court of appeal for the proper understanding of reality.

The list of attributes to be treated here had already appeared in summary form in the *Sentence Commentary*,[2] and will appear again almost literally in the *Breviloquium*.[3] But in the *Disputed Questions*, the analysis of each is carried out very extensively and in such a closely integrated way that the whole of the work appears almost as one massive argument starting from the foundation set up in the first question, moving from one attribute to the next, showing the logical structure of each, building from one to another, and culminating in the final question on primacy which, as we have seen, is a key concern of Bonaventure's trinitarian style. This provides the larger framework within which the constant dialectic described above is carried out between the two articles of each question, and even within particular articles.

---

[1] *Itin.* 5 & 6 (V, 308-312).
[2] I *Sent.* d. 2, a.un., q. 1 (I, 50-52).
[3] *Brevil.* 1, 3 (V, 211).

I. THE FOUNDATIONS

Bonaventure speaks of the existence of God and the existence of the trinity as the foundations of all certain knowledge, the first in relation to reason, the second in relation to faith.

Is the existence of God beyond doubt for the human mind? Bonaventure had treated this question in the *Sentence Commentary*[4] where he had set out the same basic position as that found in the *Disputed Questions*, though the latter treatment is far more elaborate. In his own way, Bonaventure here reveals his allegiance to the Augustinian tradition which maintained that, in some way, the existence of God is *per se notum* or self-evident. The Anselmian form of that tradition appears as a constant thread running through many variations. The necessary existence of that "being than which no greater can be conceived" appears in numerous variations.

With elaborate care, Bonaventure works out three approaches in favor of the position, arguing: 1) that it is a truth universally impressed on all human minds; 2) that it is a truth proclaimed by all created beings; and 3) that, at the level of logic, it is a truth whose non-existence is inconceivable. These arguments reveal much of Bonaventure's personal theological concerns. Concerning the first approach, he draws arguments from authors commonly cited by Medieval theologians, including John Damascene, Hugh of St. Victor, Boethius, Augustine, and Anselm. Together with these theological authorities, the authority of Aristotle is appealed to for arguments of a more philosophical tone. One notices here the presence of themes particularly dear to the Seraphic Doctor: the desire for the true and the good, for wisdom, happiness, and peace. These are brought to bear as data of common human experience which have great significance for our understanding of ourselves and hence for our knowledge of God's existence.

The underlying anthropology is alluded to in the fourth argument which deals briefly with man as an image of God. This question is more fully developed in the *Sentence Commentary*.[5] Bonaventure comments on two triads which had been introduced into trinitarian theology by Augustine. Augustine himself had seen a certain difficulty with the triad: *mens - notitia - amor*, since the members are not coordinate. Bonaventure seems to be acutely aware of this difficulty,[6] and yet he finds it possible to interpret this triad as an image of the

---

[4] I *Sent.* d. 8, p. 1, a. 1, q. 2 (I, 153-155).
[5] I *Sent.* d. 3, p. 1, a. 1, q. 1 & 2 (I, 80-87) and a. 2, q. 1-3 (I, 88-93).
[6] Loc. cit. (I, 89).

trinity in as far as it reveals "order, equality, and consubstantiality."⁷ Order is found in that the mind is like a parent, knowledge like a child, and love is that which proceeds from both as a unifying bond. Equality is seen in that the mind knows itself in a way that corresponds to its being; and it loves itself to the degree that it knows itself. The knowledge and love are consubstantial with the mind. Even while Bonaventure discusses this triad, he employs little of the Augustinian psychological interpretation, but prefers to locate the analogy in terms of the structure of order, equality, and consubstantiality. In this style of interpretation, the term *mens* can be given a meaning more akin to Bonaventure's own understanding of the Father who is the fontal source of all else. The *mens*, from which flow knowledge and love, is like the Father from whom flow the Son and the Spirit, and all of created reality.⁸

Of greater significance for Bonaventure is the triad: *memory - intelligence - will*,⁹ which appears also in the *Breviloquium* and in the *Itinerarium*.¹⁰ The human spirit may be seen as an image of God in as far as these three powers, though basically of one nature, manifest the elements of distinction, order, and origin when they express themselves in act. Again, though the triad is drawn from Augustine, the analogy which is found in it departs significantly from that of the psychological theory of Augustine. It appears to be reshaped in terms of Bonaventure's own trinitarian views.

The fact that man is an image of God has great significance in treating the question of the human knowledge of God's existence. For anything to be an image of another, it must possess a nature that is similar to that of which it is the image.¹¹ As regards man, his existence as an image of God is conceived in dynamic terms. He is structured in such a way that he is ordered to perfection and fulfillment only in the knowledge and love of God. That structure which is reflected in the faculties of memory, intellect, and will must be actuated in knowledge and love by a personal turning to God who is present to man preconsciously in human memory.¹² In as

---

⁷ Ibid. (I, 91).
⁸ M. Schmaus, "Trinitätstheologie in Patristik und Mittelalter. Die psychologischen Ternare Augustins und ihre Abwandlung bei Bonaventura," in: *Begegnung: Beiträge zu einer Hermeneutik des theologischen Gesprächs. Heinrich Fries Festschrift*. Ed. M. Seckler, O. H. Pesch, J. Brosseder, W. Pannenberg (Gras, 1972) p. 465-476.
⁹ I *Sent*. d. 3, p. 2, a. 1, q. 1-3 (I, 80-87).
¹⁰ *Brevil*. 2, 9 (V, 226); *Itin*. 3 (V, 303-306).
¹¹ I *Sent*. d. 3, p. 1, a. 1, q. 2 (I, 82-84).
¹² *Itin*. 3, 2 (V, 303-304). For Bonaventure, the term *memory* has a much wider range of meaning than in modern usage; in this regard, the Seraphic Doctor is dependent on the views of Augustine. In describing three operations of memory,

far as the finite spirit is shaped by the objects to which it turns, when it turns to God, it becomes like Him to the highest degree. Man is an image of God in terms of these faculties in as far they have God as their ultimate object. Bonaventure recognizes another level of actuation when the soul reflects upon itself. Since the soul is an image of God, when it reflects upon itself, by being conscious of itself, it becomes conformed to that of which it is the image. Hence, the image of God resides in these same faculties in as far as they have the soul itself as an object. But when the soul turns to lower creatures in such a way as to remain with them, it has turned to that which is neither God nor an image of God but only a vestige. In as far as it allows itself to be conformed to such vestiges, it looses its quality as an actual image. Surely the structure of the three faculties remains, but to the degree that they are not formed by God or by His image, they are no longer an express image. Thus, while the structure remains, the fitting actuation of the structure is not present.

Such an analysis makes it clear that when Bonaventure speaks of man as an image of God, he has in mind the basic dynamic of the human person by which the finite spirit is orientated to God as to that mystery in which it will find fulfillment and repose. The *a priori* functions involved in Bonaventure's concept of memory, and the entire epistemological structure make it clear how he can argue in favor of the position that the existence of God is indubitable. But despite all that has been said concerning the triads, still, in Bonaventure's view, reason alone cannot move from the triadic structure to an express knowledge of the trinity. The perfect understanding of the image is given not to reason but to faith alone.[13] The first series of arguments comes to an end with an argument from the soul's self-awareness and the immediacy of God's presence to the soul, a typical concern of the Augustinian tradition.

The second series of arguments (n. 11-20) represents a lengthy metaphysical reflection following the lines of the Bonaventurean method of reduction. Similar examples may be found in the *Itinerarium*[14] and in the *Collations on the Hexaemeron*.[15]

This sort of development may be seen as an indication of how,

---

Bonaventure clarifies how it is that certain *a priori* elements are present in memory. In the background stands the Platonic *anamnesis* theory, though it is clearly modified to serve the purposes of a Christian theologian. The Bonaventurean theory of memory makes it clear why this dimension of the human person can be seen as the locus of a sort of preconscious contact with God.

[13] I *Sent.* d. 3, p. 2, a. 2, q. 3, resp. (I, 93).
[14] *Itin.* 5, 2-8 (V, 308-310).
[15] *Hex.* 10, 15-18 (V, 379).

in Bonaventure's view, the reality of God is somehow involved in all human cognitive activity. The most fundamental fact that we know about any object is that it exists. As a positive state, being is the basis of the possibility of any knowledge. So crucial is the concept of being, that one cannot even affirm the non-existence of anything without moving through the positive concept of being. Being, therefore, is prior to all else and is that by which we know all else. But this must be being as first, absolute, and unlimited; it must be pure being. But such being is never found as an object of knowledge in the world. The beings which we encounter in the world are limited in many ways. They are dependent, relative, mixed of potency and act. Now, since a limit cannot be recognized precisely as a limit unless in some way we transcend it, it follows that whatever may be the form of limit we are confronted with in creatures, we do not fully understand it unless we reduce it to the pure, actual form of the positive attribute which is necessarily prior to the defective, limited form in which it appears in creatures, just as pure, actual being is necessarily prior to all limited forms of being. Thus, as non-being can be known only through being, and as privations can be known only through positive qualities, so every form of limitation must be reduced to the positive attribute which is necessarily prior. Here is the core of the arguments presented by Bonaventure; all ten reflect the same structure. And they lead to the philosophical affirmation of being as absolutely first, *a se*, etc. Since all creatures manifest the limits pointed out here, they all manifest the existence of God as the necessary, absolute, perfect, prior being.

The third series of arguments (n. 21-29) clearly bears the marks of Anselm's ontological argument. Distinguishing between the logical order and the order of real existence outside the mind, we can see the possibility of conceiving of a being than which no greater can be conceived. But if real existence outside the mind is greater than existence in the mind alone, then the concept of a being than which no greater can be conceived must contain within it the note of real existence outside the mind. For if it contained only the note of mental existence, then the concept of a greater being would be possible. If God is identified with that being than which no greater can be conceived, then the concept of the non-existence of God is self-contradictory; for it cannot be thought coherently. The Anselmian approach finds further confirmation in arguments drawn from Augustine and Boethius.

The final arguments of the series are further applications of what has been said concerning the priority of being, here seen explicitly as the foundation for the most basic principles of logic without which the human mind cannot think and which we must employ even in the act of denying them. These principles (identity, contradiction, and excluded middle) are the self-evident, irreducible principles of all coherent human thought. But they are unintelligible except in the light of the first being. Hence, the very principles that make coherent human thought a possibility lead to the conclusion that God exists necessarily.

We have dwelt at some length on the above arguments because they reflect numerous concerns which are truly characteristic of Bonaventure's personal theological style. Following the framework of the Scholastic disputation, Bonaventure now presents fourteen arguments against the thesis he is defending. These arguments are not drawn from philosophers or from heretics, but like the arguments in favor of the thesis, these also appeal to Scripture and to such respected theologians as John Damascene and Richard of St. Victor. Most of the negative arguments reflect specific problems raised against the Anselmian and Augustinian arguments given above. From many perspectives, therefore, there seems to be sufficient reason to deny the thesis, particularly since — beyond the logical questions involved — the thesis seems to empty faith of any meritorious significance.

The materials contained in the response and in the answer to the objections are an extension of what Bonaventure had already written in his *Sentence Commentary*.[16] He first clarifies what is meant by the term *indubitable* and indicates the sources that can give rise to doubt. Something is said to be *indubitable* if there are no grounds for doubt. But such grounds may arise either from some deficiency in the process of reasoning or from a deficiency in reason itself. The first possibility refers both to the object known and to the knower. Here a truth may be doubtful if the reason for its evidence is not found in the truth itself, nor in its demonstration, nor in the intellect of the knower. None of these are applicable to the question of God's existence since in Himself He is most evident, and since all creatures proclaim His existence, and since man himself is an image of God and is orientated toward God by a natural desire which, together with knowledge and memory, directs man from the core of his being to God as to that reality in which the created spirit finds its true beatitude.

If there is doubt about the existence of God, it can arise only from subjective causes; from some deficiency in the finite subject. In the *Sentence Commentary*, Bonaventure refers to this as blindness or ignorance.[17] This deficiency is explained in the *Disputed Questions*

---

[16] I *Sent.* d. 8, p. 1, a. 1, q. 2, resp. (I, 154-155).
[17] I *Sent.* d. 8, p. 1, a. 1, q. 2, resp. (I, 154) which refers not to the question of God's existence, but to His nature.

in three ways. It can mean a lack of the proper understanding of the term *God;* it can also refer to a conclusion drawn from inadequate evidence; or it can refer to the failure to reduce the objects of sense experience fully to spiritual realities. None of these deficiencies jeopardizes the evidence which Bonaventure has explained above. Therefore, for the mind that correctly understands God to be that being than which no greater can be conceived, it is impossible to doubt God's existence.

In summary, the existence of God is an indubitable truth. All of man's nature; his yearning for truth, goodness, and happiness; his knowledge of his own limitations and the limitations of all other beings in the world cry out the existence of the perfect Truth and Goodness that is God, the perfect Light that illumines our minds. Human blindness may present an obstacle to the full and deeper knowledge of God in this life, but it remains true that the existence of God is the foundation of all human certitude.

As the existence of God is the basis for all certain knowledge available to human reason, so the existence of God as trinity is the basis of all knowledge of faith. After treating of the existence of God, Bonaventure now turns to the other pillar of his development. In the *fundamenta,* fourteen positions are given in favor of the thesis that the dogma of the trinity is both congruous for the human mind and its knowledge obligatory for human salvation. Here arguments are drawn from Scripture,[18] from the theological tradition (e.g. the Athanasian Creed, and Augustine), and from theological reasons to indicate that the doctrine is obligatory in nature. The arguments for the congruity of the doctrine revolve around the idea that, though the dogma does not stand in contradiction to reason, yet it does transcend reason. It is fitting, so the arguments say, that the finite mind should be orientated to truth that is greater than itself. In as far as the mind is open to Mystery which it cannot grasp, it is liberated from the necessity of making either itself or the world around it bear the weight of ultimacy. It can, therefore, subject itself in faith to the Mystery with fitting religious dispositions.[19]

---

[18] *Mt.* 28, 19; *Mk.* 16, 16; *Jn.* 5, 23.
[19] III *Sent.* d. 23, a. 1, q. 1 (III, 470-472). Here Bonaventure elaborates on faith as the guiding light of all virtues. It is a virtue because in it is found uprightness of life in accordance with justice. Justice is nothing other than *voluntatis rectitudo,* and faith is that habit by which our intellect voluntarily comes into the captivity of Christ. Such captivity of the intellect to a truth beyond itself and greater than itself is not a denial of human nature, but is an essential component of an upright life in which alone man's nature can find fulfillment. In *ad 4* Bonaventure argues that what may appear rational from one viewpoint may seem irrational from another. It we were to accept a truth only because of the com-

This will be developed more extensively by Bonaventure in his own response.

The arguments against the thesis attempt to show first that such a doctrine is contrary to reason, and that, for this reason, it is not fitting for man to believe it (§ 1-8). Like the former, these arguments also appeal at times to Scripture,[20] at times to Augustine, and at times to theological reasoning. The arguments (§ 9-13) go on to show that the dogma is impossible for the human mind, and that therefore we are not obliged to believe it on any basis whatsoever. Finally, the question of the motive of faith is raised, the opposition seeing no adequate clarity on the issue.

Bonaventure's response argues that, as the foundation of the entire edifice of Christian faith, the doctrine is fitting, necessary, and worthy of belief. In speaking of the trinity as the foundation of faith, Bonaventure seems to contradict what he says elsewhere concerning Christ as the starting point for theology.[21] Is his theology centered around the trinity or around the person of Christ ? To answer that question, it is necessary to distinguish between the order of reality and the order of human knowledge. In terms of the order of knowledge, to which theology belongs, the Christian religious experience centers around the community's experience of Jesus Christ. From this perspective, theological methodology is Christ-centered; for it is from the historical revelation in Jesus that Christians come to discern the nature of reality. Yet, through reflection it becomes clear that, for Bonaventure, the mystery of Christ would be impossible without the mystery of the trinity. Indeed, without the trinity, there would be no creation, to say nothing of the incarnation. Such statements refer not to the order of knowledge but to the order of reality. Thus, while methodologically, Bonaventure's theology begins with the person of Christ, the prior condition in which the reality of Christ is grounded is the reality of the trinity. In this sense, it is the trinity which is the basis in the real order for the entire edifice of faith.[22]

---

pelling force of an argument, then our assent would not be voluntary but necessary. Such assent would be neither virtuous nor meritorious.

[20] 1 *Cor.* 13, 12.
[21] *Hex.* 1, 1 & 10 (V, 329-330).
[22] The position of O. Gonzalez seems incomplete or misleading in its formulation. He writes, "El cristocentrismo bonaventuriano está pues en functión de un trinitarismo anterior." (O. Gonzalez, *Misterio Trinitario y Existencia Humana* [Madrid, 1966] p. 24). While the trinity is ontologically prior, and while Bonaventure was heir to an already developed trinitarian theology, still in terms of the inner logic of his own methodological approach, it seems that the Christ-

What is it that moves Christians to believe in the trinity, and what is it that makes it an obligatory belief ? Bonaventure's reply to this question is an interesting example of his use of symbolic, philosophical, and historical thought patterns. The symbol that dominates the treatment is that of the *book*, a symbol which Bonaventure applies to the created order as a whole, to the Sacred Scriptures, and to God Himself.[23] His development may be expressed in the following schema.

Book of Creation (Efficacious)		*Book of Scripture* (More efficacious)		*Book of Life* (Most efficacious)	
Vestige in corporal beings Witness from afar	*Image* in spiritual nature Witness from near at hand	OT Implicit – in figures – in words	NT Explicit – Sacraments – Express teachings	*This life* Innate and infused light	*Heaven* Explicit & express
Appropriations	{ – Memory, intelligence, will – Mind, knowledge, love				
God as 3-fold cause	Origin, emanation, distinction				
Efficacious in state of innocence but obscured by sin.		Necessary because of darkness of sin.		Illumination from eternal light through innate light and infused light.	

While these three books appear in an apparently historical framework, this should not be taken to mean that one may render the other obsolete. Rather, it seems that the three books, read and interpreted simultaneously in the light of each other, constitute the testimony

---

mystery is the starting-point, and at the cognitive level, trinitarianism is a function of Christocentrism.

[23] For a fuller treatment of the extent to which Bonaventure uses this symbol in the whole *corpus* of his writings, cf. W. Rauch, *Das Buch Gottes. Eine systematische Untersuchung des Buchbegriffes bei Bonaventura* (München, 1961).

to the mystery.[24] What distinguishes the three books is not metaphysics but the various states in the history of grace in which man finds himself.

In its own proper reality, the order of creation is and remains a reflection of God. Every creature is a vestige of God and thus reflects His trinitarian reality in a distant and unclear way in terms of three series of attributes: measure, species, order; unity, truth, goodness; measure, number, weight. By reason of appropriations, one can recognize a distant reflection of the trinity, but not a knowledge of the three persons precisely as persons. The witness of the vestige consists primarily in its witness to a three-fold causality: efficient, exemplary, and final. Bonaventure views the material world as a medium of communication between God and man; his interpretation of its structure, therefore, is of a theological nature. The created order is the objectification of the Absolute Being's Word. It is, therefore, a means whereby the Absolute can communicate itself to the finite spirit of man. This is the structure of the world, both prior to the Fall and after the Fall.

There is yet a deeper level at which creation reflects God as triune; namely, in man who is created in the image of God. Bonaventure here employs the two Augustinian triads: memory - intelligence - will; and mind - knowledge - love. The analogy which he derives from these, and which he sees as an express and proximate witness, is that of origin and emanation leading to distinction. This corresponds fully with his understanding of the Father as described above. The analogy of origin, together with equality, consubstantiality, and inseparability constitute an express testimony to the triune character of God.

This two-fold witness of the created order was clear and adequate prior to the Fall. But sin, with its attendant darkness, has made it difficult to read the book. It is for this reason that the book of Scripture became necessary.[25] But that which is revealed in the Scriptures is not something contrary to the book of nature. Rather, the Scriptures make it possible for man to read and to interpret the divine revelation which has never been deficient nor absent from

---

[24] Gonzalez, op. cit., p. 43; K. Forster, "Liber vitae bei Bonaventura. Ein begriffgeschichtliches Aufriss," in: *Theologie in Geschichte und Gegenwart. M. Schmaus Festschrift*, ed. J. Auer and H. Volk (München, 1957) p. 397-414; H. Mercker, *Schriftauslegung als Weltauslegung. Untersuchungen zur Stellung der Schrift in der Theologie Bonaventuras* (Paderborn, 1971) p. 80.

[25] *Brevil.* prol. (V, 201-208) presents an extended treatment of how the meaning of the created order is expressed in Sacred Scripture and in the reflection on it in theology.

the beginning of the world to the end. The book of nature is not nullified but is made legible again.[26]

Scripture itself reflects varying degrees of explicitness regarding the trinity. The Old Testament witness, which is both in figures and in words, is understood as an implicit witness. As the most significant example of a figure, Bonaventure chooses the account of Abraham and his encounter with the three young men.[27] Making use of a venerable Patristic interpretation, Bonaventure sees a figure of the trinity in the fact that, though Abraham saw three men, yet he adored but one and spoke to the three as one. The clearest example of a verbal witness is *Psalm* 32, 6; *Word* and *Spirit* are expressly named, while the Father is implied by the term *Lord*.

In contrast with the Old Testament, the witness of the New Testament is explicit and is contained both in sacraments and in explicit teachings. Of the sacraments, Bonaventure singles out baptism as a clear example since it is conferred with the express invocation of the trinity;[28] for this reason it impresses the character of the trinity in the recipient. As an example of express teaching, the text of 1 *John* 5 is chosen. And Bonaventure concludes that since the witness of Scripture is so explicit, the doctrine is not only credible but necessary and obligatory as well.

The first two books of themselves are but inert realities unless they are read by human persons, for only then do they come to life in the finite spirit. They must be read in the proper light, which is found in what Bonaventure calls the *Book of Life*.[29] This term refers

---

[26] *Hex.* 2, 20 (V, 339-340); *Hex.* 13, 12 (V, 390); *Hex.* 13, 13 (V, 390).
[27] *Gn.* 18, 2.
[28] *Mt.* 28, 19. Cf. also IV *Sent.* d. 3, p. 1, a. 2, q. 2 (IV, 71-73) where Bonaventure clarifies various opinions on the form of baptism, pointing out as the common and certain opinion the view holding the necessity of a fully trinitarian formula.
[29] This term is found frequently in religious literature of various traditions. In the Bible, it is found in both the Old Testament (*Ex.* 32, 32; *Is.* 4, 3; *Dn.* 12, 1) and in the New Testament (*Lk.* 10, 20; *Phil.* 4, 3; *Apoc.* 3, 5; 17, 8; 20, 12; 20, 15), generally in an eschatological context. In later theological literature, the term is frequently given a Christological significance (St. Bernard, *Sermo in Die Paschae* [PL 183, 279]; Hugh of St. Victor, *De Arca Noe Morali* 2, 8 [PL 176, 641]). The *Summa Fratris Alexandri* recognizes three meanings for the term: 1) the knowledge of God in as far as it is the exemplar of life; 2) the human nature of the Son of God, in as far as it is the most express example of the divine exemplar; 3) Sacred Scripture, in as far as it gives verbal witness to the exemplar (*Summa* I, n. 255, p. 347). In Bonaventure, the term has a wide range of interrelated meanings all of which point to God's full and perfect knowledge in which all things in the world are known and in which the mystery of predestination resides. Cf. *Brevil.* 1, 8 (V, 216); *Comm. in Luc.* 10, 20, n. 34-35 (VII, 263-264); IV *Sent.* d. 43, a. 2, q. 1-3 (IV, 896-898); *Brevil.* 7, 1 (V, 281); *Hex.* 12, 8 (V, 385); *Lignum vitae* 12, 46 (VIII, 84-85).

here to God's own inner life of knowledge in as far as it is the source of illumination for the human mind in reading both the book of nature and that of Scripture. It is the conjunction of the innate light of the human mind and the infused light of supernatural faith that makes the proper reading of the two previous books possible. Thus, the Book of Life is not a source of knowledge independently of man's experience of the world and of history; but is the light whereby that experience may be read properly. Since illumination begins already in the innate light of the mind, and is brought to completion in the infused light, it follows that reason and faith are related to one another in a very positive manner.[30] Reason is subordinate to faith; but faith is the intrinsic perfection of reason. For if the task of reason is to know reality, and if reality is not fully known until it is known in trinitarian terms, then the task of reason is realized only partially until it finds its completion in faith.[31] Similarly, it is the conjunction of the light of reason and the light of faith that provides the basis for the unity and coherence of theology.[32]

It is in this context that we encounter a principle basic to Bonaventure's style of theology: God is to be thought of in the most exalted and most reverent terms, which is here presented as a truth taught by human reason itself and agreed on by Christians, Jews, Saracens, and even by heretics. But to think that God is not capable of perfect self-communication is a failure to think of Him in the most exalted terms. And to think that He is capable of communicating Himself fully and perfectly but does not will to do so is a failure to think of Him most reverently. Therefore, the innate light and the infused light together lead us to think of God as both capable of such communication and as actually communicating Himself

---

[30] The relation of nature to faith is raised in the seventh objection and in the response to it; it is treated also in II *Sent*. d. 18, a. 1, q. 2, ad 5 (II, 437) where Bonaventure distinguishes two ways of understanding nature. In the first sense, it refers to all that a thing is capable of being by reason of its natural origin. It is natural for creatures to become all that God wills them to become; they have a potency for perfect obedience to God's will. God never acts contrary to nature conceived in this sense. The second sense refers to the power in creatures whereby they run their ordinary course. When nature is thus understood, it is possible to say that God acts at times against nature and at times beyond nature. He acts in the first way when He produces something that is normally produced by secondary causes, the manner of production being entirely different. He acts in the second way when He produces something not found in nature, or something which nature by itself is not ordered to produce (e.g. incarnation, glorified bodies).
[31] III *Sent*. d. 24, a. 2, q. 2 (III, 520-521).
[32] J. F. Quinn, *The Historical Constitution of St. Bonaventure's Philosophy* (Toronto, 1973) p. 498-499; 679.

in this way, and hence to think of Him as a trinity.[33] Having established this foundational truth, Bonaventure indicates briefly how other doctrines of faith may be related to it.

In summary, the three books described by Bonaventure are best seen as a unity; the distinction between them is based on differing situations in the history of grace.[34] For those who existed prior to the coming of Christ, an implicit faith was possible as was fitting to their place in the history of revelation; but after Christ, the doctrine of the trinity must be believed with explicit faith since it has been revealed with such explicitness. Such faith does not stand in opposition to reason, but is in harmony with the whole of the created order and is obligatory because of the promulgation of the Gospel. That which makes it possible for us to believe is the innate light of reason brought to completion in this life by the infused light in as far as the latter leads our intellect into obedient conformity to the eternal light of God Himself. Stimulating and supporting us in this faith is the witness of Scripture, the example of the Saints and the teaching of the Doctors. The final consummation of this faith is to be hoped for in heaven where we will stand in the presence of the Light itself, no longer needing the mediation of the opaque world of our historical experience.

II. UNITY AND TRINITY

The affirmation of the unity of the divine nature may clearly be derived from the witness of the Old Testament. Bonaventure here takes up the same question from the perspective of reason. The treatment found in the *Disputed Questions* is considerably more extensive than that found in the *Sentence Commentary*.[35]

---

[33] *Brevil.* 1, 2 (V, 210-211) and I *Sent.* d. 2, q. 4 (I, 56-58). In the latter, Bonaventure argues that there are three and only three persons in the trinity from beatitude, perfection, simplicity, and primacy.

[34] This situation of grace is referred to in the tenth objection and the corresponding answer. Further light is shed on the question in III *Sent.* d. 25, a. 1, q. 2, ad 6 (III, 541). There Bonaventure argues that God's grace is present to all men. In history prior to Christ, because of the distortions introduced by sin, no one was bound to an explicit faith in Christ or in the Christian revelation. Yet, some knowledge of Christian reality was available to human beings even then from the dictates of nature, from instruction given by persons of particular religious sensitivity, and from divine inspiration by God "who offers Himself to all who seek Him in humility." This is completely consistent with Bonaventure's understanding of the *Verbum increatum, incarnatum,* and *inspiratum.* Cf. *Itin.* 4, 3 (V, 306); *Brevil.* 4, 1 (V, 241); *Hex.* 3, 2-32 (343-458).

[35] I *Sent.* d. 2, a.u., q. 1 (I, 50-52).

Arguments against the numerical unity of God can be drawn from the facts of religious and philosophical history. Polytheism is a common phenomenon in the cosmic religions; and metaphysical dualism is a recurrent temptation of philosophy. Indeed, the very arguments which are intended to persuade one of the numerical unity of the divine nature seem capable of proving the very opposite. Certainly, then, if it is reasonable to affirm the unity of God, it cannot for that reason alone be seen as a necessary truth of reason. And if we assume, for the sake of argument, that it is a truth capable of philosophical proof, how could it remain an issue of faith?

Bonaventure's approach to these questions is shaped to a great extent by the Anselmian concept of God as "that being than which no greater can be conceived," which can be seen lurking in the background of each of the particular arguments dealing with the attributes of the divine being. The attributes singled out here are: omnipotence, wisdom, goodness, influence, and causality. The analysis of the individual arguments reveals a common structure which, in each particular case, is filled with content drawn from the definition of the respective attribute. The general structure may be expressed as follows. If there were a multiplicity of separate beings, each of which possessed a divine nature, then the following would have to be reckoned with: either they agree totally in all their essential qualities, or they differ totally, or they agree in part and differ in part. Now, if they are in total agreement in all essential respects, then they are not really distinct but are numerically one and the same. If they differ totally, on the other hand, it would be a logical contradiction to say that each of two beings could be a "being than which no greater can be conceived." Therefore, if we begin by saying that one of these is God, we cannot logically make the same predication of the other. On the assumption that these beings differ totally, therefore, only one of them can logically be said to be God. The logical middle between total conformity and total difference is partial agreement and partial difference. In this case, each of the beings would possess qualities not possessed by the other together with qualities possessed in common. This would mean that each of these beings is composed of diverse parts, namely, those things possessed in common and those things not possessed in common. This would do violence to the simplicity which must characterize the divine nature. Hence, neither of such beings would be truly divine. The only logical possibility for Bonaventure is that the divine nature can be one alone. The whole analysis rests heavily on the Anselmian definition of God.

The same definition provides the key to why polytheism can and does occur so frequently. The basic problem is that of determining the proper meaning and logical function of the word *God*. If this word is taken to signify anything less than the "being than which no greater can be conceived," then it is easily possible to conceive of it in the plural. This, in fact, is what is involved in the case of those religions where anything that seems to transcend human ability and human control is readily designated as a god. What Bonaventure describes here seems to be nothing other than the "God of the gaps" made famous in the various secularist theologies of the twentieth century. Only in this sense can the term *God* be used in the plural; and in the final analysis, we are dealing with various forms of idolatry, for one is investing ultimate meaning in that which is not ultimate. But if the term is used in its proper sense, the unicity of God is seen by Bonaventure to have a self-evident quality which may be placed in parallel with the self-evident character of the foundational principles of logic. While it is self-evident to reason from one perspective, it is a matter of faith from another perspective. There is no formal contradiction in this. Indeed, it is what one might expect if one's metaphysical vision is such that it encompasses a fundamental harmony between the truth accessible to reason as such and the truth made known through the Christian revelation. Bonaventure's metaphysical vision allows for such a harmonious relation, even while recognizing the distinct functions of philosophy and theology.

The rich diversity of beings in the world, extensive as it is, is not sufficient reason for affirming a plurality of divine causal principles. It is at this point that Bonaventure's aesthetic sense appears in the argument. The world reveals an immense variety of beings; but this is not mere random difference. Rather, it is a multiplicity and differentiation which yet coheres in order and inner relatedness to form a unified cosmos. In brief, the world is not a random collection of diverse beings; it is a cosmos in the original sense of the word — an orderly, harmonious unity of multiplicity. If God is primal goodness, wisdom, and power, He is so in such richness and fullness that no single creature could sufficiently manifest the richness of the mystery of being. While God has given total and full expression to that richness in the inner-trinitarian processions, if He should freely choose to communicate Himself to something other than Himself, then it appears more fitting that He would do so in a way that would be apt to manifest both the concentration of the riches of being in one, and the fertility and fruitfulness of such being in its immense productiveness. So it is, in Bonaventure's thought, that the world, which is one and multiple, is in its entirety but a symbol of the divine nature which is supremely unified and unique in itself and simultaneously infinitely rich in being within itself, and thus is the boundless source from which flow all forms of being in the world.

At this point, it begins to appear that Bonaventure's concept of unity is verging into the direction of trinitarian thought. God must be one and supremely unified in His being, but that unity is not a static quality. It is conceived more as a dynamic power that holds multiplicity in a dynamic and harmoniously unified order. In shaping his concept of unity, Bonaventure moves from the coexistence of unity and plurality at various levels in the created world. There is a sense in which unity and multiplicity are compatible in the created world. His examples can be understood only with some definition of nature and person in mind. *Nature* is taken to refer to the form by which a being is what it is, whereas *person* is understood to be an incommunicable supposite. Thus, in a purely formal sense, the concepts of nature and person are different concepts. Therefore, in a formal sense, there is no incompatibility in the fact that one should be used in the singular while the other is used in the plural.

The coexistence of plurality and unity can be seen in the relation between a species and the individual beings in the species; while the species is one the beings in the species are multiple. Furthermore, in an individual person, the presence of multiple natures does not destroy the fundamental unity of the person, as in every human person we find both a spiritual nature and a corporal nature. The mystery of the Incarnation reveals even greater complexity since it contains in one being three different natures: both the created spiritual and corporal natures, and the uncreated nature of the divine Word as well. If there is no logical incompatibility in such a relation between natures and person, neither is there any formal contradiction in the reversal of the terms such as is found in the trinitarian dogma.

Not only is there no contradiction involved in the dogma, but the fundamental implication of the trinity points to a positive perfection. In common philosophical understanding, unity is taken to be a transcendental quality of being. But in the world of created beings, each concrete individual is but a limited concretization of the species. As such, it is unique and unrepeatable. The species is not wholly realized in any one of them, and no individual is simply a repetition of another. The full possibilities of any created nature are realized only in a multiplicity of really distinct unities, each of which involves a multiplication of the nature. In the case of creatures, each is characterized by a unity which remains unimpaired only in as far as it is totally immanent to this numerically unique individual.

Such a unity is, in Bonaventure's view, but a weak reflection of an even more perfect unity of being; namely, a unity which is capable of being distributed among various subjects while remaining fully identical with itself. Such is the unity of the divine nature which — from its own immanent richness — gives rise to a plurality without multiplying the nature.[36] Thus, it is not only non-contradictory, but pre-eminently fitting that the one divine nature, precisely because it is one in the highest degree, should give rise to multiplicity within itself such as is found in the trinity.

The coexistence of unity and plurality in creatures darkly foreshadows that pre-eminent realization of unity and multiplicity in God. But this sort of unity can no longer be understood in the monadic sense so common in Greek philosophy. It must now be understood as a unity of love which is more perfect than a mere unity of nature. But love, of its very nature, must involve a plurality. Therefore, if the unity of love is the most perfect unity, and if God is the most perfect being, then there must be an intrinsic plurality in Him, since there is nothing outside of God that is supremely lovable. Therefore, the metaphysical concept of unity which appears first of all at the philosophical level finds a new and deeper meaning at the level of theological reflection. Through reflecting on the metaphysical implications of Christian revelation, it is possible to transcend the limitations of the purely philosophical vision of reality.

III. SIMPLICITY AND TRINITY

There are three ways in which a being may be related to composition. First, it may itself be the result of composition in which prior elements are united to form something new; the composite is that being which results from the union. The second type of relation to composition becomes clear from the same example, for the prior elements are related to the composite as parts thereof. The third type of relation consists in the capacity or potentiality of entering into composition.

In none of these ways can composition be attributed to God. As that being who is absolutely prior to all else, God transcends all actual and even potential composition. Since there is nothing prior to Him, He is simple in the fullest and most proper sense. In God there is no real distinction between essence and existence, nor between faculties and activities. Though we attribute many different qualities to God, these are not separate and really distinct realities in God, but constitute one undivided divinity.

Thus, the affirmation of God's simplicity raises the question of the validity of human knowledge about Him. The fact is that human

---

[36] *Hex.* 11, 8 (V, 381).

knowledge attributes a multiplicity of qualities to God. If those concepts truly reflect something about the nature of God and are not merely logical constructs, then it would seem that God cannot be simple in Himself; for if He is, then our knowledge seems to be deceptive. On the other hand, if our concepts do not correspond to something real in God, then they appear to be mere logical fictions.

This problem shows the need for a more precise analysis of knowledge. Bonaventure understands knowledge not as mere simple apprehension, but as a process whereby an object of knowledge is reduced to two dimensions: 1) that which is; and 2) that by which it is. But any such act of reduction must take into account: 1) the knowing subject; 2) the object known; and 3) the means whereby the object becomes known to the subject. All human knowledge of God is the product of a finite mind from a limited viewpoint. Such knowledge cannot comprehend the infinite nature of God. Even though God is immense and simple in Himself, we can know Him only by means of images and concepts drawn from our experience in the world. Such experience can do no more than reflect partial glimpses of the divine reality. Therefore, while our knowledge can be truly a knowledge of God, still it will unavoidably find expression in a multiplicity of different images and concepts each of which is limited and perspectival.

Therefore, even though the object of our knowledge in this case is absolutely simple in itself, yet the limits of the human subject and the means of knowledge make it unavoidable that we know that which is simple as though it were composed. This does not totally nullify the validity of our knowledge but simply points to its limitations. For example, we conceive of God as having an intellect and will. Our tendency is to conceive of these as two really different spiritual faculties which are really distinct from each other and from the divine nature. There is a real basis for conceiving of God in this way, for to know is not formally identical with to love and to enjoy; so our concepts express something real in God. But to speak of a real basis for our concepts is not the same as saying that intellect and will are really distinct entities and really distinct from the nature of God. It would be more accurate to say that God is fully in act as pure spiritual being. But the act of spiritual being is carried out in the loving enjoyment of that which it knows. While a cognitive relation is formally different from a volitional relation, they are intimately interrelated as two intrinsic dimensions of one spiritual activity. Thus, nature, intellect, and will are at root one in God; and while there truly is knowledge and love in God, they are not present as separate entities. So, we know God in a multiplicity of concepts which seem to imply many distinctions. Such distinctions, however, arise from the limits of the human mind rather than from the divine nature.

But how can this absolute simplicity be related to the mystery of the trinity ? In answering this, it is necessary to distinguish various ways in which beings can be said to be distinct, and different types of divine attributes. Bonaventure distinguishes three ways in which persons may be said to be distinct: 1) they may be distinct because of their origin; 2) they may be distinct because they possess different qualities and properties; 3) they may be distinct for both of the above reasons. The second and third cases refer to angels and to human persons respectively, while the third refers to God in whom the persons are distinguished in origin only. But the mode of origin is not something really distinct from the person; it is identical with the person in as far as it views the person in terms of that which constitutes him in his individual personal character. There is, therefore, no composition in the person itself. Bonaventure argues further that there is no real distinction between person and essence, nor between person, property, and essence. At every level, there is total lack of composition in God, and hence there is perfect simplicity.

More difficult is Bonaventure's analysis of the divine attributes and modes of being. The modes of being are either absolute or relative. The absolute modes of being in God are identical with the divine essence. There is, therefore, no real distinction between essence, existence, and absolute modes of being in God.

But more subtle distinctions must be made with reference to relation and the relative modes of being. In any relation, we must distinguish between the *esse in* and the *esse ad;* the former refers to the inherence in a subject, the latter designates the ordering of one being to another. As relation is applied to the trinity, Bonaventure says consistently that the *esse in* passes over into substance; i.e. there is no subject of inherence distinct from the relation. The *esse ad*, on the other hand, does not pass into substance; it remains as a pure directedness to another. It is the *esse ad*, now seen as a subsistent relation, that provides the basis for speaking of three different modes in which the divine nature is possessed by the persons. The *esse* of the three persons is identical, but the manner in which each possesses divine being differs in accord with their relation to origin. The Father possesses the divine nature completely from Himself, and in no way from another. The Son possesses the divine nature as that which is communicated to Him from the Father. The Spirit possesses it as that which is communicated to Him by the Father and the Son.

These relative modes of being, also known as persons, involve no addition of new entities to the nature; but each is identical with the nature, though the relative modes stand in distinction to each other. Hence, while the relative modes do not provide sufficient grounds for speaking of composition, they do provide grounds for speaking of distinction.

The distinction resides in the persons and not in the nature. While nature and person are really identical, person is really distinct from person. Therefore, it is possible to make statements about the persons that cannot be made in the same sense of the nature. This provides the basis for distinguishing three modes of predication: 1) the essential mode, whereby things common to all three persons are predicated; 2) the personal mode, whereby things proper to one person are predicated; 3) the notional mode, whereby one predicates things that pertain to the persons, but not exclusively and properly to one. While the possibility of these different modes of predication is based on the real distinction between the persons and the distinction between the modes of possessing the one divine nature, the possibility of distinguishing the essential properties is based not on the reality of God but on the manner of human knowledge.

The distinction between *esse ad* and *esse in* is a helpful key for understanding what Bonaventure says about the properties and their relation to the essence and the persons. Parallel to the way in which *esse in* passes into substance, the property can be seen as identical with person *secundum modum essendi*. Yet, in terms of the *modus se habendi*, the property is distinct from the person.[37] From this position, the relation between property and essence becomes more clear; for person and essence are really identical. In relation to the essence, the property is only a mode of being which is really identical with the essence. Yet, parallel to the enduring status of the *esse ad* which constitutes the person and not the essence, the property differs from the essence in this relative aspect. The properties of the persons, relative to the divine nature, are modes of being. And, since in God being is radically identical with the modes of being, we can speak of distinction but not of composition.

IV. INFINITY AND TRINITY

At the beginning of his response in the first article of the question on infinity, Bonaventure, speaks of the need to be aware of how words function in dealing with the question of the infinity of God. Here perhaps more than anywhere else in the *Questions* the arguments

---

[37] I *Sent.* d. 33, a.u., q. 1, resp. (I, 572-573) carries out this parallel in express terms, and concludes: "...proprietas est persona et in persona, quia idem est per essentiam sive modum essendi, differt tamen quantum ad modum se habendi."

are based on word forms and are therefore dependent on the forms of the Latin language.

The presentation in the *Questions* is particularly difficult without the background that has been worked out in the *Sentence Commentary*.[38] There Bonaventure distinguishes various meanings of *finis* and of *negation*. Since both terms admit of two meanings, the following schema emerges which clarifies various possible meanings for the adjective forms: *finite* and *infinite*.

finis — as completion. When *finis* is understood as completion, a being is called infinite (= non-finite) to the degree that it lacks its completion (= *finis*). Understood in this sense, the term can be applied to the categories of matter, substance, and all other categories of being, but not to God who transcends the categories.

finis — as limit or boundary. The meaning of *finis* is clarified by analogy with the perimeter of a field (= *terminus* = *finis*). If the cognate adjectival form is drawn from this meaning, it applies to a being which has no boundary limiting it (= terminus), or which has no end (= status).

negation — privatively. In a privative sense, a negation signifies that a being whose nature it is to possess a certain quantity of being in fact does not realize the full potentiality of its nature. *Infinite* in this sense means incomplete, or lacking in perfection. As such, it can be applied to creatures but not to God.

negation — negatively. This refers to a being which, by nature, should have no limiting boundary and in fact does not. This applies only to God in His supreme immensity.

Thus, while the term *infinite* can be applied to creatures, it is always in the sense of a defect or a privation.[39] *Finis* may be viewed from yet another perspective which is pointed out by the Quaracchi editors[40] and which appears in Bonaventure's response to the objection: "Infinitum non finit."[41] In this sense, *finis* signifies that because of which something else exists. Relative to this meaning, the cognate form *finite* designates a being that is ordered to another as its end (= finis). Corresponding to this, *infinite* indicates a being which is dis-

---

[38] I *Sent.* d. 43, a.u., q. 2, resp. (I, 769-770).
[39] I *Sent.* d. 35, a.u., q. 5, ad 4 (I, 612).
[40] I *Sent.* d. 43, a.u., q. 1, scholion (I, 767).
[41] I *Sent.* d. 43, a.u., q. 2, ad 4 (I, 770).

orientated from its end. It is in reference to this understanding that the objection is raised that a being which is infinite cannot be the end of another; hence if God is said to be infinite, He cannot be the end or completing goal of creation. If infinite is taken to mean the lack of perfection as described above, the objection is true: "Infinitum non finit." But if infinite is understood to mean the denial of any limitation whatsoever, it is God — infinite in Himself — who is by nature the completing end of all created reality which finds its full and completing rest in Him (= status).[42]

As the term *infinite* is applied to God, it is a further specification of what has already been said concerning the unity and simplicity of the divine nature. To the extent that a being is simple, it is unified in itself and its power is more concentrated. And the more its power is concentrated, the more effective it can be and the fewer limits it has. Therefore, if God is supremely simple, His power is unified in the highest degree; and hence He is unlimited in power. But since, in God, being and power are really identical, if power is unlimited, so is being. Therefore, God is infinite both in His being and in His power. Indeed, it is that supremely unified and simple being that is the center and source of the divine power. God is infinite not in the sense that He lacks something which pertains to the fullness of His being, but rather in the sense that there is no limiting boundary to His being and His power. As such, He is supremely simple and unified, and hence supremely first; He is that being in whom all creatures have their end and goal.

If God is infinite, He is so in all respects. And if this is true, and if it is also true that there is a plurality of persons in God, then it seems that the number of persons must be infinite as God is infinite. All of the objections raise this problem in various ways. Hence, the main direction of Bonaventure's argument is to show the compatibility between the infinity of God and the fact that there are three and only three persons in God. The arguments of the first article have already shown that infinity as it applies to God involves an unlimited weight or number. Infinity, as a divine attribute, signifies not a deficiency but a fullness that knows no superfluity. Thus, in reference to the trinity, infinity means that the number of persons is neither deficient nor superfluous. The arguments given in the *Questions* are basically no different from those of the *Sentence Com-*

---

[42] I *Sent.* d. 43, a.u., q. 2, ad 4 (I, 770). The analysis of infinity and its applicability to God borrows heavily from the *Summa Fratris Alexandri* (I, q. 6, m. 1) and remotely from Aristotle (III *Phys.*, text. 63-66 [c. 6]; VII *Metaph.*, text. 40 [VI, c. 11]). The many ways in which the term may be understood are deeply rooted in the Aristotelian understanding of matter and form, and only against that background does the significance of a number of the arguments emerge.

mentary, though some new dimensions are brought out in the *Questions*.

The main arguments are based on the full perfection of God conceived in relation to His nature as productive Good; He is not only productive, but is productive in the most perfect way. As we have seen above, there are only two perfect modes of production; that of nature and that of liberality. Any imperfect types would not be found in God. Either these two modes of production are found most perfectly in God, or they are not perfect. If they are in God, and if God is perfect in all that He is, then they must be perfect in Him. The natural production proceeding from a being that is by nature the highest good would necessarily be the full and perfect self-communication of primal goodness. Though this self-communication expresses all the possible ways in which goodness can communicate itself, it does so in an immanent emanation which is but one Word. If all the possibilities were not expressed in it, then the production would not be perfect; if all the possibilities are expressed in it, then more than one would be superfluous. Similarly with the second emanation, it is the full and perfect act of pure liberality in which the lovers — seeking nothing for themselves — reach out to the other in pure liberality. From the pure, spiritual love between the two comes forth the personal love that is the Spirit. If the Spirit is not perfect, personal love, then the love of the Father and Son is defective; if the Spirit is perfect, personal love, then a multiplicity is superfluous. It is in the Spirit that the circle of divine love is closed. There can be no other perfect modes of emanation; and there can be no further immanent emanations in these two modes without implying imperfection in God.

It is in these two immanent emanations that all of God's actions *ad extra* are grounded. That there is some truth in the objections can be seen in the fact that when the self-expression of God reaches beyond the one immanent Word to the world of creation, it takes the form not of one creature but of a rich multiplicity of creatures which, in their very richness, express something of the inner fecundity of God. Yet, because the immanent Word bears the weight of the fullness of the divine fecundity, the world is liberated to be itself; it need not bear the weight of such total perfection.

The work of God *ad extra* finds its goal not simply in the existence of creatures, but in the indwelling of God in His personal creatures. For Bonaventure, the divine indwelling is mediated from the Father through the two persons who are produced; it finds its fullest realization in that the human person truly returns to the Father from whom it comes in the most radical sense. Since this relation between the soul and the Father is mediated through the two persons who emanate immanently and through their visible missions in history, the impossibility of an infinite number of produced persons appears in the doctrine of grace. For if there were an infinite number of produced persons, and if the soul returns to the Father through the produced persons, then it would be necessary for the created soul to traverse the infinite. Since this is a clear impossibility for Bonaventure, it follows that the number of produced persons cannot be infinite.

Thus, when the question is approached from each of three perspectives — from the nature of God, from the mystery of creation, and from the divine indwelling — the conclusion is that an infinity of persons is impossible, while a trinity of persons is fully in harmony with the infinity of God.

V. ETERNITY AND TRINITY

Boethius defined eternity as the "simultaneous and total possession of interminable life." Accepted in this form by Bonaventure, the definition is given greater clarity through its relation to other divine attributes, particularly simplicity and immensity.

As we have seen above, because God is absolutely simple, there is nothing prior or posterior in Him since these would imply some composition. On the other hand, immensity means that God has no beginning or end. Supreme simplicity implies full simultaneity, since it denies any prior or posterior; immensity implies complete interminability. When these two attributes — simultaneity and interminability — are brought together they constitute eternity. And since immensity and total simplicity are properties of God alone, so also eternity can be an attribute of God alone. Bonaventure sees this as a necessary conclusion since the two attributes which enter into it are necessary attributes of God. Necessary as it may be, it can be understood only by one who sets aside his imagination and sense-imagery and who approaches the question in terms of reason.

Yet certain analogies may help shed light on the question. Bonaventure takes up the example of God's presence to place. As was seen above, God is supremely simple and immense. He is totally one and unified in His being and power, knowing no hint of composition; and yet He is totally present to places which are distinct and physically separate from each other without suffering violence to His unity and simplicity. A similar relation may be seen between His immensity and time. Parallel to the unity and simplicity described above, the immensity of eternity means that what we experience in a time framework as past, present, and future is concentrated and compacted into one *now*. In the language of time, the attribute of eternity is clearly parallel to what unity and simplicity say in the language of space; namely, the total concentration of all the dynamism of being.

Thus, as the simple God is present to many separate places, so the eternal God is present to the many separate and distinct moments of time. Time itself may be seen as a vestige of eternity; for present, past, future are so rooted in the fluid movement of time that what was future later becomes present and then past. If, on the other hand, the present were understood to be rooted in unchangeable and stable being, we would be approaching the meaning of eternity by negating the defects of the vestige.

A more striking example is found in Bonaventure's view of memory in the human soul. Memory is here understood much in the Augustinian sense.[43] It is not simply the retention of past experiences, but involves a number of *a priori* functions in human knowledge. It is particularly in what Bonaventure calls memory that the human soul is in contact with the Ideas, the first principles of reason, and with God Himself. In the present instance, Bonaventure singles out three functions of memory; namely, the recall of the past, the knowledge of the present, and the foreknowledge of the future. Though these occur in real temporal succession, they are present to the soul simultaneously. Thus, a certain type of simultaneity is present in the soul, though, because of the soul's dependence on sense-experience, it is not a perfect simultaneity; for the soul's experience is bound up with the flow of time.

Limited as these examples are, they show the possibility of arriving at a proper understanding of eternity. Eternity is not an endless extension of time; rather, it is the fullest concentration of life in one point. Eternity is the mode of God's being as time is the creature's mode of being.

If God is necessarily eternal, how is it possible to see eternity in relation to the trinity ? The problems involved here are concerned primarily with the relation of production to simultaneity. Production seems to involve priority and posteriority just as cause is prior to effect. If there is no priority in the trinity, then all three persons are equally first, and hence none can proceed from another; production would seem to be impossible. But if there is priority and posteriority among the persons, then they are not equally eternal.

Bonaventure's analysis of this question revolves around three points: 1) the relation among essential attributes; 2) the proper understanding of the emanations of origin; 3) the nature of the personal relations. We have already seen how Bonaventure comes

---

[43] Cf. note 12 above.

to affirm unity, simplicity, and immensity as necessary attributes of God and as related to the mystery of the trinity. In the first article of the present question he has shown that God is necessarily eternal. But if the essential attributes are fundamentally one in God, though conceived separately by us, then if there is a harmonious relation between the trinity and the attributes of unity, simplicity, and immensity, so must there be harmony between the trinity and eternity. That there is true eternity in God is related to immensity; that there is supreme eternity is related to simplicity; and that there is one eternity is related to unity. If unity, simplicity, and immensity do not exclude the trinity, neither should eternity.

How this relation should be conceived can be seen better through reflection on the emanations which may be approached in terms of each of the three elements involved in the concept of production: 1) the person producing; 2) the person produced; and 3) the mode of production. Concerning the first, the person producing is really identical with the act of production; and in the act of production, he is totally engaged with the full extent of his power. As the person is really identical with the nature, and mode of being is really identical with being, it follows that the person in its mode of being as productive is eternal as is the nature; for they are at root one and inseparable. Simply stated, they are simultaneous. But if the person exists eternally as productive, then both the act of production and the term of production must likewise be eternal; they must be simultaneous with the eternal nature and person. Since the productive person produces with the full actuality of his power, the person produced bears the fullest conceivable likeness to its source, and hence is fully equal. And since the first production is one that flows necessarily from the nature of the supreme Good, the actual emanation can be no less eternal than the Good itself.

The emanations are the basis of the relations which distinguish the three persons. But the relations in God are not added subsequently to His being from without. On the contrary, they are intrinsic to the fullness of His being, and therefore are fully simultaneous with His nature. As relations that pertain to the fullness of being, they in no way conflict with His perfect infinity.

Though there is no prior or posterior in God, this does not mean that there is no order. There is, indeed, order; but it is the order based on origin. As origin need not be seen in terms of temporal sequence, though it is always found that way in the created world, so the order based on origin need not be a temporal order. It is the order based on the modes in which the divine nature is possessed. In the first person, it is possessed as in no way being from another and as being totally communicative; in the second person, it is possessed as being communicated from another, and as being itself communicative; in the third person, it is possessed as being totally communicated and in no way communicative. This is the order of the divinity. It must be pointed out further that the common tendency to equate *being from another* with a cause-effect relation must be transcended. The creature is from God as from its cause. But the concept of cause is here transcended by the trinitarian concept of principle. The causal relation between God and creation involves an essential difference between them as well as a relation of total dependence of the creature on God. The trinitarian concept of principle involves neither, but only personal distinction. Principle, therefore, refers to source or origin only and not to a relation of inferiority or dependence.

Thus Bonaventure hopes to have shown that the essential components of eternity are in full harmony with the trinity. The simultaneity involved in simplicity may be seen here in the full actuality of God's nature as productive Good, which emanates eternally and thus exists eternally in four intrinsic relations founded on the two perfect modes of emanations. The simultaneity of eternity is bursting with the dynamism of goodness and life. The interminability involved in immensity is seen in the fact that these relations are not accidental features that would add to an otherwise limited deity. Rather, as intrinsic relations, they express in a fuller way the limitless nature of the divine.

In speaking of these issues, we unavoidably make use of the language of time; language that can easily conjure up the image of temporal duration in God. Bonaventure recognizes such language as both useful and inadequate. It is useful, because it can be a means of expressing God's transcendence of whatever perfection is realized in time and expressed in temporal language. On the other hand, to the positivist who may be inclined to a one-dimensional understanding of language, Bonaventure points out the highly analogical quality of such language in which the sound of time attempts to express the silence of eternity. If we are to gain any deeper understanding, it can only be by transcending the images of sense-experience and even the possibilities of reason, and allow reason to be led beyond its limitations by the light of faith.

VI. IMMUTABILITY AND TRINITY

Concerning the immutability of God, Bonaventure speaks of unanimity among all who think correctly, whether they be philosophers or theologians. The Old Testament speaks of God in these terms, and reason can clarify that religious claim by showing that immutability is implied in the concept of God as the absolutely first being to which all mutable being must be reduced and in whom the entire created order finds its resting-point.

The meaning of immutability is clarified by showing its relation to the necessary attributes that have already been discussed, particularly the attributes of simplicity, immensity, and eternity. When the nature of God is approached in terms of simplicity, any possibility of change would have to be viewed as a change of form. Since any change of form is impossible in a being who is absolutely simple, no change of this sort can be envisioned; as simple being, possessing nothing accidental to itself, the divine nature is incapable of change in itself. As immense being, God is present in His totality to each point of space. It is therefore inconceivable that He should be transported from one place to another; as immense, He can undergo no change in reference to place. Eternity involves a similar relation to time; God is present to each separate moment of time just as He is present to every distinct place. Hence, as eternal, He can undergo no change in reference to time. Citing Augustine and Hugh of St. Victor, Bonaventure argues that all change can be reduced to one or the other of these three possibilities: change in form, in place, or in time. Since the three attributes have already been seen as necessary qualities of the divine nature, the affirmation of immutability seems unavoidable.

But a serious objection seems to arise from God's external works, especially the works of creation, historical mission, and indwelling. If creation means that the world of created reality begins to exist after non-existence, it seems that God must become Creator in actuality after being only potentially a Creator. It seems, further, that He performs distinct acts in succession, such as creating, conserving, sparing, and punishing. Finally, the act of creation certainly seems to imply that God enters into a relation to creation, as do other relative attributes such as those expressed in the titles Lord, Refuge, and King. All of this seems to imply change in God.

Bonaventure's response to such questions lies well within the framework of classical metaphysical concepts. He replies that change is indeed involved; but it is to be understood in terms of a non-mutual relation. The change is in the creature only and not in God. God's action is totally identical with His being; and like His being, it neither begins nor ends. The divine action has effects in time, but eternity and time are essentially different modes of existence corresponding to the nature of God and the nature of the creature respectively. A logical error occurs when this is overlooked and God's eternal being is conceived as if it had extension in time that differs only in being longer than that of the creature. The difference between these two modes of existence must be respected consistently at the logical level. In Bonaventure's view, this takes the form of direct signification and connotation. In speaking of God in terms of relative attributes, our predications signify directly God who is eternal and immutable; but at the same time, they connote an effect in the order of temporal changeable beings. Thus, God Himself is eternally identical with His act; there is neither beginning nor end, nor any plurality of actions. But the external effect exists only in its proper mode of being; and hence it is multiple, mutable, and temporal. Any statements which seem to imply that God begins to do something which He was not doing before must be understood only and exclusively of the external effect.

The same problem arises but in an even more acute form when we turn our attention to the history of salvation. The New Testament seems to have no hesitation in speaking of the mission and descent of the Son of God. The effect of the mission of the Son is the incarnation, the assumption of a human nature which He did not possess prior to the incarnation. The doctrine of grace affirms the indwelling of God in human souls in such a way that the divine presence begins to exist in the repentant person just as it ceases to exist in the sinner. But how is it possible to make such statements without affirming change in God, at least of an accidental sort ? Yet if the history of salvation obliges us to make such statements, does it not require us to affirm some sort of change in God ?

The response to such questions follows the same fundamental pattern as we have seen above. Here as elsewhere in his works, Bonaventure emphasizes the metaphorical character of terms such as *descent* and *mission*. The Son does not embark on a space odyssey, leaving the Father for a period of time, literally coming down, and later returning to His proper abode in the trinity. Such an understanding arises from taking a metaphor too literally. It must be understood that God, precisely as a trinity, is present to all times and places. To speak of a mission of one of the divine persons is to say that the eternal emanation is made manifest in time and has a particular temporal effect. The purpose of any such mission is to deepen the reality of the indwelling of God in human souls. Thus, when we say that the Son is sent, or that He descends, this does not indicate something new on the part of God, but designates that the temporal effect of the eternal emanation has a beginning and endures in time. Similarly, in speaking of the assumption of a human nature by the Son of God, the language of incarnation should be understood to involve a change in the created nature but not in the Word Himself.

Finally, the indwelling of God is effected not by a change in God but by a change in the human person.

The relation of immutability to the trinity is developed largely through its relation to eternity and simplicity. Eternity, as we have seen, excludes any change; simplicity excludes even the possibility of change, since it excludes any sort of composition. Thus, if the trinity is understood in terms of supreme simplicity, eternity, and immutability, it appears that the convergence of all these attributes points to the fact that the trinity is being in its fullest possible actualization. The question of the trinity, then, is the question of being, viewed from a particular sort of religious experience. Here the deeper metaphysical dimensions come to the fore. Being at its highest and fullest actualization is realized in the two dynamic moments of knowledge and love; knowledge which gives rise to a word of self-expression, and love as a unifying power. Thus, that which we conceive of and speak of in terms of our temporal experience and categories is in reality the total, full dynamism of spiritual being at its apex of actuality. It is being that is totally luminous to itself, and fully unified within itself through the power of love. It is in this way that God exists immutably and actually; and thus He is actually and immutably a trinity. God is always, actually and unchangeably in full conformity with what He is.

Hence, while we use the language of generation and production to speak of the origin of the Son and the Spirit, this language is analogical and must be purified of all the limiting elements which are involved in generation among creatures. Production and generation, therefore, do not involve any emergence of new being in God, but express the eternal actuality of the fecund nature of the mystery of the divine being.

VII. NECESSITY AND TRINITY

As we have seen earlier, Bonaventure distinguishes three types of necessity; one that is totally extrinsic to a being, another that is totally intrinsic, and a third that is partly intrinsic and partly extrinsic. Each of these, in turn, includes sub-categories, the differences arising from the source of the necessity. Some types of necessity are brought to a being from factors outside itself, while others arise from a relation of one being to another upon which it depends for its full actualization. But of all the types which may be distinguished, it is only a completely intrinsic necessity springing from the very nature of the being in question that can be applied to God.

It is that type of necessity which Bonaventure calls a necessity

---

7 St. Bonaventure, Disputed Questions

of immutability or independence. By it he wishes to say that God is in no way necessitated by anything outside Himself and is in no way dependent on others for His fullness of being. He is fully and completely self-sufficient and completely true to His own nature. He can be in no other way than He is. Such an understanding of necessity does not conflict with the freedom of the divine will, as would be the case with the other types of necessity. It is precisely because God is fully self-sufficient in Himself that He can communicate Himself freely to others without any loss or any threat of loss. Necessity of this sort is what is meant when it is said that God exists in and of Himself. Existing in Himself, He knows no composition of any sort in Himself; existing of Himself, He is neither made nor sustained by any other. Lacking all composition, He is incapable of change; lacking any creative or sustaining cause, He neither comes into being nor ceases to be. His being is permanent, stable, self-sufficient; it is unchangeable and independent of all others, free of all need and of all forms of coercion from without. God exists not for the sake of anything else, but simply for His own sake. He is that necessary being to which all contingent being must be reduced. As the being that exists in and of itself and for its own sake, God is the absolute source and the fulfilling end of all else. In the words of the New Testament, He is the Alpha and the Omega.

What can this mean in relation to the trinity? It must be recalled that for Bonaventure, the dominant category for conceptualizing God is the category of the Good, but the Good conceived in personal terms. As the Good that is necessarily (= necessity of immutability) in full accord with its own nature, it must be supremely communicative. But since He is Good that is supremely personal, liberality and generosity must be a dimension of the communicativeness of God. It is, therefore, precisely in the trinitarian conception of God that it becomes possible to transcend the dilemma: either necessitated or free; either totally self-sufficient or dependent on creation in order to be God. There is a sense in which necessity applies to God. For Bonaventure, it is in the sense of the necessity of immutability and independence. As this type of necessity is seen in relation to the nature of the Good, it provides the context for understanding the necessary (= *per naturam*) emanation of the Son as the necessary, immanent self-communication of the Good. As we have seen above, when this neo-Platonic viewpoint is extended through the personal category of love, the circle of divine self-communication is completed through a communication whose proximate principle is the will. Thus we see the significance of the two technical phrases used by Bonaventure to express the role of nature and will in both the divine processions: "natura, concomitante voluntate," and "voluntas, concomitante natura." The will is present in the first procession as concomitant and approving though the procession emanates from the nature of God as Good and therefore has a prevoluntary dimension. The second procession is immediately from the will as generous and liberal; it is a communication of fully personal love. Conceiving of God in this way places the full burden of being God in the Godhead itself; for it is there that the full communication of the Good takes place as both necessary and free. But if God is thus conceived, it follows that any other communication is not necessary for the sake of God's existence as God. And if that be the case, then it follows that when God does in fact communicate being to creation, the created world need not be made to bear the weight of being God. As the world, it is the contingent and limited participation in being, goodness, and truth. It need not be a perfect world or the best possible world; it is sufficient that it be a world of limited goodness that is apt for the working out of God's loving purpose.

So as the dialectical relation of necessity and will is seen in God, it becomes possible to see both the nature of God and His relation to the world with far richer theological depth. If necessity is to be affirmed of God as regards His nature as self-communicative Good, then necessity must be an attribute of all that is really identical with that nature. Since the three persons, while distinct among themselves, are really identical with the divine nature, they are necessary as the nature itself is necessary. They are really simultaneous with the nature, though generally conceived in temporal categories. Hence, they all exist equally and immutably. And since, for the fullness of the divine self-communication, the will is required, Bonaventure can conclude that trinity, necessity, and will coexist. Not only are they not contradictory; but when properly understood, they reveal a remarkable coherence and inner harmony with each other.

The relation of necessity and will in God helps clarify in what sense God is the end and goal in which His creation is to find its beatifying rest. The intellect of the human person is carried throughout life by a constant search for truth, never to find rest from its quest unless it should find truth that is infallibly necessary; for only in such truth will it find security. But the spirit-life of humankind is not only a cognitive adventure, for cognition itself is not complete without the inner drive for union with the object known. This involves the area of affectivity and will. As the intellect does not find rest in the truths to be discerned in creatures but only in the Truth that is necessary and infallible, so the will does not come to rest in its reach for the good until it embraces the supreme Good. But the supreme Good, if it is to transcend the impersonal categories of neo-Platonism, must include the personal dimensions of love and will. It is only when these dimensions are taken into account that we can speak of God in terms of pleasure and happiness. Thus, through the two most basic moments of its spiritual life, the created spirit is orientated to a being that is both necessary and free, for only when the supreme security which flows from the divine necessity is united with the supreme pleasure that flows from the divine goodness and will can the human spirit find supreme happiness and fulfilling rest. Our affection rests only in that good which is supremely lovable, and our mind rests only in that truth which is supremely infallible and certain; we can be beatified, therefore, only in a being that is both necessary and voluntary. Since, as we have already seen, necessity and will exist in God only in as far as He is a trinity, it is only in a trinitarian God that the journey of the created soul will come to rest.

When we are lead to speak of necessity with respect to the trinity, it does not follow that either the fact of the trinity or its necessity must be fully evident to us. Evidence must be considered both from the objective and from the subjective side. Objectively, God's existence as a trinity is most evident in itself. As we have seen in the first question, such a mystery is not fully evident to the human mind in the limitations of its historical existence. But when the natural light of the mind is illumined by the eternal light of God, the evidence for the trinity is such that we may speak of certitude, albeit a certitude of faith. Such a certitude transcends even the certitude of reason, and it directs the created spirit to that mystery in which alone it will find the fulfillment of its quest for truth and goodness.

VIII. PRIMACY AND TRINITY

It is in the treatment of primacy that the entire development of the *Questions* finds its high-point. Not only is primacy the climax of this particular work, but it is fundamental to Bonaventure's approach to God in general and to the trinity in particular. It is, indeed, a very personal development of the Seraphic Doctor and is found in this form in none of his predecessors. In the present context, Bonaventure brings his entire lengthy discussion of the divine attributes to a close with his attempt to prove that primacy, when properly understood, demands the existence of the trinity. By the mere fact that God is the first principle, He is necessarily a trinity.

We are here at the heart and center of Bonaventure's trinitarian system from which he explains both the mystery of the trinity and the nature of God's relation to creatures. God is first not only in the sense that His nature is prior to all created natures, but the concept of primacy must be drawn into the very life of God where it finds its absolute roots in the person of the Father, who is source and origin of all, within and without the Godhead. The origin of all from the Father through the Son and Spirit, and the return of all to the Father through the Son and the Spirit constitutes the "intelligible circle" of created existence which, in its own way, reflects the "intelligible circle" that is the life of God.

As the absolutely first being, God is being in its fullness. This we have seen at work over and over in the arguments of the preceding questions. A lack or privation can be known only through the corresponding positive quality which is prior not only in the logical order, but in the real order as well. To the degree that something is prior, to the same degree it is more full of the positive qualities and perfections of being. Since God is absolutely prior to all else, He is the full actuality of being in all its necessary perfections.

From this, it follows that God is cause of others to the degree that He is first; for to be first is the same as to be principle.[44] To be principle with respect to the world is to be cause or source from which all emanates and to which all returns. The productive fecundity of God is in proportion to His primacy;[45] His absolute primacy, therefore, designates Him as the universal fountain of all origin, or in Bonaventure's suggestive terms, the *fontalis plenitudo*. He is the absolute source and cause of all that exists.

Not only does primacy illumine God's nature as fountain of all created being, but — as Bonaventure argues — if God is eternal, then He is principle from eternity. But, since He is pure actuality in all that He is, He must be eternally productive as principle. But if we are not to be forced to conclude that the world is necessary and eternal, we must conclude that the primacy of God requires perfect, intrinsic production. We are, therefore, lead into the realm of trinitarianism. Primacy demands not only that God be cause of the world, but also that He be perfectly and eternally productive within Himself; for if He is eternally first, He is eternally principle, most perfect, most actual and productive prior to the production of the world. Indeed, it is precisely because He is productive within that the production of the external world is possible; for the world is not equal with God, but the production of something unequal is necessarily posterior to the production of something equal. The necessary prior condition for the production of the world, therefore, is the eternal production of another who is fully equal with God.

---

[44] I *Sent.* d. 28, a. 1, q. 2, ad 4. Also, in the present *Question*, fundament 1.
[45] I *Sent.* d. 2, a. 1, q. 2, fund. 4: "quanto aliquid prius tanto fecundius."

Primacy with respect to the world, consequently, requires primacy within God Himself.

Thus far, we have seen the relation between primacy and production in God. The question of the productions may be further clarified through the basic movements of spiritual, intellectual beings which are active as principles through an inner word of knowledge and the intrinsic gift of love. Such a principle first conceives an inner word and breathes love within before it produces an external effect. The analogy may be applied to God as a spiritual principle; before He can be productive externally, He must be productive internally in this two-fold way. These two modes of intrinsic productivity may be further specified as productions *per modum naturae* and *per modum voluntatis* as clarified above. But these two immanent modes of production must have a proportionate term, which is found in the hypostatic Word and in the hypostatic Love. The divine fecundity, which lies most radically in the Father but is possessed in common by the three persons with respect to creatures, is the fount from which flow the inner-divine emanations as well. Creation itself is but the radiation in space and time of the eternal inner-trinitarian life.

Primacy, then, is the central trinitarian concept for Bonaventure's system. As the eighth *argument* shows, all the necessary attributes discussed in the previous questions are brought together around this concept. That which is abolutely first is prior in all respects to that which is not first. Since creation is the production of that which is imperfect, lacking in unity, composed, finite, in potency, temporal, changeable, lacking in actuality and necessity, such a production is necessarily posterior to a production which brings forth the perfect, supreme, undivided, simple, infinite, eternal, immutable, and necessary. A study of the previous arguments shows that, to a great extent, they are but variations on this theme. This indicates the density and compactness of Bonaventure's thought which is guided by a relatively small number of keenly perceived insights.

For centuries of Christian literary history, Rachel had been known as the symbol of the contemplative life. Reaching to that tradition, Bonaventure can appeal to the symbolic figure of this Old Testament woman to bring his reflections to a close, and to trace in a few bold strokes the relation of the trinity to the mystery of the human person. It is not in the contemplation of an abstract, impersonal first principle that we find rest and fulfillment, but only in the contemplation of that mystery of the most holy, personal God of goodness and love. As the trinitarian life of God may be symbolized by a circle, so also human existence is a going-out from the triune God and a return to the same God after the manner of an intelligible circle through memory, intelligence, and will. The human soul will find its full completion and its rest in that it becomes conformed to the triune God Himself as a true similitude of the trinitarian mystery which has stamped its creation with the indelible sign of its origin. And this is eternal life which flows from the eternal Fount of Life, sweeping like a great river through time and history and the spiritual development of humanity, and closing back on its point of origin. He is the Alpha aud the Omega; the Beginning and the End.

THE DISPUTED QUESTIONS
ON THE MYSTERY OF THE TRINITY

The Text of St. Bonaventure
in Translation

With the help of divine grace, we intend to offer some reflections concerning the mystery of the trinity beginning with two questions as a preamble. The first of these is the foundation of all certain knowledge; the second is the foundation of all the knowledge of faith. The first is whether the existence of God is an indubitable truth; the second is whether it is a truth of faith that God is a trinity.

QUESTION I

CONCERNING THE CERTITUDE WITH WHICH THE EXISTENCE OF GOD IS KNOWN, AND CONCERNING THE FAITH BY WHICH THE TRINITY OF THE SAME GOD IS BELIEVED

ARTICLE I

WHETHER THE EXISTENCE OF GOD IS AN INDUBITABLE TRUTH

In the first place, the question is raised as to whether the existence of God is an indubitable truth. There are three ways of arguing in favor of this. The first way says: Every truth that is impressed in all minds is an indubitable truth. The second way says: Every truth proclaimed by all creatures is an indubitable truth. And the third way says: Every truth which, in itself, is most certain and most evident is an indubitable truth.

The first way shows both from authority and from proofs that the existence of God is impressed in all rational minds, and it proceeds in the following manner.

ARGUMENTS IN AGREEMENT

1. In the third chapter of the first book, Damascene writes: "The knowledge of God's existence is naturally implanted in us."[1]

2. Again, Hugh writes: "God has tempered the knowledge of Himself in man in such a way that while man can never totally comprehend what God is, yet at the same time, he can never be totally ignorant of the fact that God exists."[2]

3. Again, Boethius writes: "The desire for the true and the good is implanted in the minds of men."[3] But an inclination toward the true and the good presupposes knowledge thereof. Therefore, there is impressed in the minds of men a knowledge of the true and the good and a desire for that which is most desirable. But that good is God. Therefore, etc.

4. Again, in many places in his work *On the Trinity*,[4] Augustine says that the image consists in mind, knowledge and love; and the concept of image is applied to the soul because of its relation to God. If, therefore, it is impressed in the soul by nature that it is an image of God, it follows that the soul has knowledge of God implanted in it by nature. But the first thing knowable about God is that He exists. Therefore, this is naturally implanted in the human mind.

5. Again, the Philosopher says that "it would be inappropriate for us to be in possession of the most noble habits and yet to know nothing of them."[5] And since the truth of God's existence is the most noble truth and the one most present to us, it would be inappropriate that such a truth should remain hidden to the human intellect.

6. Again, the desire for wisdom is implanted in the minds of men since, as the Philosopher says: "By nature all men desire to know."[6] But that wisdom which is most desirable is the eternal wisdom. Therefore, there is implanted in the human mind a desire for such wisdom above all else. But as we said earlier, love cannot exist unless there is some knowledge of the object loved. Therefore, it is necessary that some knowledge of that highest wisdom be impressed in the human mind. But this is first of all to know the existence of God, who is that wisdom. Therefore, etc.

---

[1] *De Fide Orthod.;* cf. also c. 1.
[2] *I De Sacram.*, p. 3, c. 1.
[3] *Lib. III de Consol.*, prosa 2.
[4] IX, c. 2, n. 2 ff.; XII, c. 4, n. 4 ff.; XIV, c. 8, n. 11 ff.
[5] *Lib. II Poster.* c. 18 (c. 15).
[6] *Lib. I. Metaph.* c. 1.

7. Again, the desire for happiness is implanted in us in such a way that no one can doubt that other men wish to be happy, as Augustine writes in many places.[7] But happiness is found in the highest good, which is God. Therefore, if such desire is impossible without some knowledge, it is necessary that the knowledge by which we know the existence of God as the highest good be implanted in the soul itself.

8. Again, a desire for peace is implanted in the soul to such an extent that peace is sought even through its opposite, and the desire cannot be removed even from the damned and the demons, according to the *City of God*, 19.[8] But if there can be no peace for the rational mind except in a being that is eternal and immutable, and if desire presupposes some notion or some knowledge, then a knowledge of the eternal and immutable being is implanted in the rational spirit.

9. Again, a hatred of falsehood is implanted in the soul. But every hatred takes its origin in love. Therefore, the love of truth is even more firmly implanted in the soul; and this is especially true with reference to that truth in whose likeness the soul is made. But if that is the first truth, it follows necessarily that some knowledge of the first truth is implanted in the rational mind. The fact that the human mind has an innate hatred of falsehood is apparent in the fact that no one wants to be deceived, as Augustine writes in the tenth book of his *Confessions*.[9] In the fourteenth book of the *City of God*,[10] Augustine shows that hatred is caused by love; for no one hates something unless he loves its opposite.

10. Again, the rational soul naturally has knowledge of itself whereby the soul is present to and knowable to itself. But God is most present to the soul and is knowable in Himself. Therefore some knowledge of God Himself is implanted in the very soul. If you say that there is no similarity here since the soul is proportional to itself whereas God is not proportional to the soul, I reply on the contrary that there is no parallel, because if proportionality were necessarily required for knowledge, the soul could never come to a knowledge of God since it can be proportioned to Him neither by nature, nor by grace, nor by glory.

These arguments show that the existence of God is indubitable for the human mind as a truth that is naturally impressed. One cannot be in doubt except in matters about which there is no certain knowledge.

---

[7] *De Trin.* XIII, c. 3, n. 3; c. 4, n. 7 ff., c. 20, n. 25.
[8] C. 13, n. 1 ff., also c. 11 & 12.
[9] C. 23, n. 33 ff.
[10] C. 7, n. 2.

Again, the same point is shown in a second way as follows: Every truth that is proclaimed by all creatures is an indubitable truth. But all creatures cry out the existence of God. Therefore, etc. That every creature proclaims the existence of God is shown from ten self-evident postulates and their presuppositions.

11. The first is this: If there is posterior being, then there is prior being, because there is nothing posterior except it be from something prior.[11] But if the sum total of posterior being exists, there must necessarily be a first being. Therefore, if it is necessary to say that among creatures there is both posterior and prior, it is necessary that the sum total of creatures infers and cries out that there is a first principle.

12. Again, if there is being that exists from another, there is also being that does not exist from another, because nothing can bring itself from non-being to being.[12] Therefore there must necessarily be a first principle of eduction, and this is found in the first being which is not educed from another. Therefore, if that being which exists from another is called a created being, and that being which does not exist from another is called uncreated being — and this is God, then every category of being infers the existence of God.

13. Again, if there is possible being, there is a necessary being since that which is possible implies indifference as to being or non-being. But nothing that is indifferent to being and non-being can exist except through something that is entirely determined with respect to being.[13] Therefore, if that necessary being in which there is no possibility of non-existence is none other than God, and if everything else has some degree of possibility, every category of being infers the existence of God.

14. Again, if there is relative being, there is also absolute being, because the relative is never terminated except in the absolute.[14] But an absolute being which depends on no other can only be a being that receives nothing from another. This is the first being, and all other being is in some way dependent. Therefore it is necessary that every category of being infers the existence of God.

15. Again, if there is diminished being or qualified being, there is a being that exists absolutely, because qualified being can neither exist nor be understood unless it is understood through unqualified being. Neither can diminished being exist or be understood except through perfect being, just as a privation cannot be understood

---

[11] Aristotle, *IV Phys.* text. 7 (c. 1); *II Metaph.* text. 10 (I brevior c. 2) & V text. 17 (IV, c. 11).
[12] Aristotle, *II De Anima*, text. 47 (c. 4).
[13] Cf. Avicenna, *Metaph.* tr. 1, c. 7.
[14] Aristotle, *I Ethic.* 6.

except with respect to a habit.[15] Therefore, if every created being is being only in part, and if the uncreated being alone is absolute and perfect being, it is necessary that any category of being infers and leads to the conclusion that God exists.

16. Again, if there is being that exists because of another, there is also being that exists because of itself, otherwise nothing would be good.[16] But that which exists because of itself is none other than that being than which none is better, and this is God Himself. Therefore since the sum total of other beings is ordered to Him, the sum total of beings infers God both as to being and as to understanding.

17. Again, if there is being by participation, there is also being by essence, since one cannot speak of participation except with respect to some essential property which is had from another, since everything that exists accidentally is to be reduced to that which exists of itself.[17] But every being other than the first being — which is God — has being by participation; the first being alone has being by essence. Therefore, etc.

18. Again, if there is being in potency, there is being in act, because a potency can be reduced to act only through a being in act, and there would be no potency unless it were capable of being reduced to act.[18] If that being which is pure act and has no potency is none other than God, it is necessary that everything other than the first being infers the fact that God exists.

19. Again, if there is composite being, there is simple being, because a composite does not have being of itself.[19] Therefore it is necessary that it take its origin from something that is simple. But the most simple being, having no trace of composition, is none other than the first being. Therefore, every other being infers God.

20. Again, if there is changeable being, there is also unchangeable being, since — as the Philosopher proves — movement takes its origin from a being at rest and terminates in a being at rest.[20] If, therefore, that being which is entirely unchangeable is none other than the first being — which is God — and if all others are created, and in as far as they are created, they are changeable, it is necessary that the existence of God is inferred by any category of being.

---

[15] Averroes, *III De Anima*, text. 25.
[16] Boethius, *De Hebdomadibus;* Aristotle, *XII Metaph.* text. 52 (XI, c. 10).
[17] Aristotle, *II Phys.* text. 66 (c. 6.).
[18] Aristotle, *IX Metaph.*, text. 13 (VIII, c. 8).
[19] *Lib. de Causis*, prop. 21 ff.; Rich. of St. Victor, *De Trin.* V, 4; Alan of Lille, *I De Arte seu Articulis Cathol. Fidei*, n. 3.
[20] *Lib. VIII Phys.*, text. 33 ff. (c. 5); *XII Metaph.*, text. 35 ff. (XI, c. 7); *Lib. de Causis*, prop. 18.

From these ten necessary and manifest postulates it is inferred that all categories or divisions of being infer and proclaim the fact that God exists. But if every such truth is an indubitable truth, it follows necessarily that it is true beyond doubt that God exists.

The same thing can be demonstrated in a third way as follows. Every truth which is so certain that it cannot be thought not to be is indubitably true. But the existence of God is such a truth; therefore, etc. The first premise is self-evident; the second can be shown in a number of ways.

21. For Anselm writes in the fourth chapter of the *Proslogion:* "Good Lord, I give you thanks, because that which I first believed through your gift, I now understand through your illumination, so that even if I did not wish to believe in your existence, I could not fail to understand its truth."

22. Again, Anselm proves the same thing in the following way: God is that than which nothing greater can be conceived.[21] But since it is true that that which cannot be thought not to be is more true than that which can be thought not to be, therefore, if God is that than which nothing greater can be conceived, God cannot be thought not to be.

23. Again, that being than which nothing greater can be conceived is of such a nature that it cannot be thought of unless it exists in reality. For if it exists only in thought, then it is not that being than which no greater can be thought. Therefore if such a being is thought to be, it is necessary that such a being, which cannot be thought not to be, exist in reality.

24. Again, Anselm writes: "You alone are whatever is better to to be than not to be."[22] But every indubitable truth is better than a doubtful truth. Therefore being is to be attributed to God indubitably rather than doubtfully.

25. Again, Augustine writes in his *Soliloquies* that no truth can be seen except through the first truth.[23] But that truth through which every truth is seen is the most indubitable truth. Therefore, the existence of God is not only an indubitable truth, but it is impossible to think of something more indubitable. It is, therefore, a truth of such a sort that it cannot be thought not to be.

26. Again, he proves the same thing as follows.[24] Whatever can be thought of can be stated. But it is in no way possible to say that God does not exist without saying simultaneously that God does

---

[21] *Proslog.*, c. 3, 4 & 15; *Libro contra Insipientem*, c. 1 ff.
[22] *Proslog.*, c. 5.
[23] *Lib. I*, c. 8, n. 15.
[24] *Soliloq.* I, c. 15, n. 27 ff., II, c. 2, n. 2; c. 15, n. 28; Anselm, *Monolog.*, c. 18.

exist. This becomes clear in the following way. If there is no truth, then it is true to say: "There is no truth." But if this is true, then something is true. And if something is true, there is a first truth. Therefore, if it is not possible to say that God does not exist, neither is it possible to think it.

27. Again, to the degree that a truth is prior and more universal, to that degree it is more evident.[25] But that truth by which the existence of the first being is affirmed is the first of all truths, not only in reality but also in our knowledge of reality. Therefore, it is necessarily the most certain and most evident truth. But the truth of the axioms or the first concepts of the mind are so evident because of their priority that they cannot be thought not to be. Therefore no intellect can think that there is no first truth, nor can it be in doubt about this.

28. Again, "No proposition can be more true than that sort in which something is predicated of itself."[26] But when I say that God exists, the existence predicated of God is totally identical with God, because God is His very existence. Therefore, nothing is more true or more evident than that proposition in which the existence of God is affirmed. Therefore no one can think that it is false or can be in doubt about it.

29. Again, no one can be ignorant of the truth that "the best is the best," and no one can think that this is false. But that which is best is the most complete being, and every being that is complete to the highest degree by that very fact exists in actuality. Therefore, if the best is the best, the best exists. It can be argued in a similar way: If God is God, then God exists. But the antecedent is so true that it cannot be thought not to be. Therefore it is indubitably true that God exists.

But on the other hand, the objection is raised that it is possible to think that God does not exist, and that it is a truth that can be doubted. That God can be thought not to be is shown in the following way.

OBJECTIONS

1. The *Psalm* says: "The fool has said in his heart there is no God."[27] But "to say in one's heart" is to think. Therefore it is possible, at least for a fool, to think that God does not exist.

2. Again, in the third chapter of the first book Damascene writes:

---

[25] Aristotle, *I Poster.*, c. 2; *I Phys.*, text. 2 ff.
[26] Boethius, *II Periherm. Arist.*, c. 4 (c. 14).
[27] *Ps.* 13, 1.

"The pernicious evil of human nature has prevailed to such an extent that it has led some men to the most irrational and most evil abyss of perdition of saying that there is no God."[28] Therefore, it is possible at least for evil men to think that there is no God.

3. Again, according to 1 *Cor.* 8, an idol is nothing.[29] Therefore, to think that God is an idol is the same as to think that He does not exist. But it is possible to think that God is an idol, and this does happen at times. Therefore it is possible to think that God is nothing.

4. Again, whatever can be signified can be thought also. But it is possible to signify the non-existence of God as happens in the statement: "God does not exist." Therefore, it can also be thought.

5. Again, an objection is raised against Augustine's argument which proved that the proposition "there is no truth" implies that there is some truth. For if it is true that "something is true," then this proposition has a contradictory. But no proposition entails or assumes its contradictory statement. On the contrary, it assumes it is not the case. Therefore, from the statement that there is no truth, one does not conclude that there is some truth.

6. Again, an objection is raised against the argument by which Anselm proved the existence of God from the fact that a being, than which no greater can be conceived, exists in thought. For the same reason, if someone conceives of an island than which no greater can be conceived, one can argue that such an island exists in reality.[30] If the latter argument is invalid, so is the argument of Anselm.

7. Again, the question is raised: In what sense is it said that it is impossible to think that God does not exist? It is manifestly false if it is taken to mean that this can be thought in no sense whatever. But if it is taken to mean that it cannot be thought truly, then the same argument shows that every necessary truth is of this sort.

Again, it is shown that the existence of God is a truth that can be doubted.

8. Richard of St. Victor writes: "We hold nothing with greater certitude than that which we apprehend by faith."[31] But there can be doubt about those things which we apprehend by faith. Therefore even more so is it possible to doubt concerning all other objects of knowledge.

9. Again, that which is supremely hidden admits of a very great degree of doubt. But God is supremely hidden, since "He

---

[28] *De Fide Orthod.*
[29] Verse 4.
[30] The example of the island is raised against Anselm's *Proslogion* by Gaunilo in *Pro Insipiente.*
[31] *De Trin.*, I, c. 2.

dwells in inaccessible light."[32] Therefore a very great degree of doubt attaches to the reality of God and all things concerning Him. If doubt is possible concerning the existence of other things, even more so is it possible concerning God.

10. Again, there is doubt about realities that are below or on a par with the soul. But such things are more accessible to the soul than those things which are superior to it. But if the truth of God's existence is beyond human understanding, it seems that there can be great doubt about it.

11. Again, in the case of God, to exist and to be just are identical. But it is possible to doubt whether God is just. For the same reason, it is possible to doubt whether He exists.

12. Again, it is pointless for anyone to attempt to prove that about which no doubt is possible.[33] Therefore, if the existence of God can be doubted by no one, it is pointless to try to prove it. But if the Saints and Doctors who attempted to prove it were not working in vain, it is clear that it must be possible to doubt it.

13. Again, no one knows the principle "The whole is greater than its part" unless he knows what a whole is.[34] Therefore, no one knows whether God exists unless he knows what God is. But if doubts are possible concerning God's essence, they are also possible concerning His existence.

14. Again, if there could be no doubt concerning the truth of the existence of God, there would be no merit in belief. But the source of all merit is to believe that God exists, as it is written in *Hebrews* 11: "Anyone who comes to Him must believe that He exists, etc."[35] Therefore, if this is to be reckoned as meritorious, it is also something that can be doubted.

CONCLUSION

That God exists cannot be doubted if dubitable is understood as a truth for which evidence is lacking in itself, or in its proof, or in the intellect that apprehends it. Nonetheless, doubt can arise from the viewpoint of the knower; namely, by reason of a deficiency in the acts of apprehending, judging, and reducing.

Response. In order to understand the foregoing, we must note that a thing is indubitable by reason of the absence of anything that

---

[32] 1 *Tim.* 6, 16.
[33] The first principles, which cannot be demonstrated. Aristotle, *I Poster.*, c. 3.
[34] Aristotle, *I Poster.*, c. 3.
[35] Verse 6.

could be doubted. A thing is said to be doubtful in two ways: either because of the process of reasoning or because of a defect in reason itself. The first way involves something on the part of the knower and on the part of the object known; the second way refers only to the knower. In the first sense, a truth is said to be doubtful if the reason for its evidence is lacking either in itself, or in its demonstration, or in the intellect that apprehends it. Concerning the existence of God, certitude is not lacking in any of these ways.

Indeed, it is certain as far as the knower is concerned, for the knowledge of this truth is innate to the rational mind in as far as it possesses the nature of an image. By reason of this, there is innate to the mind a natural desire for, together with a knowledge and memory of that reality in whose image it is made, and to which it naturally tends for its beatitude.

It is even more certain in terms of its demonstration. All creatures, whether they are viewed in terms of their defects or in terms of their perfectibility, in voices most loud and strong, cry out the existence of God whom they need because of their deficiency and from whom they receive their completion. Therefore, in accordance with the greater or lesser degree of fullness which they possess, some cry out the existence of God with a loud voice; others cry out yet louder; while still others make the loudest cry.

Moreover, it is a truth that is most certain in itself, in as far as it is the first and most immediate truth. In it not only is the cause of the predicate included in the subject, but it is the fullness of being itself which is predicated and which is the subject about which the predication is made. As a union of beings that are extremely distant from each other is entirely repugnant to our mind, because no mind can think that one and the same thing both exists and does not exist at the same time, so also the division of something that is entirely one and undivided is truly repugnant. Hence to say that a being which possesses the highest degree of existence is non-existent involves a most evident fallacy, just as is the case in saying that to exist and not exist are one and the same. Thus, the existence of the first and highest being is a truth that is most evident.

Therefore, if the term *indubitable* is taken to mean the absence of doubt because of the process of reasoning, the existence of God is indubitably true, because — whether the intellect turns within itself or outside itself, or whether it looks above itself — if it proceeds rationally, it knows that God exists with certitude and without doubt.

But if the term *indubitable* is taken in the second sense namely, as the removal of that doubt which comes from the deficiency of reason, it can be conceded that, because of human weakness, it is possible that some one might doubt the existence of God because of a three-fold defect in the mind of the knower; that is, a defect in the act of apprehending, or in the act of judging, or in the act of fully analyzing. Concerning the act of apprehending, doubt arises when one does not correctly and fully understand what is signified by the term *God*, but understands it only in terms of a particular element. Thus the gentiles thought that God signified whatever was superior to man and could foresee future events. Therefore, they believed that the idols were gods and adored them as gods since they gave some true information about future events.

Relative to the act of judging, doubt arises when the argument is based on partial knowledge, as when the foolish man sees that justice is not apparent in the case of the wicked, and he concludes from this that there is no law in the universe; and from this he concludes that there is no first and highest ruler in the world who is the glorious and high God.

In like manner, doubt arises because of a defect in the act of analysis when the carnal mind is not capable of resolving beyond those things which are evident to the senses, as are corporeal realities. For this reason, some have thought that the visible sun — which holds the highest place among corporeal creatures — was God since they did not know how to resolve things further to an incorporeal substance nor to the first principles of things.

In this way, doubt may arise concerning the existence of God from the deficiency of the intellect itself that apprehends or compares, or resolves. According to this understanding, the existence of God can be doubted by some intellect if it has not sufficiently and totally understood the meaning of the term *God*. But for the intellect which fully understands the meaning of the word *God* — thinking God to be that than which no greater can be conceived — not only is there no doubt that God exists, but the non-existence of God can not even be thought. Therefore the reasons given to prove this should be conceded.

REPLIES TO THE OBJECTIONS

1.2.3. Concerning the first objection raised against the *Psalm* and Damascene, the response is clear. The objection proceeds from that doubt which arises from the defect of reason in the mind of the fool. Obscured by darkness, he neither sufficiently resolves, nor rightly judges, nor fully apprehends the meaning of the word *God*. The intellect itself, by reason of its proper condition, has sufficient light within itself to dispel such doubt and rescue itself from such foolishness.³⁶ Therefore, in this defective consideration of the foolish man, the mistake of the intellect arises more from the will than from necessity; it comes from a defect in the knower rather than from a deficiency in the object known.

From this our response to the objection about idols becomes clear. The gentile considers an idol to be God because his apprehension of God is defective. He does not conceive of God as the highest and best, but merely as whatever is capable of doing what man cannot do. From this, deceptive error and vacillating doubt arises in him. He throws himself into his error with stubbornness so that his position becomes wholly inexcusable.³⁷ And yet, he is not entirely lacking in knowledge of God, because, even though in his perversity he desires to worship an idol, yet he has a natural instinct to worship the God against whom he fights by throwing himself into voluntary error.

4. Concerning the objection which argued that whatever can be signified can be thought also, we reply that something can be thought in a two-fold sense; either as mere thought, or as thought accompanied by assent. In terms of mere thought, that which is false can be thought of as true, and that which is manifestly false can be thought of as manifestly true. But in terms of thought accompanied by assent, only that which is true or similar to truth is thought. The first meaning of *thought* is as extensive as speech. But the second meaning is not so extensive. It is of this kind of thought that both Anselm and Augustine speak, and in this sense it is said that God cannot be thought not to exist.

5. To the objection which maintained — against the argument of Augustine — that contradictory realities do not mutually imply each other, we reply that this is true in as far as they are contradictories. But it must be understood that an affirmative proposition contains two affirmations; one by which the predicate is affirmed of the subject, and another by which the proposition itself is affirmed as true. In terms of the first affirmation, such a proposition is distinguished from a negative proposition which denies the predicate of the subject. The second affirmation is similar to a negative proposition, because both the negative and the positive proposition assert that something is true. The contradiction arises in reference to the first proposition and not to the second. When it is stated that "there is no truth," in as far as this proposition denies the predicate of the subject, it does not infer its opposite, which is the proposition that "there is some truth." But in as far as it asserts that it is true,

---

³⁶ *Ps.* 4, 7.
³⁷ *Rm.* 1, 20.

it infers that something is true. Nor is this surprising; for, just as every evil presupposes a good, so every falsehood implies a truth. Therefore the error which affirms that there is no truth includes both parts of a contradiction, since by negating the predicate of the subject, it denies any truth whatever, but by asserting that it is true, it posits the existence of some truth. Therefore, in view of both of these affirmations it can be inferred that this is intrinsically false and unintelligible to any mind that apprehends correctly. And this is what Augustine wishes to say.

6. About the objection against Anselm's argument concerning the island than which none greater or better can be conceived, we respond that there is no comparison, because when I speak of that being than which nothing greater can be conceived, there is no repugnance between the subject and its implication. Therefore, it can be thought of in a rational way. But when I speak of an island than which none better can be conceived, there is a repugnance between the subject and its implication. For an island is a limited being, while the implication is proper to the most perfect being. Therefore, since there is a contradiction in the adjunct,[38] it can be conceived only irrationally, and the mind contradicts itself in its own thought. Therefore, it is not surprising in such a case that one cannot infer the real existence outside the mind of that which exists in thought. But the situation is different in the case of being or of God, for whom such an implication is not repugnant.

7. Concerning the question "In what sense are we unable to think of God as not existing," our response is already clear. It is not a question of being unable to understand what the words signify,[39] or of understanding what is meant by the statement: "God does not exist." Rather, it means that it is so self-evident and so certain to the knower if he desires to think correctly, there is nothing that could separate him from this truth. It is, therefore, a truth that is supremely evident and present, which is absent to no place, time, thing, or thought. Such is not the case with other created truths.

8. To the objection that we hold nothing with greater certainty than that which we comprehend by faith, it should be said that this is true concerning the certitude of adherence, but not about the

---

[38] Aristotle, *II Periherm.*, c. 2 (c. 11); Anselm, *Contra Insipientem*, c. 3. Adjunct refers to terms which are accidents with respect to the subject and do not combine to form a unity. When such opposite elements are present, a full logical resolution is not possible.

[39] Aristotle, *II Poster.*, c. 7 & 10 (c. 9).

certitude of understanding, as is apparent to anyone who thinks about it.[40]

9. In reference to the objection that since this is a hidden truth, it is open to a great degree of doubt, it must be said that even though God is simple and of one form in Himself, nonetheless He is in a certain way hidden and in a certain way manifest; as the Apostle implies in *Romans* 1: "What can be known of God was manifest to them."[41] To some, the trinity of appropriations is manifest, but not the trinity of persons. And to others the unity of essence is manifest and not the trinity of appropriations. To yet others the trinity of God Himself is manifest but not the unity of essence. But that which is primarily manifest about God is His very existence, and in this regard, He is not hidden but manifest. Therefore, it is not doubtful but indubitable.

10. To the objection about the soul doubting things which are either below itself or on the same level with it, we reply that the objection is not valid, since, even though the existence of God of its nature is above the soul, yet it is within the soul in the form of knowledge, and outside the soul in the form of representations and persuasions which all creatures contain in themselves, since this truth is contained in and understood in every truth.

11. Concerning the objection that in God *to be* and *to be just* are identical, we respond that the conclusion does not follow, since, though these are the same in and of themselves, they are not the same in terms of the notions by which they are grasped, nor in terms of the effects in which they are reflected. Therefore, it is possible that one aspect be manifest and not the other.

12. To the objection that it is pointless to try to prove something that no one doubts, it should be said that this truth, as is clear by now, does not need proof because of any lack of intrinsic evidence, but rather because of faulty reflection on our part. Hence, arguments of this sort are exercises of the intellect rather than proofs that provide evidence and make the truth manifest as proven.

13. To the objection that no one knows principles unless he knows the terms of the principles, we reply that this is true. But the knowledge of some terms is hidden while that of others is manifest. Furthermore, the knowledge of that which is signified by a term can be more or less complete or most perfect. It is in this way that we must understand the possibility of knowing what God

---

[40] "Certitude of adherence" pertains to the affective domain while "certitude of understanding" pertains only to the intellect (III *Sent.* d. 23, a. 1, q. 4 [III, 480-483]).

[41] Verse 19.

is with perfect, full, and comprehensive knowledge; but this sort of knowledge is possessed by God alone; or the possibility of knowing Him clearly and plainly as He is known by the Blessed; or the possibility of knowing Him "imperfectly and as in a mirror,"[42] in the way that God is known to be the first and highest principle of all things in the world. Of itself, this can be manifest to all, since anyone who knows that he has not always existed, knows also that he comes from another; the same is true of all others. Since this knowledge is available to all, and since once this is known, the existence of God is known; therefore the existence of God in itself is indubitable for all.

14. To the objection that to believe the indubitable is not meritorious, it can be said that to believe the existence of God in itself is not meritorious. It is meritorious only in as far as it is the basis for an article of faith, such as God is a trinity, which rests upon it. It is because of the latter that there can be merit, since if this truth alone were believed, it would not produce merit. The Apostle speaks about the existence of God in as far as it is the foundation of the other articles of faith. And this foundation is innate to the nature of man, lest, if the human intellect were to know nothing of God by means of its proper nature it might excuse itself on grounds of ignorance. And this is what Master Hugh says: "Wherefore from the beginning, God willed to be neither totally manifest to the conscience of man nor totally hidden, lest — if He were totally manifest — faith would have no merit and infidelity would have no place; infidelity would be seen to be erroneous because of the evidence, and faith could not be exercised with respect to the hidden. If He were totally hidden, faith could not be helped by knowledge, and infidelity would be excused of its ignorance. For this reason, it was necessary that God present Himself even while remaining hidden, lest if He were totally hidden, He should be totally unknown; so that even as He manifests Himself to be known, He remains hidden lest He be totally manifest; this He does so that man's mind might be stimulated by what is known and challenged by what is hidden."[43]

---

[42] 1 *Cor.* 13, 9.
[43] *I De Sacramentis*, III, c. 2.

ARTICLE II

WHETHER IT IS A TRUTH TO BE BELIEVED THAT GOD IS A TRINITY

Supposing that the existence of God is an indubitable truth, it is now asked whether it is a truth to be believed that God is a trinity. By credible, I mean that which is congruous for belief and which ought to be believed. That it ought to be believed is shown as follows.

ARGUMENTS IN AGREEMENT

1. The final chapter of *Matthew*: "Go forth, therefore, and teach all nations, baptizing them in the name of the Father and of the Son and of the Holy Spirit."[1] In the last chapter of *Mark* the following is added to these words: "Whoever believes and is baptized shall be saved; and whoever does not believe shall be condemned."[2] But a truth without which salvation is impossible is most worthy of belief. The fact that God is a trinity is a truth of this sort; therefore, etc.

2. Again, in his *Symbol*, Athanasius writes: "But this is the Catholic faith, that we venerate one God in trinity and trinity in unity." A little before this he says: "Unless one preserves this whole and inviolate, without doubt he will perish for eternity." Therefore, if salvation is impossible without this faith, the conclusion is the same as above.

3. Again, in the third chapter of the first book *On the Trinity* Augustine writes: "When one inquires about the unity of the trinity, Father and Son, and Holy Spirit, nowhere is error more dangerous, inquiry more difficult, or the results more rewarding."[3] But every truth in which there is danger of error together with salvation in correct thinking is a truth most worthy of belief. Since the fact that God is a trinity is a truth of this sort, the conclusion is the same as above.

4. Again, in the third chapter of the first book of the *Hypognosticon* Augustine writes that "no one can be saved without faith in the Mediator."[4] Therefore, it is necessary for salvation to believe

---

[1] *Mt.* 28, 19.
[2] *Mk.* 16, 16.
[3] I, 3, 5.
[4] I, 3, 4.

in the Mediator. But the Mediator cannot be known unless the distinction of persons is known; therefore it is necessary for salvation to believe in the distinction of perons. But this distinction of persons is in the trinity. Therefore it is necessary for salvation to believe the truth that God is a trinity.

5. Again, no one in whom the trinity does not dwell can be saved, for the entire trinity indwells simultaneously in man by reason of grace. But the trinity does not dwell in anyone who does not believe. Therefore, no one can be saved except in as far as he believes in the most blessed trinity. The major premiss is clear. The minor is proved as follows by what is said in *John* 14; that "the world cannot accept the Spirit of truth, because it neither sees nor knows Him. But you know Him, for He remains with you and dwells in you."[5]

6. Again, it is impossible for anyone to be saved if he is not a member of Christ. But it is impossible to be a member unless one is united with Him; and such a union is impossible except through faith, hope, and charity. Therefore, no one can be saved without faith in Christ. But faith in Christ includes faith in the eternal generation, and accordingly it involves distinction in the trinity. Therefore, without faith in the trinity, it is impossible for anyone to be saved.

7. Again, it is impossible for anyone to find salvation who does not believe that God is the creative principle. Indeed, unless one believes this about God, it is impossible for man to worship and venerate God in a proper manner. But it is more noble to be the principle of generation than to be the principle of creation, since the offspring that is begotten is more noble than the creature that is made. Therefore, no one can be saved who does not believe that God is the principle of generation, and for the same reason, that He is the principle of spiration, and therefore no one can be saved unless he believes that God is a trinity.

8. Again, it is impossible for anyone·to be saved who does not love and honor Him who is supremely worthy of love and honor. But the Son and the Holy Spirit are to be loved and honored supremely as is the Father, according to *John* 5: "He who does not honor the Son does not honor the Father who sent Him."[6] Therefore, no one can be saved who does not love and honor the Son and the Holy Spirit just as he does the Father. But no one loves and honors anyone unless in some way he knows and believes. Therefore, etc.

---

[5] Verse 17.
[6] Verse 23.

From these arguments it is clearly shown that it is necessary and is required for salvation to believe that God is a trinity.

It will now be shown that this is also fitting.

9. Rightly ordered affection clings to the highest good more than to itself. Therefore the rightly ordered intellect assents to the highest truth more than to itself. If, therefore, our intellect is to be justified in believing, it is necessary that some truth which exceeds its judgment be proposed to it. But the fact that God is one and a trinity is the first thing proposed among the truths worthy of belief. Therefore however much it is hidden to the human mind, it is rightly and fittingly proposed for belief.

10. Again, as charity captures the affections in obedience to Christ, so faith captures the intellect.[7] But it would not be captive if it were not brought to assent to some truth that exceeds its judgment. Therefore it is fitting that the first among the truths proposed for belief should exceed human understanding.

11. Again, "that which is apparent to all or to many or to the wise by the mere fact that it is apparent is rendered capable of proof."[8] Therefore that which is believed by many or by the wise, by the mere fact that it is believed, is rendered believable. But the fact that God is a trinity is believed by many and by the wise. Therefore it is fitting to believe that He is a trinity.

12. Again, it is more irrational to affirm that an innumerable multitude believes the unbelievable than to affirm that what is believed by a multitude is believable. But most certainly, a multitude believes that God is a trinity. Therefore it is reasonable to believe this.

13. Again, as we owe understanding to reason, so we owe faith to authority.[9] But nothing is more authentic than Sacred Scripture which is steadfast not only because of the truth it contains and because of its antiquity, but also because of miracles and prophecies. Therefore, if the divine Scriptures testify to this truth commonly, it is fitting and reasonable to believe this truth, namely, that God is one in trinity.

14. Again, there are three classes of truths that are believable, according to Augustine: "Some things are believed and known at the same time; some things are first believed and then known by understanding; some things are believed and never known by reason, as is the case with the history of human deeds."[10] That which is believed in such a way that it can be understood by reason is

---

[7] 2 *Cor.* 10, 5.
[8] Aristotle, *I Topic.*, c. 1.
[9] Augustine, *De Utilitate Credendi*, c. 11, p. 25.
[10] *Lib. 83 Qq.*, q. 48.

more credible than that which cannot be understood. But the fact that God is a trinity is a truth of this sort. Therefore, since some of the historical facts narrated by the authentic Scripture are credible — for it is not incredible that 'Abraham begot Isaac;' indeed, it is very credible; and there are other similar cases — therefore it is credible that God is one and a trinity.

OBJECTIONS

1. Whatever is contrary to all the dictates of reason is incredible for reason. But all reason dictates the contrary of the statement that a being which is one is really a trinity. Therefore, it is incredible for reason.

2. Again, whatever is contrary to that which created nature indicates is incredible. But all created nature indicates the contrary of the fact that something which is one and not multiplied in form is multiplied in supposites. For in every created nature, when the supposite is multiplied, the form is multiplied as well. Therefore, if our intellect is led through creatures to recognize the existence of God, as is stated in 1 *Cor.* 13: "We see now through a mirror and dimly,"[11] since every created nature indicates the contrary of the truth that God is a trinity, this is necessarily an incredible truth.

3. Again, whatever is believed is believed either by means of reason or beyond reason. Therefore, if it is a credible truth that God is a trinity, it is so either by means of reason or beyond reason. But if it is by means of reason, it is not meritorious, since "that faith for which human reason offers a proof has no merit."[12] If it is believed as something beyond reason, it is irrational to believe it because anything beyond reason believed by one who has the use of reason is believed irrationally; it is not a credible truth. Therefore the fact that God is a trinity is not a credible truth.

4. Again, whatever is believed is believed either because of itself or because of something else. If the fact that God is a trinity is a credible truth, it is such either in the first way or in the second. If it is believed because of something else, then it is not itself the object of true faith. If it is believed because of itself, just as nothing is lovable because of itself unless it is of itself adequate for our affections; therefore nothing is credible in itself unless of itself it is apparent to the intellect. But the fact that God is a trinity is not of itself apparent to the intellect. Therefore it is not a credible truth.

---

[11] Verse 12.
[12] Gregory, *II Homil. in Evang.*, homil. 26, n. 1.

5. Again, a virtue is consonant with nature, since as Tullius says and as Augustine agrees, "a virtue is a habit that is by nature consonant with reason."[13] Therefore, whatever is incredible to a natural virtue is incredible to the virtue of faith. But the fact that God is a trinity is not credible to nature itself. Therefore it is not credible to a virtue superadded to nature.

6. Again, grace is the perfection of nature,[14] and perfection is not repugnant to a being which is capable of perfection, but rather in harmony with it. Therefore, if by nature it is not credible that God is a trinity, then neither is it credible by reason of any added grace.

7. Again, "The creator of nature does nothing contrary to that nature which cooperates with Him."[15] Therefore, He who is the teacher and inspirer of nature does nothing contrary to the natural dictates of reason. Therefore, if the fact that God is a trinity is not credible through the natural dictates of reason, neither is it credible through an additional inspiration.

8. Again, a principle of scientific knowledge should be very easily known, as is clear with the principles of demonstration which are self-evident to the intellect.[16] Therefore a principle of the knowledge of faith should be readily accessible to faith. But the fact that God is a trinity is not readily accessible to faith; indeed it is very difficult, as is clear in the case of those who do not yet have faith. Therefore, it is not the first among the truths of faith; nor is it the middle nor even the last among those truths, as is evident. Therefore, in no way is it a truth of faith.

From these arguments it appears how it can be shown that the fact that God is a trinity is neither a truth of faith, nor a truth which is fittingly believed.

Next it is shown that it is not a truth of faith that must be believed.

9. No one is obliged to that which he cannot do, since Jerome says: "Let him be anathema who claims that God has commanded the impossible."[17] But to believe that God is a trinity is not in our power, since faith is a gift of God. But if no one is obliged to that which is not in his power, no one is obliged to believe this.

10. Again, if we are obliged to believe this, it is either because of the law of nature, or the law of Scripture, or the law of grace. It is not because of the law of nature since that law is inscribed in

---

[13] Cicero, *Lib. II Rhet.* c. 54; Augustine, *Lib. 83 Qq.* q. 31, n. 1.
[14] Ambrose, *Expos. in Ps. 118*, serm. 14, n. 42.
[15] Augustine, *XXVI contra Faustum*, c. 3.
[16] Aristotle, *I Poster.* c. 2, and *IV Metaph.* text. 8 (III, c. 3).
[17] *Expositio Symboli ad Damasum.*

the heart of man and is most evident to all;[18] but this truth is concealed and hidden from human strivings. It is not because of the law of Scripture, since it was a credible truth before Scripture began. On the other hand, if it were believable only because of Scripture, then it would not pertain to all times and all persons. It is not because of the law of grace, because that faith existed before the law of grace began. And furthermore, the law of grace is not burdensome. Therefore, if it is difficult to believe this, we are not obliged to do so by the law of grace, nor by the law of nature nor by the law of the Scriptures, as we have shown. Therefore, in no way are we obliged to believe it.

11. Again, if we are obliged to believe this truth, this is either because it is true or because it is a truth that is commanded. The reason cannot be that it is true, since we are obliged to believe everything that is true in the same way. But if the reason is that it is commanded, it must be either by a moral precept or by a sacramental precept. It is certain that it is not a sacramental precept. Neither is it a moral precept, since all moral matters are reduced to the ten precepts of the decalogue; and no one is commanded in any of these to believe that God is a trinity. Therefore in no way are we obliged to this.

12. Again, if we are obliged to believe this, it is because it is either a truth that is seen, or one that is heard, or one that is inspired. It is not a truth that is seen, for no one in history sees this truth. Neither is it to be believed because it is heard, since only he who has heard such a truth is obliged to believe it. But if it is an inspired truth, then only those in whom it is inspired are bound to believe it. Therefore, no one is bound to it except those who believe it. But this is false, therefore the first is false.

13. Again, I ask what is it that moves the Christian to believe this truth. If you say that the divine Scripture moves you, so that if the divine Scriptures did not teach this, you would not believe it, it can be said to the contrary that even if the whole of Scripture were burned, yet neither the Church nor the Christian soul would give up faith in the trinity. Therefore, the principal reason moving us to this belief is not Scripture. If you say that you are moved by miracles, it can be said to the contrary: "That faith has no merit for which human reason offers a proof."[19] Faith such as that which comes from miracles is a faith that is forced rather than voluntary, and such faith is not meritorious. If you say it is grace that moves you, it can be said to the contrary that no one knows whether he

---

[18] *Rm.* 2, 14 ff.
[19] Gregory, *II Homil. in Evang.*, homil. 26, n. 1.

possesses grace. Therefore, no one knows whether he ought to believe this truth. But in the case of an article of faith which we are obliged to believe, we are certain that we ought to believe. Therefore we are not moved to believe this by reason of grace. If you say that the eternal truth itself moves you to believe this, it can be said to the contrary that only a truth which is seen can move to belief. Since this truth is not seen by the soul, it seems that the soul must be moved to believe this in some way other than by the eternal truth itself.

The question remains, therefore, if this is a truth of faith, by what are we moved and by what are we obliged to believe it?

CONCLUSION

It is a credible truth that God is a trinity, since to believe this is fitting, obligatory, and worthy.

Response. The fact that God is a trinity is a truth of faith of such a sort that it is fitting, necessary, and worthy of belief.

To understand this, we must note that since this article of faith is the foundation of the entire Christian faith, there is a threefold testimony by which we are led, obliged, and elevated to believe it, so that foundation might remain unshaken. This threefold testimony is the concern of a threefold book; namely, the book of creation, the book of Scripture, and the book of life. The first provides a testimony that is efficacious; the second, a testimony that is more efficacious; and the third, a testimony that is efficacious to the highest degree. The book of creation, which I call the first book because it appeals first to our senses, offers a twofold witness, since "every charge requires the testimony of two witnesses."[20] Every creature is either a mere vestige of God — as is corporeal nature — or an image of God, as is the intellectual creature. Each of these gives witness to the trinity. However, that which is but a vestige does so, as it were, from afar. Every creature has measure, species, and order; or unity, truth, and goodness; or measure, number, and weight, which by appropriation correspond to the trinity of persons, and thus give witness to the fact that God is a trinity. This is what Augustine says in the book of *83 Questions:* "For everything that exists there is one thing by which it is; another by which it is known; and another to which it conforms. Therefore, every creature manifests a threefold cause by reason of which it is; and by reason of

---

[20] *Dt.* 19, 15; *Mt.* 18, 16; *2 Cor.* 13, 1.

which it is this; and by which it is in conformity with itself. This cause of creation — which is its author — we call God. It is necessary therefore, that the trinity exist; and the perfect mind can discover nothing more excellent, more intelligible and more blessed."[21] From this Augustine shows that creation is a vestige which gives witness to the fact that God is a trinity.

But that creature which is an image — such as the intellectual creature — testifies to the threefold character of God, as it were, from near at hand, because an image is an express similitude. The intellectual creature has memory, intelligence, and will; or mind, knowledge, and love; mind, like a parent, knowledge like an offspring, and love like a bond proceeding from both and joining them together. For the mind cannot fail to love the word which it generates. Therefore, these not only indicate origin and emanation which leads to distinction among them; but they indicate also quality, consubstantiality, and inseparability, from which an express testimony is given to the fact that God is a trinity. For since He is spirit and intellect, He can lack neither a word that is begotten nor a love that proceeds. Among these there is distinction by reason of origin, and emanation of one from another; and together with this, there is equality, consubstantiality, and inseparability. This is what Augustine intended to add toward the end of the ninth book *On the Trinity*, showing how testimony to the eternal trinity is given by the created image.[22] This twofold witness of the book of creation was efficacious in the state of innocent nature, when that book had not been obscured; nor had the eye of man been darkened. But when the sins of man had weakened his sight, then that mirror was made dark and obscure, and the ear of our inner understanding was hardened against hearing that testimony. For this reason, divine providence saw fit to provide the testimony of another book; namely, that of the book of Scripture which was written in accord with the divine revelation which has never been deficient nor absent from the beginning of the world to the end.

This book, moreover, in accordance with its two parts, testifies in a twofold way that the trinity exists. In the Old Testament, an implicit witness is given, while in the New Testament, the testimony is explicit. The testimony concerning the trinity in the Old Testament is given both in figures and in words. The most authentic among those figures is the one which was shown to "Abraham, the father of our faith." Concerning him, *Genesis* 18 says that in the three men who appeared to him, he saw three but adored one, wherefore he

---

[21] *Lib. 83 Qq.* q. 18.
[22] I *Sent.* d. 3, p. 2, q. 1 & 2 (I, 80-93).

spoke to the three as to one.²³ In this, he himself understood the mystery of the trinity and made it known to others. That which David, the most distinguished of the prophets, said in the *Psalm* seems to be the most efficacious among the testimonies given in words: "By the word of the Lord the heavens were established, and by the breath (= Spirit) of His mouth all their strength."²⁴ Here the trinity of persons is implied in such a way that two persons are explicitly mentioned by the names *Spirit* and *Word*, and one implicitly by the name *Lord*. In many places, indeed in almost all the figures and words of the Old Testament, witness to the trinity is given at least implicitly.

Similarly, testimony is given in the New Testament, but explicitly both in the sacraments and in express teachings. For the first of the sacraments, which is baptism, is conferred with the express invocation of the divine trinity, according to what is written in the final chapter of *Matthew*.²⁵ There it is written: "Teach all nations, baptizing them in the name of the Father, and of the Son, and of the Holy Spirit." Therefore the character of the trinity is imprinted in that fundamental sacrament. Among the many words that testify to the same truth, that which was written only by the friend of the Spouse in 1 *John* 5 is an express statement: "There are three who give testimony in heaven; the Father, the Word, and the Holy Spirit. And these three are one."²⁶ This testimony is so express and efficacious that it renders this truth not only credible — i.e. congruous for belief — but necessary as well, since it obliges us and constrains us to believe it.

But because "not all listen to the Gospel"²⁷ and since this is a truth beyond reason, therefore the divine wisdom has provided an eternal testimony, which is the book of life. This book of life by itself and in itself explicitly and expressly gives incontestable witness to the eternal trinity to those who see God in heaven with "unveiled faces."²⁸ For those on earth, it provides a testimony through the influence of light, since while on earth, the soul is capable of receiving such an influence, as it is written in *John* 1: "The Life was light for men;"²⁹ because that book of life is "the true light which illumines every man coming into the world."³⁰ Illumination is

---

²³ Verse 2.
²⁴ *Ps.* 32, 6.
²⁵ Verse 19.
²⁶ Verse 7.
²⁷ *Rm.* 10, 16.
²⁸ 2 *Cor.* 3, 18.
²⁹ Verse 4.
³⁰ *Jn.* 1, 9.

given in two ways, namely, by an innate light and by an infused light. From these two lights, concurring with the habit of faith, the argument that God is a trinity arises for our belief, and eventually every truth which pertains to the practice of the Christian religion. This becomes clear in the following manner. By reason of that light given naturally to man by God and known as the light of the divine face,[31] human reason dictates to each individual man that we are to think of the first principle in the highest and most reverent way; in the highest way because He proceeds from no other; in the most reverent way, because other things proceed from Him. In this there is agreement among Christians, Jews, and Saracens, and even heretics. But to think that God can and does wish to produce one equal to and consubstantial with Himself so that He might have an eternal beloved and cobeloved is indeed to think of God in the highest and most reverent way; for if one thinks that He is not capable of this, one does not think of Him in the highest way; and if one thinks that He is capable of this but does not will to do it, one does not think of God in the most reverent way. That God exists in this way and that He is to be thought of in this way, I say, is not dictated by the innate light by itself, but by the infused light from which — together with the natural light — one concludes that God is to be thought of as one who generates and spirates one co-equal to and consubstantial with Himself, and thus one thinks of God in the highest and most reverent way. To think this of God is to honor, venerate, and worship Him in the highest degree. From this it is clear how faith in the trinity is the foundation and root of divine cult and of the entire Christian religion.

From this root, by which we believe that God is to be thought of in the highest and most reverent way, and that therefore He is both one and three, it follows as a consequence that we should believe that God is the creator of all things, that He punishes the wicked, rewards the good, and relieves those in misery. Because He is most high, His dignity requires that His deeds be great and just. Because He is supremely compassionate, His dignity requires that He look upon the humble and lift up the fallen.[32] And thus we believe that He became incarnate and suffered because of His supreme compassion, and that He will judge the world in His supreme dignity and equity.

From what has been said, we may infer what the root of the Christian faith is; what witness there is to it; what articles of faith flow from it; and what is the principle and first of all the articles

---

[31] *Ps.* 4, 7.
[32] *Ps.* 137, 6.

of faith which pertain to the service of God; namely, to believe that God is one and a trinity. And since Jesus Christ was the highest and supreme worshipper of all, it was He who first commanded that this truth be preached clearly and openly throughout the entire world, thereby obliging all men to believe it. Therefore, while prior to His coming, men were obliged to believe in the trinity only implicitly, now after the promulgation of the New Testament, all are obliged to believe it explicitly, so that it is a truth of faith not only because it is worthy of belief or fitting for belief from the testimony of creation; but it must be believed by reason of the promulgation of the truth of the Gospel. The promulgation of the Gospel takes its origin in the Savior, as we read in *Hebrews* 2 where the Apostle,[33] in speaking of the Christian faith, says: "It was announced first by the Lord to those who heard Him, and it was confirmed for us by signs, miracles, and various works of power, and the distribution of gifts of the Spirit as He willed."

Therefore if it is asked what it is that moves us to believe this — is it Scripture, or miracles, or grace, i.e. the eternal truth itself — the answer should be that that which moves us principally is the illumination which begins in the natural light and finds its consummation in the infused light, for this leads us to think of God not only in a lofty manner but also in a reverent manner, because this illumination proceeds from the eternal light itself which takes our intellect into obedient captivity;[34] in capturing the mind, it subjects it to God in worship and veneration and renders it ready to believe whatever pertains to the divine honor and veneration, even though such things be beyond our reason. This becomes clear from experience if one turns to the secret things of his own mind. There are many things that move us and support us, and in a certain way lead us to believe this. The authentic testimony of Scripture moves us as do the examples and witness of the Saints; the arguments of the Doctors, and the judgment of the universal Church move us as well as unquestionable miracles. Therefore Richard writes in the second chapter of the first book *On the Trinity:* "We hold nothing more unshakeably than that which we apprehend by faith; for these things were revealed by heaven to the Fathers and divinely confirmed by so many great and marvelous signs and prodigies that it would seem to be a great mental aberration to have even a little doubt in these matters. Therefore innumerable miracles and other deeds that can only be of divine origin lead to faith of this sort and do not allow for doubt. Therefore we use signs for arguments

---

[33] Verse 3.
[34] 2 *Cor.* 10, 5.

and prodigies for proof in attesting and confirming these matters. Would that the Jews and the pagans would pay heed to the great peace of conscience with which we can stand in this matter before the divine judgment. Can we not say with full trust in God: 'O Lord, if this is an error, we have been deceived by you since these things have been confirmed for us by great signs and prodigies such as could be done only by you.' Certainly these things have been given to us by men of the greatest sanctity and have been approved by the highest and most authentic testimony; and you yourself 'worked with them and confirmed their message with the signs that accompanied it.' "[35]

Thus, it is clear how we would respond to the four issues raised in the last objection: Namely, what is it that moves the faithful to believe that God is one and a trinity ?

REPLIES TO THE OBJECTIONS

1. To the first objection which said that whatever is contrary to all the dictates of reason, etc., we reply that reason can be understood in three ways; as fallen, as innocent, and as elevated. When it is said that whatever is contrary to all the dictates of reason is incredible, if this is understood in particular of fallen reason it is false, because it is possible that something which is repugnant to fallen reason is consonant with innocent or elevated reason. But if it is understood universally of reason in all three senses, then the first proposition should be conceded as true, but the minor is false and should be denied; since — while reason dictates the opposite of the fact that God is one and three, innocent reason dictates something consonant with this, and elevated reason dictates this very truth itself, as is clear from what has been said.

2. To the objection that whatever is contrary to the indications of all created nature is incredible, we reply that created nature can refer to something in two ways: either in itself or in its cause. Created nature refers to something that is temporal, changeable, and composed, but that has a cause which is eternal, immutable, and most simple. Since in the case of creatures supposites are distinguished by matter and by the form appropriate to the matter, unity of form cannot exist in the creature together with a trinity of supposites. Yet in the case of the Creator — in whom there is indeed no matter but true fecundity — while there is oneness of form and substance, there is distinction among the supposites by reason of origin. Now,

---

[35] *De Trinitate*, I, 2; *Mk.* 16, 20.

since the creature does not in every way indicate the contrary of the fact that God is a trinity, indeed, when understood correctly, it is in conformity with this truth; therefore, it is more credible than incredible.

3. To the objection that everything that is believed is believed either by means of reason or beyond reason, it should be said that there are two ways to believe something by means of reason; either by means of reason alone or by means of reason aided by grace. Therefore, although it may not be credible from reason alone that God is a trinity, yet it is credible for reason aided by grace and by the light poured in from above. What is credible in this way is not believed irrationally since the grace and light infused from above do not pervert reason but rather direct it.

4. To the objection that whatever is believed is believed either because of itself or because of something else, we respond that the fact that God is a trinity is believed because of itself since it is the highest and first truth pertaining to divine cult. To the objection that whatever is credible in this way is evident of itself to the believer, we respond that this is true of that believer in whom there is no impediment and who has that disposition which makes him ready to assent to uncreated truth itself. And such is the case in what has been proposed, since the true Christian believes this truth without any further persuasion when it is proposed to him.

5.6. To the objection that a virtue is in harmony with nature, we respond that this is to be understood of political virtue.[36] But, if it is understood with respect to a virtue given by grace, it is not true that such a virtue is in harmony with nature in as far as nature is fallen, but only in as far as nature is reformed and elevated; and this is effected by divine grace infused from above.

And in this way our response becomes clear to the objection about grace; namely, that grace is the perfection of nature. Grace is the perfection of nature not only in as far as it equips nature but also in as far as it both reforms and elevates it. But in reforming and elevating it, grace does not destroy nature itself nor any part thereof, but only the defects surrounding the nature.

7. To the objection that the Author of nature does nothing contrary to nature, we respond that nature has two meanings; either the natural course of events, or the natural obedience of the creature. In the first sense, God frequently acts in works beyond nature or even contrary to nature, as in miraculous works; but in the second sense He does nothing contrary to nature. Similarly, we should understand that our natural intelligence may be spoken

---

[36] Macrob., *I Somn. Scipion.*, c. 8.

of in two ways; either in as far as it is created so as to think in accordance with its own proper light, or in as far as it is created to subject itself to the eternal light. In this last sense, nothing is dictated to us contrary to our intelligence. But in the first sense, something is dictated which — though it seems to be contrary to reason — becomes consonant with reason after the light has been infused; for what at first seemed impossible for reason or difficult to believe afterwards becomes very easy to believe to such a degree that the true believer says to the eternal Teacher: "Your testimonies are indeed worthy of belief."[37]

8. To the objection that a principle of scientific knowledge is known most readily etc., we reply that the knowledge of faith is the knowledge of piety, as it is written in *Titus* 1.[38] And even though for the mind that proceeds according to the dryness of speculation it may seem very difficult to believe that God is one and a trinity, yet to the mind filled with piety, it is very easy to think that the Highest Father should have an Only-Begotten whom He loves as Himself, and whom He gives for the salvation of man.[39]

9. To the objection that no one is obliged to the impossible we reply that even though man is not sufficient of himself, yet he is capable with the divine assistance which is offered him provided he does what he himself is capable of doing. And since man is capable of doing those things which prepare the way for the possibility of faith, therefore he should be considered capable of belief; and, above all other things, he ought to be obliged to believe since neither interior nor exterior incentive is lacking, which indeed is the case in the time of revealed grace.

10. To the objection which said that we are obliged either by the law of nature, or of Scripture, or of grace, we reply that properly speaking, it is according to the law of grace that we are obliged and held to believe this truth specifically. Nevertheless, both in the law of nature and in the law of Scripture there is an obligation to believe it at least implicitly. For in every age, anyone who stubbornly denies that God is a trinity is judged to be estranged from truth and from divine cult. But above all is this the case now in the age of grace when this virtue is revealed and preached and approved expressly and in many ways. And if you raise the objection that this ought not to be, since the law of grace ought to be easy, we reply that to love one's enemy is not easy except to one who has charity;

---

[37] *Ps.* 92, 5.
[38] Verse 1.
[39] *Jn.* 3, 16.

so also to believe that God is a trinity may seem difficult to the unbeliever, but it is easy for one who has faith.

12. To the objection that we are held to believe it either because it is seen as true or because it is heard, or because it is inspired, we reply that we are held to it because it is a truth which above all pertains to divine worship and has been publicly preached. Therefore man is not excused by a lack of hearing nor by a lack of interior light, because he can do those things which precede the inspirations of faith in him.

11. To the objection that if we are obliged to believe this, it is either because it is true or because it is a truth of precept, we respond that it is because it is a truth of precept. And if you ask under which commandment, I reply under the first commandment in which it is said: "Hear, O Israel, the Lord, Your God, is one. You shall adore the Lord, your God; and Him alone shall you serve."[40] Indeed, in this command we are obliged expressly to believe that God is one, but implicitly to believe that God is a trinity. This may be clarified as follows: because by this command we are obliged to honor God with the cult of *latria*, which is here called *service*. But the term *to cultivate* is used in spiritual matters by way of analogy with material things. In the material realm, to cultivate a field means to uncover the tender shoots that take their origin there and grow from the earth. Similarly, to give cult to God means to confess with heart and mouth and deed that He is principle in such a way that He is not perfectly honored unless we confess that He is the principle of all other principles not only as efficient cause in creation, but also as restoring cause in our redemption and as perfecting cause in our glorification. Neither is He confessed perfectly if He is believed to be principle in reference to time and not also to be the principle of all principles from eternity. Nor is He confessed perfectly unless He is believed to be the principle of all principles who exists from eternity as the principle of another. And this is what we believe when we believe that the Father eternally generates a Son and together with Him breathes the Holy Spirit, so that from eternity there is in God a principle that proceeds from another principle as well as a principle that does not proceed from another principle.

The perfect honor of God, therefore, necessarily means to think and to believe that He is that principle which from eternity is the principle of another principle so that the manifestation of the temporal productions may be clear. And whoever fails in any of these does not give perfect worship to God. Since this is revealed per-

---

[40] *Dt.* 6, 4 & 13.

fectly and not haphazardly in the time of grace, it is necessary to believe all these things explicitly if we wish to be counted among the number of the true worshippers of God. We are obliged to this by reason of the command of the divine law itself, which bound man implicitly prior to the coming of Christ, but now obliges explicitly since this is the time for worshipping God perfectly.

From this it becomes clear why sacrifices were pleasing to God in the time of the written Law and why they pertained to divine cult in as far as they were all signs prophesying and prefiguring the repair of mankind which was effected through the sacrifice of the immaculate Lamb and the outpouring of the blood of Jesus Christ.[41]

It is also clear why it is that in the time of grace no figurative sacrifice is offered, but Jesus Christ Himself in His flesh and blood, in as far as this is the time for worshipping God truly and perfectly; and therefore it is necessary that the truest and most perfect sacrifice be offered, which is indeed only one, namely, Jesus Christ Himself. It is also clear why unbelievers are justly condemned. If, indeed, a man does dishonor to an earthly king by offering him only a portion of his kingdom and is therefore rightly expelled from the kingdom, all the more does he do a dishonor to the eternal majesty who denies that God is principle of all other principles of all things existing in time or that He is eternally active as principle from within, and such a man is worthy not only of being expelled from the kingdom of God, but also of being cast into the punishment of hell together with the devil and his angels.

It is also clear why we worship God in faith. For in thinking of God in this way, as the Christian faith does, we think of Him as the most high and most loving principle, who is to be both feared and loved. Because of these two things, man is recalled from evil and incited to every good. This is perfect justice, and he who possesses it is worthy of the eternal inheritance.

---

[41] 1 *Pt.* 1, 19.

QUESTION II

WHETHER A TRINITY OF PERSONS CAN EXIST TOGETHER WITH UNITY OF NATURE

Supposing that it is a truth of faith that God is a trinity, it is then asked whether a trinity of persons can exist together with unity of nature. Two questions are raised concerning this matter. The first is whether the divine being is supremely one. The second is whether the highest unity of nature can exist together with a trinity of persons.

ARTICLE I

WHETHER THE DIVINE BEING IS SUPREMELY ONE

Concerning the first question, we will proceed to show that the divine being is supremely one. That this is so is sufficiently proclaimed by faith and by the divine Scriptures, in *Exodus* 20: "God, your God, is one";[1] and in *Deuteronomy* 32: "See, therefore, that I alone am God, and there is no other God beside me";[2] and David in the *Psalm*: "There shall be no strange God among you, and you shall not worship any foreign God."[3] The divine Scriptures give sufficient instruction on this matter. It is now our intention to demonstrate the same thing by arguments. For every mind that makes use of reason supposes that God is that than which nothing greater or better can be conceived; He is therefore most excellent in nature and power, in wisdom and goodness, in influence and causality. For if He suffered a defect in any of these, then He would not be the highest, and consequently He would not be God. Therefore these six qualities are supposed as true and most certain.

---

[1] *Ex.* 20, 2.
[2] *Dt.* 6, 4; 32, 39.
[3] *Ps.* 80, 10.

ARGUMENTS IN AGREEMENT

1. The argument from sublimity of nature is as follows. That which excels all others is more sublime than that which does not. Therefore, if it is impossible for more than one being to excel all others, then it is impossible and even unintelligible that God should not be one.[4] For if we were to suppose a plurality here, it would follow that one and the same being both excels the others and is excelled by them. Therefore if several beings were God, none would be God. Therefore, either God does not exist, or if He exists, He is one.

2. The argument from omnipotence is the following. A being is truly omnipotent not only if it can do all things, but also if it is the source from which all power is derived. But to be able to do all things and to be the cause of all power can belong only to one being — if it belonged to many, it would belong to none. If, therefore, omnipotence is an attribute of God, it is impossible and unintelligible that God should not be one; because if several beings were omnipotent, each of them could annul the power of the other. Therefore, if several beings are omnipotent, none of them would be omnipotent.[5]

3. The argument from the highest wisdom is as follows. It is proper to the supremely wise being to know all things.[6] Therefore, if there were several gods, either they would be mutually ignorant of each other, and thus neither of them would be supremely wise; indeed, they would be truly foolish; or they would know each other either through a species, or through the other's essence, or through themselves. If one knows the other through a species or through the other's essence, then it would be informed by receiving something from the other. If it knows the other through itself, then it would be the principle of the other; hence one of these would not be God. Therefore, the highest wisdom does not allow that there be a plurality of gods, nor can we think of such a plurality. For if several gods are thought to exist, their wisdom would be either identical or distinct. If they have distinct wisdoms, then either one of them excels the other or both of them are imperfect. If they have the same wisdom, they would not have different natures, since each of them would be the highest wisdom. Therefore, they would not be two.

---

[4] Aristotle, *V Topic.*, c. 3 (c. 5).
[5] Rich. of St. Victor, *De Trin. I*, c. 25; II, c. 15.
[6] Aristotle, *I Metaph.*, c. 2.

4. The argument from the highest good is the following. That which is the highest good is to be loved supremely and for its own sake. Therefore, if there were several supremely good beings, either each of them would love the other for the other's sake, or not. If not, then neither of them would be good. If yes, then each of them beatifies the other; therefore, neither would be the highest. Therefore, it is impossible that the highest good be multiplied. Indeed, this would also be contrary to reason, because each of these would either be or not be the greater good. If not, then one of them is superfluous. If yes, then neither is the highest. Therefore, if a multiplicity of highest goods is thought to exist, they are not understood to be supremely good.[7]

5. The argument from influence is the following. God influences all things in a most perfect manner. Therefore, He confers the whole of being and not a part thereof.[8] But if there were several gods, either one would give nothing, and hence would not be God; or each would give either part of being or nothing at all, and neither would be God; or each would communicate the same being, and then each would be simultaneously in the same effect by way of essence, power, and presence, since this is proper to the highest influence. Therefore, either one would be in the other, or both would be circumscribed, and thus neither would be God.

6. The argument from the highest causality is the following. God is the first, ultimate, and most perfect cause; and hence He is the cause in whom all things come to rest fully in terms of efficient, exemplary, and final causality.[9] Therefore, if there were several gods, one would be reduced to the other, and none would be first, highest, or most perfect. Hence, none would be God.

7. The argument from all the qualities given above is the following. If there were a plurality of gods, either they would be totally identical in all these qualities, or they would differ totally, or they would agree in part and differ in part. If they were totally identical, there would not be a plurality of gods; if they differed entirely, then if one were God the other would not be God. If they agreed in part and differed in part, then they would both be composed of parts. Therefore, neither of them would be simple; hence, neither would be God.

From the above, it is argued that the divine being cannot be multiplied, either in reality or in thought.

---

[7] Rich. of St. Victor, *De Trin. II*, c. 19.
[8] *Lib. de Causis*, prop. 1.
[9] Aristotle, *II Metaph.*, text. 5 ff.

OBJECTIONS

In opposition to this, arguments are raised first of all against the proofs given above.

1. The arguments do not appear to draw a true conclusion. Since the fact that God is one is a matter in which pagans, unbelievers, and heretics have erred, all of whom had the use of reason, not only can it be thought, but it can be judged and believed that there are many gods. Or if the contrary cannot be judged, then it is not an article of faith.

2. Again, the arguments do not seem to draw necessary conclusions because the same arguments can be used to prove that there are not several persons in God. This is clear for anyone who reflects further on it, whether from the sublimity of nature, or of power, or of wisdom, or of goodness, or of influence, or of causality. But if the arguments proceed from the same means to arrive at false conclusions, they do not lead to necessary conclusions.

3. Again, if by means of the arguments given above it is necessarily proved and demonstrated that God is one, then the faith seems to be emptied of merit, since "that faith for which human reason provides a proof has no merit."[10] Therefore arguments are either weak or useless.

Objections are raised against the proofs from the same attributes.

4. First, from sublimity. It is of greater sublimity to excel things of a similar nature than to excel things of a different nature; and to excel great things rather than to excel small things. Therefore, if the creature is not of like nature with God, and if creation is, as it were, nothing in comparison with God, then God is not understood to be highest and most excellent if He excels created being only. Therefore it seems that it pertains to the divine excellence to posit a plurality of uncreated natures, and then to posit one above the others.

5. From omnipotence, the argument is the following. As Hilary says, "It is proper to perfect power that the nature in which it resides can carry out whatever the speaker has declared."[11] And again, reason dictates that a certain degree of power can accomplish only so much; a greater degree is capable of more; and the highest degree of power is capable of the most. But God is omnipotent in the highest degree. Therefore, since it is possible for us to say that there are many gods, God can bring it about that they should exist. And since He can cause lesser things to be, He can also cause greater

---

[10] Gregory, *II Homil. in Evang.*, homil. 26, n. 1.
[11] *De trin.* V, n. 5.

things, and even the greatest things. Therefore, He can produce something distinct from Himself that would be as great as Himself. It is, therefore, consonant with omnipotence that there be a multiplicity of gods.

6. From wisdom, it is argued that it is proper to the highest wisdom to know that which is other than itself; and the more perfect the object known, the more perfect is the wisdom. If nothing is entirely perfect except that being which is God, and if divine wisdom eternally knows something distinct from itself with a most perfect knowledge, it seems that from eternity there would be something distinct from God which, nonetheless, would be divine. Therefore, the divine wisdom does not exclude but rather requires several divine essences.

7. From goodness, it is argued: "Goodness is diffusive to the highest degree";[12] and "many good things are preferable to fewer."[13] Both of these propositions are self-eviden ttruths. Since the highest diffusion of the divine being cannot take place in a creature, it must take place in another uncreated nature. Having posited this, the whole divine essence is better because of the multiplicity of goods. Therefore, if all that is better is to be attributed to God because of His supreme goodness, it seems that the highest goodness does not exclude but rather demands the existence of many divine natures.

8. From the highest influence, it is argued that the perfect influence necessarily demands that such influence not take place without the divine essence, presence, and power. Therefore for the same reason, it cannot be multiplied without the multiplication of essence, power, and presence. Therefore, since there is a plurality of divine influences, there is also a plurality of essences.

9. From causality, the following argument is made. The first cause is the most perfect cause; it is first and immediate, and therefore cause in the proper sense. But if the effect is multiplied, it is necessary that the proximate and proper cause be multiplied. Therefore it is necessary to affirm multiplicity in the first cause, since multiplicity is affirmed and exists in the effects caused by it.

10. Again, from all these properties an objection is raised against all the above; for the most perfect sublimity in nature and power, wisdom and goodness, influence and causality is the reason for positing a multitude in the effects that are caused. Therefore, if the same being is not to be the cause of opposite effects,[14] it seems that

---

[12] Ps.-Diony., *De Caelest. Hierarch.*, c. 4, p. 1; *De Div. Nom.*, c. 4, p. 1.
[13] Aristotle, *III Topic.*, c. 2.
[14] Aristotle, *II De Gener. et Corrupt.*, text. 56 (c. 10).

these qualities lead us to posit multiplicity rather than unity in the efficient cause; and thus rather than favoring the proposition defended here, they favor the opposite thesis.

CONCLUSION

That God is one is a truth that is not only believable but also intelligible.

Response. The fact that God is one is a truth that is not only believable but intelligible as well since it is both necessary and certain not only from the testimony of Scripture and the illumination of grace which is received in faith, but its truth is self-evidently certain from the testimony of creation as well.

It is certain of itself, therefore, because the divine being possesses unity in every way by reason of its singular sublimity and its sublime singularity. Since God has every perfection in Himself, and this in the highest and most excellent degree, He is proved to be one not only from the sublimity of nature and wisdom, power and goodness, influence and causality, but also from all His qualities and from the noble properties which are attributed to Him in the highest way. Therefore, all these qualities attest to the unity of the highest essence.

It is certain also from the testimony of created beings, because every creature is seen to possess unity just as it possesses a natural goodness. "Nothing can exist unless it be one," as Boethius[15] and Augustine[16] say, and as both sense and intellect teach us. As each creature, by reason of its goodness, proclaims that the true and highest goodness is in God, so by reason of its unity, it proclaims that the cause of all things is one in itself.

Nor does the diversity among beings run counter to this testimony. For all the diversity among beings is comprehended within one universe, which in itself is finite and limited, and perfect. But that would not be the case unless that plurality were reduced to some being in which it comes to rest. And therefore it is necessary that all be reduced to one final end and one first principle, otherwise an infinite series would arise. Therefore, the very universe of beings testifies that God is one. Whence, as it is impossible to reasonably think of one circumference except in reference to a single center from which all lines flow and to which all are reduced as to their end, so in the one universe, we should not speak nor think of God except as one alone.

---

[15] *De Consol.*, III, prosa 11.
[16] *De Moribus Manich.*, II, c. 6, n. 8.

Therefore this is both necessary and evident; and it is known in such a way that no one who has the use of reason can doubt it if he knows "what it is that is expressed by this name." For if the word *God* signifies the first and highest principle of all things thereby encompassing the entire universe, anyone who understands this affirms as a consequence that God is one. Whence, just as principles are self-evident because they are known immediately in the knowledge of their terms,[17] so for anyone who understands what is signified by the terms, it is clear without doubt that God is one.

However, many have erred concerning the number of the gods, for ignorance of the significate begets deception concerning the supposite, and this leads to the heresy which affirms a plurality of gods. Because men believe that God is that which exceeds human power or human knowledge, when they see that demons can do such things, they believe that demons are gods. And they are led into error and blindness and fall into the worship of idols. This is indeed most absurd, but it is not to be marveled at, since "an error that is small at the beginning becomes great at the end." Philosophy can rescue us from such an error, but the Christian faith does so even more effectively; and both of these agree that the divine being is supremely one. Therefore the arguments which prove this should be conceded, because they arrive at a true conclusion through a necessary middle term.

REPLIES TO THE OBJECTIONS

1. To the objection that the conclusion is false because many men are of the opinion that there are many gods, the response is clear since they use the supposite and the significate of the term *God* in a way that differs from its proper meaning. Therefore, there is no contradiction. While the name *God* has no plural according to its proper meaning, it may have a plural when it is taken in an improper sense. So it should be understood in the present case. And the illumination of faith was necessary because of the blindness of the mind, which frequently accepts as true something which is false. Nonetheless, it can be maintained that reason is capable of proving that God is one in as far as His unity is taken in an absolute sense; but the illumination of faith is necessary in as far as the unity is related to a plurality of persons.

2. To the objection that the same conclusion can be drawn concerning the persons, it should be said that there is no parallel

---

[17] Aristotle, *I Poster.*, c. 3.

since in all the persons there is one nature and power and wisdom and goodness and influence and causality. This would not be so if there were different divine natures; therefore a plurality of persons involves no contradiction.

3. To the objection that faith is emptied of its merit, it must be said that this would be true if assent were given only because of the arguments. However, since assent is given because of truth itself and not principally because of the arguments, merit is possible because of the assent of faith. Nothing excludes the possibility that the same matter be both known and believed in terms of different aspects and considerations.

4. To the objection concerning sublimity in relation to great things and things of a similar nature, it should be said that there would be a point to this if something were to accrue to the divine sublimity from the subjection of others. But it is not true, since God is just as sublime in Himself and existing alone as He would be if He ruled over a thousand worlds. Furthermore, it would not add to His sublimity to have something of like nature existing in a servile condition. Thus, even though sublimity of this sort might seem, in a way, to increase His glory, in reality it would decrease it.

5. To the objection concerning power, it must be said that every word must be understood in terms of what is truly possible for a power, for certain possibilities involve weakness rather than sublimity. The possibility of having a nature equal to but different from oneself pertains to the dignity of a limited power, and therefore it is repugnant to omnipotence. Therefore, even though this can be said in words, yet it cannot be attributed to God, for the extent of the divine power is not to be judged according to the degree of this possibility, but rather according to the dignity of its own proper act which is immense; therefore the power is immense.[18]

6. To the objection from wisdom, namely, that it knows another, it must be said that though God knows eternally that which is other than Himself, and this is in accord with the highest wisdom, nonetheless, it is not fitting for God to know the other through the other but through Himself. But this is not possible unless the other being, which is of such a nature as to proceed from God Himself, is in God as in its causal principle. For even if evil is known by God, this is by means of the idea of the opposite good. Therefore the perfection of divine knowledge does not require that the object of knowledge be an actual being, nor that it be the highest being, since God knows earthly realities in the best and highest manner

---

[18] Rich. of St. Victor, *De Trin.* I, c. 21.

through Himself. The objection has its place in that sort of knowledge which takes its origin from things, but God does not have that sort of knowledge.

7. To the objection that the highest diffusion and multitude of goods pertains to the highest good, it must be said that, if *highest* is understood absolutely, then the highest communication within is appropriate to the highest good, but not the highest communication to something outside itself. For there ought to be but one highest good which indeed cannot be added to by a multitude of goods. When it is said that the highest good is supremely diffusive, it should be understood that this is true in as far as *highest* refers to that which is diffusive in power and not in act. And when it is said that a multiplicity of goods is better, we reply that this is true in reference to finite goods where one adds something to the other, and where something of the good is lacking to each one and this is supplied for by a good added to it.

8. To the objection concerning influence, namely, that it cannot exist without God and therefore it cannot be multiplied unless God be multiplied, it must be said that this does not hold, and there is no parallel because it pertains to the perfection of the agent that an effect cannot exist without the presence of the agent since the effect depends totally on the agent; and that agent which acts immediately acts in a more noble manner than one which acts through another. However, this is not so in the case of number and multitude. For it does not pertain to the perfection of an agent that it be multiplied in a multiplicity of effects, but quite the contrary, namely, that while remaining one in itself, it is the cause of diverse effects.

9. To the objection that the proximate and immediate cause is multiplied, it must be said that this is true of a cause which operates by way of nature and whose power is limited. Thus it is a cause in the proper sense, but not a universal cause. But in the production of creatures, the first cause acts by way of art and will. For this reason, it is supremely free as a cause and is limited by nothing; and it is simultaneously a proper and universal cause because whatever perfection exists in the creature must necessarily be posited in the creative essence.

10. To the objection that these are means of proving multitude and diversity, it must be said that they prove not just any sort of diversity among creatures, but rather a diversity with order and connection and an inclination to unity; and thus a diversity in unity. And by reason of that unity, they infer a unity in their cause. Moreover, they do not lead to the opposite conclusion because unity in the cause is not contradictory to multiplicity in the effects; as

is clear in that sort of unity from which infinite species of numbers proceed. So it is that the supreme wisdom and power and goodness — though they are one — are not sufficiently manifested through one effect. Therefore, they imply a diversity in the effects caused by them. Thus our response to all the objections is clear.

ARTICLE II

WHETHER UNITY OF NATURE CAN EXIST TOGETHER WITH A TRINITY OF PERSONS

Supposing that the divine being is supremely one, it is then asked whether the unity of nature can exist together with a trinity of persons. Their incompatability appears in the following.

OBJECTIONS

1. To be one both in form and in supposite is more perfect than to be one in only one of these. Therefore, if the divine being is one in form and not in hypostasis, it would seem that it is not supremely one.

2. Again, to be one both in substance and in property is more perfect than to be one in only one of these. But the trinity cannot exist without a plurality of properties. Therefore it necessarily involves some lack of unity. Therefore these two cannot exist simultaneously.

3. Again by reason of the definition of *one*,[1] the more a thing is undivided, the more it is one. Therefore, there must be total lack of division and total lack of distinction in that which is supremely one; and therefore there can be no plurality. Therefore, either there is no trinity there, or the supreme unity is not found there.

4. Again, that which is one both as a real unity and as a unity of reason is more perfect than that which is one only in reality. But a trinity of persons cannot coexist with a unity of reason. Therefore, the highest and most perfect unity is lacking. Therefore, they cannot exist together.

5. Again, there is a rule that "Two things that are equal to a third are equal to each other."[2] If that third being is simply one, it

---

[1] Aristotle, *III Phys.*, text. 68 (c. 7).
[2] Aristotle, *I Elench.*, c. 5 (c. 6).

follows that either the divine substance is not supremely one, and the persons do not communicate in it, or one person does not differ from the other. But if either of these is granted, then trinity and unity are incompatible.

6. Again, there is a rule that when two things are so related to each other that what is predicated of one is predicated formally of the other, then if one is multiplied the other is multiplied also; as is apparent in man and animal, and white and color.[3] But formally, person is the essence. Therefore, if there are several persons, there are several essences. And thus the same conclusion follows as above.

7. Again, the syllogistic form does not err in the case of propositions that are self-evidently true and in which no accidental reality is found.[4] But these propositions are self-evidently true, namely, each person is distinct; and each person is the essence. Therefore, the essence is distinguished, and it is therefore numbered. Therefore the essence is not one in a trinity of persons.

8. Again, there is a rule that when the object defined is multiplied, then the definition is multiplied together with its defining elements. But substance and nature are contained in the definition of person. Therefore, if there are many persons, there are many essences, substances, and natures. Therefore, the plurality of persons is incompatible with the highest unity of the divine nature.

9. Again, person is defined either by reason of substance or by reason of relation. If it is defined by reason of relation, then a plurality of persons would be identical with a plurality of relations. If it is defined by reason of substance, then the multiplication of persons is identical with the multiplication of substance and nature. Therefore, unity in nature is incompatible with a trinity of persons.

10. Again, when I say that the person is one and the essence is one, this refers either to the same unity or to a different unity. If it refers to a different unity, then there is a plurality of unities, and therefore, it would not be supremely one. If it refers to the same unity, then if one is multiplied so is the other, and if one is not multiplied, neither is the other. Therefore, trinity and highest unity are incompatible.

11. Again, a person is capable of producing only by reason of its nature; but there is no plurality in God except by reason of production. Therefore, if production multiplies person, in the same way it will multiply the nature. Therefore, in God plurality cannot exist together with the supreme unity of nature.

---

[3] Aristotle, *IV Topic.*, c. 5.
[4] Aristotle, *I Prior.*, c. 1 ff.; *I Poster.*, c. 4 ff.

12. Again, the supreme simplicity of God excludes composition not only in nature but also in person. Therefore, since unity is related to plurality as simplicity is to composition, if the highest unity exists in the divine nature, there can be no plurality, neither in nature nor in person.

13. Again, in the divine being, either there is no distinction or there is the most perfect distinction. But the most perfect distinction is that which exists by reason of the form. Since this cannot exist together with the highest unity,[5] it remains either that the highest unity is not found there, or plurality is not found there.

14. Again, unity and truth are convertible and are attributed to every nature. Therefore, if there is a true plurality in God, then truth is multiplied in God; there are, then, multiple truths in God and therefore a plurality of entities. Therefore there is not true unity. And thus the same conclusion follows as above.

15. Again, that the "Father generates" and that the "Holy Spirit proceeds" are two true statements if there is a trinity in God; therefore there are two truths. Therefore if a plurality of truths is repugnant to the highest unity, so also is a plurality of persons.

16. Again, the trinity is constituted either by the repetition of the same unity or by the addition of diverse unities. If it is the repetition of the same unity,[6] then there is no real plurality; and the result would be a superfluous triviality. If it is by addition of diverse unities, since any multiplication or aggregation of diverse unities is repugnant to the highest unity, it is clear, etc.

17. Again, all plurality can be reduced to unity. But in God nothing should be posited that is reducible to something else. Therefore, etc.

18. Again, many properties existing in many subjects bespeak the highest distinction. Contrariwise, therefore, one property existing in only one subject bespeaks the highest unity. Therefore, if the highest unity is found in God, it follows that there is no plurality.

19. Again, God has nothing that is not of Himself. Therefore, every person that is God has whatever it possesses of itself. But only one person can be of itself. Therefore, a plurality of persons cannot exist together with the unity of the divine being.

20. Again, where there is plurality, there is diversity. And where there is diversity, there is a lack of identity. And where there is a lack of identity, supreme unity is lacking.[7] Therefore, etc.

But, on the contrary, objections are raised against this from authority and from reason. From authority in the following way.

---

[5] Boethius, *De Trin.*, c. 2.
[6] Boethius, *De Trin.*, c. 3.
[7] Aristotle, *V Metaph.*, text. 16 (IV, c. 9).

ARGUMENTS IN AGREEMENT

1. 1 *Jn.* 5: "There are three who give testimony in heaven, the Father, the Word, and the Holy Spirit. And these three are one."[8] I call that thing one in an absolute sense to which nothing else is added. Therefore, they are one in an absolute sense. Therefore, trinity does not destroy unity.

2. Again, Bernard to Eugene: "Among all the unities, the unity of the trinity holds first place."[9] But that which holds the highest place among many has being in the highest degree. Therefore, the unity of the trinity is the highest unity. Therefore, a true trinity stands together with the highest unity.

3. Again, a plurality of individuals is not repugnant to the unity of a species; indeed, they coexist. Therefore, if nature designates the common form and person designates the individual or the supposite,[10] a trinity of persons is in no way derogatory to the unity of essence.

4. Again, a plurality of nature is not repugnant to unity of person; indeed they coexist, as is clear in the case of man. Therefore, by reason of a logical conversion a plurality of persons in God is not repugnant to the unity of essence or nature. Therefore they can exist together without diminution.

5. Again, we find one nature in one person, as in the case of the angels; and we find three extremely diverse natures in one person, as in Christ. Therefore, it seems that it is not only possible, but, indeed, very fitting to find a trinity of persons in one nature. And this is the case in God; therefore, etc.[11]

6. Again, that unity which can remain one in many subjects is more excellent than that unity which can maintain its unity only in one person. But the divine unity is the most excellent unity. Therefore it must stand together with a plurality of persons. Therefore, there is no contradiction.

7. Again, as the Philosopher says: "That which generates does not generate another except by means of matter."[12] But in God, there is no matter. Therefore, the one who generates is not distinguished from the one generated. Indeed, moreover, one cannot generate oneself. Therefore, if in God there exists generation without matter, then there exists a plurality of persons without the multiplication of form.

---

[8] Verse 7.
[9] *De Considerat.*, V, c. 8, n. 19.
[10] Boethius, *De Persona et Duabus Naturis*, c. 1-3.
[11] Bernard, *De Consideratione*. c. 9, n. 20.
[12] *VII Metaph.*, text. 28 (VI, c. 8); *II De Anima*, text. 47 (c. 4).

8. Again, as Damascene says, "To generate is to produce a similar being from one's own substance."[13] But the divine substance is not capable of division. Therefore, it is necessary that the one who generates gives his entire substance to the one that is generated. Therefore they cannot be distinguished according to substance. And yet they are distinguished. But neither are they distinguished accidentally because in God there is no accident. Therefore they are distinguished in person; for there remains the distinction in person together with total indistinction in nature.

9. Again, that unity is more perfect in which, together with the unity of nature, there remains the unity of love. But "love tends toward the other."[14] Therefore it includes the distinction of the lover and the beloved. Therefore, if the most perfect unity exists in God, it is necessary that He possess an intrinsic plurality for He has nothing outside Himself that is supremely lovable.

10. Again, likeness, equality, and identity include in their concepts both plurality and unity. This is clear because "likeness is the same quality existing in diverse beings."[15] Therefore, since the highest likeness can exist both in reality and in the mind, and since the highest likeness and identity cannot be or be conceived except with unity and plurality, therefore either it is necessary that the highest unity exist together with true plurality, or else the highest likeness can neither exist nor be conceived. And as a result, no sort of likeness could exist or be conceived. But if these conclusions are impossible, it remains that in God the highest unity coexists with true plurality.

CONCLUSION

The highest unity and trinity in God are not repugnant to each other, but manifest marvelous concord and harmony.

Response. In God the trinity and the highest unity are not contradictory, but manifest a marvelous concord and harmony, according to what the most saving faith says. And the soul purged and elevated by faith can grasp this to some extent; in general, it is difficult and impossible to understand anything unless one first assents to it.

The Christian faith, therefore, says that the divine nature is one and supremely one, and nevertheless there are three persons, one of whom proceeds from the other and through the other; and

---

[13] *De Fide Orthod.*, I, c. 8.
[14] Gregory, *I Homil. in Evang.*, homil. 17, n. 1.
[15] Boethius, *III De Differentiis Topic.*

therefore they communicate in essence and form while their properties are truly distinct. While to the non-believer these seem to be incompatible, to the believer, they seem to be not only compatible but harmonious. However, two things must be considered if we are to understand this. The first is what person and nature signify; the second is how they are related to production. The first removes any contradiction; the second shows the harmony.

It must be recognized, therefore, as Boethius says in *Concerning Two Natures and One person*,[16] that "nature is the specific difference informing a particular thing"; "person, however, is an individual substance of a rational nature"; or as Richard says, "incommunicable existence."[17] The difference, therefore, is that nature refers to the form itself by which each thing is what it is; while person refers to the individual or incommunicable supposite. Because they were ignorant of these definitions, heretics have said that in Christ there are two persons as there are two natures; others have said that there is one nature as there is one person. If they had known the difference between these, they would have seen how it is possible for a plurality of natures to exist with a unity of person, as is clear in any human being.[18] Therefore if a plurality of natures of itself is not contradictory to unity of person, for like reason the reverse is not contradictory — namely, the plurality of persons in a unity of nature. If it is not contradictory, then it can exist in God.

Not only do they have a different meaning, but they are related differently to production. Since it is proper to the supposite to act through the form,[19] it is proper not to the nature but to the person to produce and to be produced, while it is proper to the nature to be communicated through production. Therefore, since the divine nature is entirely indivisible and without any matter, therefore it is not multiplied or numbered by division or partition. Therefore it is entirely one in the produced and in the producer. But because no one can produce himself, it is necessary that there be a plurality at the level of person. Since in the emanation of persons, the nature is communicable while the person is that which produces, emanation requires that there be plurality at the level of persons and unity at the level of nature in such a way that there is no contradiction here but rather the highest harmony.

Therefore, since the plurality does not divide the unity, nor does the unity confuse the plurality, it becomes apparent that the divine

---

[16] C. 1 & 3.
[17] *De Trin.* IV, c. 18 & 22 ff.
[18] Boethius, *De Persona et Duabus Naturis*, c. 4, 5 & 7.
[19] Aristotle, *I De Anima*, text. 64 (c. 4).

being is singularly admirable and marvelously singular. And this is proper to it alone because of the highest simplicity which does not allow that the nature have parts nor that it be associated with matter. Therefore this is proper to it alone; and this in a most admirable way because nothing can be found that is entirely similar to this. Therefore to be one in many with no multiplication or diversification of essence is the exclusive property of the divine nature and is its singular privilege. And that which is one in the first and highest degree ought to have this privilege because it is first and highest. Therefore, it is one in such a way that it cannot be formally multiplied; and it is one in such a way that it can be neither limited nor restricted to only one supposite; it is one in a way which does not impede it from being the eternal principle with respect to that which is coequal with itself, and coeternal and most perfect. Hence no man praises the divine unity perfectly unless at the same time he recognizes the trinity, nor does anyone render perfect worship to the one God unless in faith he confesses that God is a trinity. Hence, those arguments that demonstrate this are to be conceded.

REPLIES TO THE OBJECTIONS

1. To the first objection, it must be said that form is twofold. One type of form is multiplied in many supposites,[20] and in such a form perfect unity cannot coexist together with a plurality of supposites. The second type is that kind of form which is not multiplied in a plurality of supposites, and such is the form of the deity. And since such a form is in no way multiplied by reason of the plurality of supposites, therefore in it there exists simultaneously true plurality and highest unity. This is what is expressed in the name *trinity* in which the unity of nature is included with plurality.

2. To the objection that it is more perfect to be one both in substance and in property, etc., it must be said that property is twofold; namely, absolute and relative. If the objection is understood of an absolute property, it is true; but if it is understood of a relative property, it is not true, since plurality in terms of a relative property does not posit diversity in the thing or in the nature, neither with respect to the essence nor with respect to existence; but it asserts only a different relation which is not incompatible with the highest unity, as can be shown by examples in the case of a point and unity.

3. To the objection that the more a thing is undivided, the more it is one, it must be said that the indivisibility in the definition

---

[20] Aristotle, *I Periherm.*, c. 5 (c. 7).

of unity excludes that sort of division which divides a whole into its parts. But the unity of the trinity is not related to the plurality of persons as is a whole to its parts because the entire deity is in each of the persons most fully and perfectly. Therefore, personal distinction does not contradict that sort of indivisibility which is to be found in the highest unity.

4. To the objection that whatever is one both as a real unity and as a unity of reason is more perfect, etc., it must be said that the word *reason* can be understood in two ways. In the first sense, it adds something really distinct from the essence, such as is the case with essential elements of a being. In the second sense, it does not add anything over and above the essence, but adds only a relation. If the proposition is understood in this way, it is not true, because the plurality of such reasons in no way diminishes the highest unity of the essence or nature.

5. To the objection that two things which are equal to a third are equal to each other, it must be said that this is to be understood of identity in the supposite. Hence it is that — though there is in Christ a unity of dignity that is less than the unity of trinity which is in God — nevertheless man is predicated of God, and God of man, by reason of the unity of person. However, Son is not predicated of Father, nor Father of Son, by reason of the unity of nature since the distinction of the supposites stands in the way of this.[21] Or it can be said that this rule is not violated if it is understood of one and the same genus of unity; but if it is applied to different types of unity, the understanding of this rule is neither correct nor sound. For it does not follow that if different things are equal to a third in generic terms that therefore the persons are numerically identical. In this case, therefore, it is to be so understood that even if essence and person are essentially one, yet it does not follow that they are personally one. It suffices that there be an essential unity between them.

6. To the objection that in formal predication when the subject is multiplied, the predicate also is multiplied, it must be said that this is true when the multiplication of the subject takes place by addition or by formal difference. For in that case it is necessary for the multiplication of the subject that the predicate be multiplied. But this is not the case in the present question; for the multiplication of persons is not a formal multiplication nor is it one that takes place by the addition of any absolute quality; but by reason only of origin and the respective emanation.

7. To the objection that the syllogistic form does not err in

---

[21] Bernard, *V De Consideratione*, c. 8, n. 18 and c. 9, n. 20 ff.

self-evident propositions, it must be said that even though in God there is nothing accidental inhering in Him, nonetheless, there are various levels of predication used to speak of God, namely, predication in reference to substance and in reference to relation, so that "substance contains unity, and relation unfolds the trinity."[22] From this it follows that each of these modes of speech and predication is extraneous to the other; and this is sufficient to cause that sophism known as the fallacy of accident.

8. To the objection that when the object defined is multiplied, the defining elements are multiplied also, it must be said that this is true concerning those things that fall under the formal definition directly. But nature falls under the definition of person indirectly; and substance — in as far as it falls under the definition of person — is identical with hypostasis, which is multiplied in God without any multiplication of the essence.

9. To the objection that person is defined either by reason of substance or by reason of relation, etc., it must be said that person is nothing other than an "hypostasis distinct by reason of a property."[23] Therefore it is predicated by virtue of an intrinsic relation and by virtue of the substance that is not common but proper. Therefore, it does not follow that there is only a plurality of relations, nor that there is a diversity of natures because of the plurality of the divine persons.

10. To the objection that when person and essence are one, they are such either by the same unity or by diverse unities, it must be said that it is neither absolutely identical nor absolutely diverse; rather it is one and the same according to a real unity, but diverse because of a distinction introduced by reason, according to what Augustine says, "It is one thing for Him to be God, and another thing for Him to be Father."[24] He is called Father not because there is an essential or real distinction between deity and paternity, but because Father involves a relation to another which is not included in the essence.

11. To the objection that a person is capable of producing only by reason of the nature, it must be said that production involves the person as subject and principle and as object or term. And therefore true production necessarily effects a multiplication of persons. But production involves nature as the principle of production and as the very reality which is communicated by means of the production. And since in that production the whole nature is com-

---

[22] Boethius, *De Trin.*, c. 6.
[23] Cf. I *Sent.* d. 25, a. 1, q. 2, ad 4 (I, 441).
[24] *De Trin.*, VII, c. 6, n. 11; *Enarrat. in Ps. 68*, serm. 1, n. 5.

municated and nothing is lost in the communications; therefore, even though person is multiplied, yet the nature is not multiplied.

12. To the objection that the highest simplicity excludes composition in nature as well as in person, it must be said that the highest simplicity excludes composition out of diverse elements and with another being; and therefore it can coexist neither with a composition of nature nor with one of person. But the highest unity of nature excludes only essential diversity, and therefore it is not incompatible with a plurality of persons. And thus the two cases are not similar.

13. To the objection that in the divine being there must be either the most perfect distinction or no distinction at all, it must be said that a perfect distinction may be understood in two ways, either intensively or in terms of completion. In the first sense, it should not be predicated of God; in the second sense it is predicated of God because the less a thing deviates from unity the more perfect it is. Therefore because that plurality does not deviate from the highest unity, it follows that such a plurality alone is at the same time true and most perfect.[25]

14. To the objection that unity and truth are convertible, it must be said that this refers to truth in the singular and not in the plural. But when truth and plurality are put in relation to each other, and *vice versa*, then a single object is related not to another single object but to a plurality. Therefore, in this case the consequence is not necessary. When one speaks of a true plurality in God, the word *true* is nothing else but an expression of the plurality that is in the supposites. But on the contrary, when truth is said to be multiplied, a multiplicity is implied in truth itself and in the divine essence.

15. To the objection that it is one truth for the Father to generate and another for the Holy Spirit to proceed, it must be said that if this is understood to refer to the truth of complex judgments, such as in the truth of prayer and of speech, then there are many truths and many articles of faith. But if this is understood to refer to the truth of simple terms, or to the truth of reality, then to say that the Father generates and that the Son is generated, and that the Holy Spirit proceeds is to say nothing else than that the Father, the Son, and the Holy Spirit exist, and that there is but one act of being in them. Thus, the truth of reality is abolutely one.

16. To the objection that there is either a repetition of the same unity or not, it must be said that it is a repetition of the same unity, not however in the same respect but in different respects.

---

[25] Ps.-Dionysius, *De Div. Nom.*, c. 13, p. 2-4.

Therefore it is not a superfluity nor an aggregation of unities. Therefore the multiplication which is found here is not incompatible with the highest unity. It is in this sense that the statement of Boethius, *On the Trinity*,[26] is to be understood when he says that "God is a trinity in this sense, as if one were to say three times: sun, sun, sun." There is a similarity because of the repetition of the same unity. There is a dissimilarity because the unity of the trinity is repeated in reference to different subjects whereas the unity of the sun is repeated in reference to the same subject. Therefore, the trinity in God is real while that in the sun is not.

17. To the objection that plurality is reducible to unity it must be said that a plurality which bespeaks a defect in the highest unity is related to that unity as to its principle and cause; and this is reduced to unity by a proper reduction, which is the reduction of an effect to its cause; and there is no such plurality in the divine being. But a plurality which does not bespeak any defect in the highest unity does not need to be reduced in this way since it is itself the highest unity. Nonetheless, in as far as in God the emanation of divine persons is affirmed from the first person as from a principle, in this sense it is not repugnant that there be a reduction to the first person as to the principle from which the others are produced.

18. To the objection that many properties existing in many subjects bespeak highest distinction or diversity, it must be said that even though, in terms of an extrinsic reason, a plurality of nature in a plurality of person seems to be quite repugnant to the highest unity, nonetheless, in reality and in terms of an intrinsic reason, there is greater repugnance in the case of a plurality of natures in one supposite which is constituted by the natures, since the supposite is made into a composite and is less one than if a plurality of natures were found in a plurality of supposites, as is clear in the nature of angels and of man. And therefore, since the highest unity is found in God, therefore unity is to be affirmed of Him in a more noble and more excellent way, as when we affirm one nature which is not multiplied in the plurality of supposites, instead of affirming one nature in only one person.

19. To the objection that whatever God has, He has of Himself, it must be said that this is true because the divine essence cannot be derived from any other principle. But from this it does not follow that whatever a person has it has of itself. Likewise it does not follow that if the essence is not produced therefore the person is

---

[26] C. 3.

not produced. Thus the argument cited does not come to a true conclusion.

20. To the objection that where there is plurality there is diversity, it must be said, as is clear from the above, that a plurality which relates to form, substance, and nature does not lead to diversity in the proper sense of the word. Therefore nothing is lost from the highest unity and identity, which consists in this; namely, that three persons have the highest unity of essence and nature.

QUESTION III

WHETHER THE TRINITY CAN EXIST TOGETHER WITH THE HIGHEST SIMPLICITY

Next it is asked whether the trinity can exist together with the highest simplicity. In this matter two questions are raised. The first is whether the divine being is most simple. The second is whether the trinity and the highest simplicity can exist together.

ARTICLE I

WHETHER THE DIVINE BEING IS MOST SIMPLE

Concerning the first question, one can proceed to show in the following way that the divine being is most simple.

ARGUMENTS IN AGREEMENT

1. Augustine, in the second book of the *Confessions*, "Nothing more simple than you can be found."[1] Since it is simple in the fullest sense, therefore it is simple in the highest degree. Therefore it is most simple.

2. Again, in the thirteenth book of the *Confessions*, "You alone are simple for whom to live is the same as to live in blessedness."[2] Therefore in God, to be is the same as to live in blessedness. But there is no composition in that being in whom these are the same, but only highest simplicity. Therefore, etc.

3. Again, that being which is absolutely first is most simple. But the divine being is of this sort. Therefore, etc. The proof of the major is: that which is composed is posterior to the elements of which it is composed, and that which is simple is prior to that which is composed. Therefore, the cause of the predicate is contained in the subject of the stated proposition; therefore it is self-evident.

---

[1] C. 6, n. 13.
[2] C. 3, n. 4.

The minor is evident because God exists of Himself; for if He had His being from another, then He would not be God, but the other would be God. And, again, if we are to come to an end, and not to proceed into infinity, it is necessary to affirm that some being is the first of all.

4. Again, that being which is absolutely necessary is most simple. But the divine being is absolutely necessary. Therefore, etc. Avicenna and Algazel prove the major in their *Metaphysics*.[3] For that which is absolutely necessary is totally independent and incorruptible. But everything that is composed depends on its component parts, and in as far as it depends on them by nature, it can be resolved back into its components. The minor is evident because the more perfect of contrary qualities is to be attributed to God. Therefore since that which is absolutely necessary is more perfect than that which is possible or contingent, it is evident, etc.

5. Again, that being which is most perfect is most simple; but the divine being is of this sort, therefore, etc. The minor is evident. The major is proved in that the quality of perfection is to be attributed in the highest degree to that which is most perfect; otherwise it would not be the most perfect. But, as is clear, simplicity is a quality of perfection. Therefore it must be affirmed necessarily that simplicity is in God in the highest degree.

6. Again, that being which is most powerful is most simple; but the divine being is most powerful; therefore, etc. The minor is evident since He is called *God* because He is omnipotent. The major is proved in that "the more unified a power is, the more infinite it is," according to the *Liber de causis*.[4] Therefore the power which is most infinite is most unified, and therefore most simple. But no power is most simple unless its substance is most simple. Therefore, etc.

7. Again, that being for whom to be and to possess are identical is most simple.[5] But God is identical with whatever He possesses; therefore, etc. The major is clear, because if there is any composition, one of the component elements is distinguished from the other. The minor is evident through induction and reasoning; since God has wisdom, therefore either He is wisdom or He is not; and thus it can be argued concerning the other attributes except for the relative attributes. If He is wisdom, then my position stands. If He is not, and if He is wise by reason of wisdom, then He is wise by

---

[3] Avicenna, *Metaph.*, tr. 1, c. 8 & tr. 8, c. 4 ff., Algazel, *I Philos.*, tr. 2, c. de esse possibile et esse debitum.

[4] Propos. 17.

[5] Augustine, *De Civ. Dei*, XI, c. 10, n. 2.

reason of something other than Himself. But, therefore, if He has wisdom from another, then He has perfection from another; therefore, He is not God, etc.

8. Again, that being which is most perfect is most simple; but the divine being is of this sort. Therefore, etc. The minor is clear because no attribute is more consonant with the divine being than perfection. The major is proved because that which is itself perfection, totally and completely and according to itself, is more perfect than that which contains something perfectible within it. But everything that is composite or capable of being composed has something perfectible within it. Therefore it is impossible that any being possess the highest perfection unless it be most simple. Therefore, the same conclusion as above.

9. Again, that being which is composed is mutable. Therefore, from the negation of the consequent,[6] whatever is immutable is simple, and whatever is absolutely immutable is absolutely simple. But the divine being is totally immutable, because it can be changed neither to something better, nor to something equal, nor to something worse, since it is entirely the highest good. Therefore, the divine being is most simple.

10. Again, to the degree that a thing is simple, to that degree it is one. But the divine being is one in the highest degree, as has been shown in the preceding arguments.[7] Therefore it is necessary that the divine being is absolutely most simple.

OBJECTIONS

1. Anselm says, whatever corresponds to God corresponds to Him in the highest degree.[8] But the divine being differs from created being; therefore it must differ in the highest degree. But, the greater the number of differentiating qualities, the greater is the distinction between beings, and the more they are composed. Therefore, it is necessary that the divine being be composed in the highest degree.

2. Again, that being which is entirely abstracted from a supposite is more simple than concrete being. But the divine being is not abstract but concrete with a supposite, because in the divine being there is true deity and a true hypostasis possessing deity. Therefore, etc. If you say that these are only logically different, either there is something real that corresponds to reason or there is not.

---

[6] Boethius, *III De Differentiis Topic.*
[7] Q. 2, a. 1 above.
[8] *Monolog.*, c. 16.

If there is something, then the conclusion follows. If there is not, then it is entirely pointless and false.

3. Again, whatever perfection is found in the creature is to be attributed to the Creator as well.[9] Now, in the case of the creature, the more it is composed, the more it approaches perfection, as is clear in man who is the most perfect of the creatures in the universe, and who is also the image of God. Therefore, it is evident, etc.

4. Again, among ordered forms, that form which arises from some addition is more actual, as is clear in generic and specific forms, because the form of the species is more actual. But that which exists because of an addition is composed. Therefore, composition attests to greater actuality and completion. Therefore, since the divine being is most actual and most complete, it is composed in the highest degree.

5. Again, the properties of the divine being are unity, truth, and goodness. Therefore, either truth is identical with the substance or not. If they are entirely the same, then truth is no more a property of substance than the reverse; which is absurd. If they are not entirely identical, then the property adds something; therefore there is some composition.

6. Again, either truth and goodness are identical, or they are not. If they are identical, then the vestige of goodness is a vestige of truth, which is false. If they differ in some way, then that in which they exist is in some way composed. If you say that they differ only logically, then it is asked what is the basis for distinction.

7. Again, acts are diversified by reason of their objects.[10] But the soul is turned to God as the truth by means of knowledge, and as the good by means of love. If therefore those are formal objects, and if those acts are formally different, it is evident, etc.

8. Again, in the divine being there is power, wisdom, and will. Therefore either I say something more by these three qualities than by one of them, or I do not say more. If not, then he who says that God has power only, does not detract from God, which is false. But if I say something more, then that is totally in God. Therefore, there is composition.

9. Again, either power is identical with knowledge, or it is not. If it is not, then there are diverse realities in the divine being. If they are identical, then to know is the same as to be able. But God knows evil; therefore He can do evil. But this is absurd. Therefore the contrary is true. Therefore it seems that God is composed.

---

[9] Anselm, *Monolog.*, c. 15.
[10] Aristotle, *II De Anima*, text. 33 (c. 4).

10. Again, the divine will places limits to its power, for God does not do all things which He knows and can do, but only those things which He wills to do. However, no being places limits on itself. Therefore, power, wisdom, and will are different from one another. Therefore, the divine nature is composed.

11. Again, that which is completely simple cannot be shared; neither to a greater nor to a lesser degree. But the divine being is shared to a greater and a lesser degree not only by wayfarers but also by the blessed, who participate in His life and contemplate Him in Himself. Therefore, it is impossible that the divine being be entirely simple.

12. Again, that which is completely simple does not have a multiplicity of operations, because "the same being, which remains always identical with itself, is ordained to the same effect."[11] And again, a multiform action is either identical with the agent itself — in which case the agent is not simple — or it is not identical with the agent — and in this case also the agent would not be simple. But God does carry out a multiplicity of operations; namely, He creates, He governs, and He remunerates. Therefore, etc. If you say that these differ only by reason of the effect, it can be replied that the action does not flow from the effect, but the contrary. Therefore, this diversity takes its origin in a diversity of action rather than in a diversity of effects.

13. Again, that which is completely simple does not perform operations simultaneously which are completely different and infinite, because when a simple being turns itself to something else, it does so totally,[12] and no power less than the infinite is sufficient to realize an infinite action. But God simultaneously creates the soul of one man and justifies the soul of another. These actions are distinct and infinite. Therefore, etc.

14. Again, that which is totally simple is not multiple in its idea nor in the cognitive assimilation thereof. But in the divine being, there is a plurality of ideal reasons, because "a man is created by one reason and a horse by another."[13] Therefore, the divine being is not supremely simple. If you say that a plurality of ideas is a plurality of relations, it is said in reply that the likeness among certain beings is sought not in their relations but in their form. Therefore, if the ideas are said to be likeness in the divine mind, and if one and the same being viewed under the same aspect cannot possess a likeness with diverse things, it is necessary that there be composition in the divine art and wisdom.

---

[11] Aristotle, *II De Generat. et Corrup.*, text. 56 (c. 10).
[12] Aristotle, *III De Anima*, text. 36 (c. 7).
[13] Augustine, *Lib. 83 Qq.*, q. 46, n. 2.

CONCLUSION

The Divine Being Is Supremely Simple.

Response. The divine being is most simple. For the evidence of this, we must study two things; namely, the perfection of the divine attributes and the ways in which we know.

If we consider the modes of the divine attributes, the divine being, in as far as it is first, is most simple. For in as far as it is the first being, all things flow from it; and in as far as they flow from it, they flow back and are reduced to it as to their final end. Thus, God is alpha and omega, first and last, principle and end.[14] Since these qualities — which seem to be most distant from each other — concur in every way in one being, it is necessary that the divine being be most perfect and, as it were, like a certain intelligible circle. It is also necessary that it be most simple.

A being can fail to realize the highest unity for three reasons: either because it is composed of different elements; or because it is a component part of another being; or because it has a capacity for entering into composition. In as far as the divine being is first, it is not composed of prior elements; for there is nothing that is prior to itself. In as far as it is most perfect, it cannot be a component part of another being, for that which is perfect does not enter into the constitution of another being. In as far as it is the ultimate being, all other beings are ordered to it as to that end in which they find repose. Thus it is most absolute; and hence it lacks not only actual composition but potential composition as well. Thus, the most simple being befits God truly and properly for none of these three qualities is found in any other being.

It befits Him perfectly by reason of the same three attributes. Since He is most perfect, He has all the qualities of perfection: since He is the ultimate and the best being because of which all things exist, He possesses those properties in the highest degree. Since He is the first, in whom there is no diversity, it is necessary that all that is in Him should be one and most simple, excluding all composition and including all perfection. Therefore, in God there are all the qualities of perfection; namely, power, wisdom, will; goodness, truth and unity; being, life and understanding; and other similar qualities; all these are in God truly, perfectly, and in the highest degree, in their proper and perfect reality. Nonetheless, they are identical to such a degree that they involve no composition nor do they diminish His simplicity.

---

[14] *Apoc.* 1, 8.

No one will see this truth clearly unless he understands in a similar way that in the divine being the highest simplicity coexists with supreme immensity. How this can be understood will be investigated in what follows,[15] but now it must be supposed as certain and indubitable so that we might rightly understand the divine simplicity in accord with the requirements of the divine attributes.

We should also consider the different ways in which we know. Since three elements concur for any knowledge; namely, a knower, a thing known, and medium or cause of knowing, knowledge can be viewed in three ways. It can be considered in terms of the object, and then knowledge is true if it discerns those things which are really there, as when it understands spiritual things in a spiritual way; or it can be considered in terms of the subject knowing, as when it understands abstractly things which are united with it, and this is not a falsehood, for — as the Philosopher says — "abstraction is not a lie";[16] or it can be considered in terms of the cause through which the subject knows, as when it knows one being in many ways through a multiplicity of ideas.

It should be recognized, therefore, that our intellect resolves an object of knowledge totally when it reduces it into the understanding of that which exists and that by which it exists; and when it understands a composite thing, then it carries out that resolution in reference to itself as well as in reference to the object. But when it does this in relation to something that is totally simple, then it carries out the resolution in reference to itself but not in reference to the object, since otherwise it would not be able to understand. Therefore, when our intellect knows God, it knows full well that in Him there is total simplicity, no composition and no concretion, yet it understands this in terms of that which is and that by which it is. And this is not false, since it does not posit that modality in reference to the object; nor is it pointless, for it truly refers to a reality on the part of God, even though these are not diverse realities in God. For in God there is truly essence and supposite, yet they are one reality; there is truly will and power, yet these do not constitute a plurality of entities but are known through a plurality of ideas.

And thus, as Augustine says, "God is truer than what we understand of Him; and what we understand of Him is truer than what

---

[15] Q. 4, a. 1 below.
[16] *II Phys.*, text. 18 (c. 2.).

we say of Him."¹⁷ Therefore, every intellect is limited in its understanding of the divine being, and yet — nonetheless — the intellect that is faithfully turned to Him knows but one thing even though it understands that one thing in multiform ways. It knows the abstract concretely, the simple complexly, the immense finitely, the eternal temporally, because — as has been said — it does not attribute those modalities to the intelligible object itself, but only to itself or to the medium of its knowledge. Therefore a true intellect confesses the divine being to be entirely simple by means of its own proper light of reason. Therefore those arguments that prove this should be conceded.

REPLIES TO THE OBJECTIONS

1. Concerning the first objection in favor of the contrary, that the divine being differs in the highest degree from created being, it must be said that this is true. But concerning what is inferred from this — namely, that it differs because of a great number of differing qualities — it can be said that this does not follow; for the first categories of being differ greatly, and nevertheless they differ of themselves.¹⁸ Also, the differences which immediately divide the genus itself differ of themselves, and yet their difference is very great.

But if you object that beings resemble one another to the degree that they share many qualities, and that therefore the difference between them would correspond to the number of qualities in which they differ; it can be said in response that the divine being differs from created being because of many differences which place the plurality and real difference on the side of the creature rather than on the side of God, since those qualities which are in the creature by way of multiformity and real difference are found in God even more perfectly in the form of the most simple identity, as is clear from what has already been said and from what will be said below.

2. To the objection that that being which is entirely abstracted from a supposite is more simple than a concrete being, it must be said that *supposite* is to be understood in two senses, one that adds something beyond nature and another that does not. In the case of the first understanding of supposite, that which adds beyond nature so as to limit and distinguish the being, the objection is true. But we do not affirm a supposite in God in this sense, because in Him

---

¹⁷ *De Trin.*, VII, c. 4, n. 7.
¹⁸ This refers to the ten predicaments: substance, quantity, etc. Cf. Aristotle, *V Metaph.*, text. 17 & VIII text. 15, or IV, c. 12 and VI, c. 4.

there is no distinction coming from any addition beyond nature, but only distinction by reason of origin of one person from another. Hence in God there is no concretion through real inherence but only in terms of our understanding. And if it is objected that either there is something in the object that corresponds to our understanding, or there is not, the response is clear that there is something that corresponds to our understanding. For in God there is both true nature and true supposite; that is, there is deity and that which possesses deity. Whence, even though the intellect understands this after the manner of a difference, such an understanding is not false since the distinction is made either because of the mind or because of the medium of knowledge, and not because of the object known. Or, if it is attributed to the object, some real difference is affirmed between the supposite and the nature, but of such a sort that it involves no composition, as will become more clear in the following question.

3. To the objection that whatever perfection is found in the creature is to be attributed to the Creator, it must be said that there is perfection in an absolute sense and there is perfection in a qualified sense. Whatever in the creature bespeaks perfection in an absolute sense is to be attributed to the creative essence truly and properly. But that which bespeaks perfection in a qualified sense is not fittingly attributed to God.[19] When it is argued, therefore, that a greater composition in the creature leads to a greater perfection, as is clear in man, it must be said that this is a diminished perfection which arises from the aggregation of many because what a being cannot have in itself by reason of its oneness it can have through union with others. Therefore, such a perfection is not to be attributed to the divine being, which is the most noble and which stands at the summit of all perfection.

4. To the objection that among ordered forms, that form which arises from an addition is more actual, it must be said that there is actuality which is intrinsic to a particular genus and actuality that is extrinsic to any genus. Actuality intrinsic to a genus is an actuality mixed with potency, which potency resides in the nature of the genus and is reduced to act through the addition of the specific difference which distinguishes it. The proposition is true in the case of this sort of actuality. Beyond this, there is an actuality extrinsic to any genus which has no mixture of potency; and this is the actuality of pure act. In this case, therefore, there is no addition of one thing to another as act is added to a particular potency.

---

[19] Anselm, *Monolog.*, c. 15.

Such actuality is affirmed of God. Therefore, it does not follow that any addition or composition is to be attributed to Him.

To the objection that the highest good results from adding to that which is good, it must be said that the addition exists only in the intellect since the concept of the good is included in the concept of the highest good. But there is no addition in the object, both because the created and uncreated good do not share any common nature, and because the highest good is of a greater simplicity than that common reality signified by the word *good*, and because the highest good exceeds every created good by an improportionate excess. Therefore when *good* is affirmed in reference to the created and to the uncreated good, this is done only by reason of a certain analogy because every created good flows from the uncreated good as from the first cause. Therefore, that which is posterior to the first cause, by that very fact, lacks the highest simplicity; but the first cause — by reason of the fact that it is first, is most simple. Therefore, as the quality of simplicity, when added to being, does not involve any composition in being, as when I say *simple being*, neither does the term *highest* posit any composition when it is said of the good.

5. To the objection that the properties of the divine being are unity, truth, and goodness, it should be said that truth is a property of the divine being in as far as, of itself, it expresses a mode of being. But since in the divine being there is no difference between essence and power,[20] therefore there is no difference between the essence and its modalities because it is impossible that it exist in two different ways. And therefore, since essence and the modes of being are identical in God, there is no composition. Since a mode of being is a property of the essence itself, and not the contrary, it follows that unity, truth, or goodness are said to be properties of the divine essence; however, the divine essence cannot be said to be a property of truth or goodness because it does not designate a mode of being as the other terms do.

6. To the objection that either truth and goodness are identical in God or they are not, it must be said in reference to the principal significate or the object understood by these terms that what they express is really one reality in the divine being, since God is not good because of one distinct reality and true because of another, but in as far as He is good, He is also true. But, in terms of the cause of knowledge by which the intellect ascends from creatures to an understanding of the Creator, there is a difference, because as un-

---

[20] Aristotle, *III Phys.*, text. 32 (c. 4).

created truth and goodness is understood through the created truth and goodness, and as these differ in creatures in some way; therefore they are said to be different in some way with respect to the cause of knowledge, even though they are identical in reality.

This is not false, nor is it an error in understanding because these are found in God most truly and most perfectly even though in God they are not really distinct among themselves as they are in created being. And this is sufficiently clear if one understands what was said in the principle of the solution concerning the multiple modes of our knowledge.

7. To the objection that acts are distinct by reason of their objects, the response is already clear because even though those objects are really identical in God, they are said to be distinct in reference to our mode of knowledge. Therefore, just as distinct representative properties correspond to different acts in the created vestige which has a representative meaning, since goodness and truth are not identical in created nature, so there are distinct powers that correspond to these in the image that apprehends them. These consist in the intellective and the affective powers. This is the case because both in the vestige and in the image there are found certain distinct qualities that correspond to certain realities which are totally identical in God.

8. To the objection that power, wisdom, and will taken together either do or do not say more than one of them alone, it must be said that they say more explicitly, but implicitly each of these is included in the others. For there cannot be highest power where there is not will and wisdom. Therefore, if one is attributed to God without the other, it is attributed in a limited sense; not because they are really distinct, but because the same reason that makes it impossible for them to be separated makes it impossible for them to be distinct. Therefore, just as they cannot be distinct, neither can they be separated.

9. To the objection that power is either identical with knowledge or it is not, it must be said that we can speak of power and knowledge in two senses, either with reference to the principal signification or with reference to the connotation. In terms of the principal signification they are really identical, but in terms of the connotation they differ. For, to be knowable by God is not the same as to be possible, just as to be known is not the same as to be produced. The term *possible* designates a thing in as far as it does emanate or can emanate. But the word *knowable* refers to a thing in as far as it is present to the mind of the knower. And because there is not one reality in God by which He is powerful and another by which He is capable of knowledge — since both of these are properties of God

in Himself, therefore even though they are distinct in terms of connotation, they are identical in reality.

10. To the objection that the will places limits to its power, it must be said that we can speak about power and will in three ways: either in reference to affect, or in reference to effect, or in reference to relation. In the first sense, they are identical and equal, because whatever God does will He can will; or whatever He can do, He wills to be able to do. In the last sense, they are not equal, since power is predicated in relation to that which is possible whereas will refers to that which is willed; and more things are possible than are effectively willed. But in the second sense, they are equal, namely, in as far as they are related to the effect, since, even though power extends to more things than does will, nevertheless since God produces nothing unless He wills it, power and will are said to be equal in relation to the effect. Therefore, will is said to be limited by power not by reason of their own nature, but by reason of that to which they are related.

11. To the objection that whatever is completely simple cannot be shared, neither to a greater nor to a lesser degree, it must be said that participation can be understood in two ways; namely, in terms of formal participation as the species participates in the genus,[21] or in terms of influence, as effects participate in their cause. In the first sense, the objection is true. But the divine being is not said to be shared to a greater or lesser degree in this way, but only in the second way. But this does not imply diversity in that which is shared, but in that being by means of which participation arises, namely, in some created good.

12. To the objection that whatever is completely simple does not have a multiplicity of operations, it must be said that operation refers both to the action itself and to the work produced, or to the act in the active sense and to the effect produced. In the first way, the operation of God is identical with God Himself. Therefore it is not multiplied in itself by reason of itself, but it is multiplied on the part of the creature by reason of the effect produced. In the first sense, therefore, the proposition is true; but not in the second, for the more simple a being is, the more powerful it is, and hence the more it is the principle of a multiplicity of effects.[22]

13. To the objection that whatever is completely simple does not simultaneously perform operations which are distinct and infinite, it must be said that a being can be simple in two ways; in the first way simplicity excludes immensity; and in the second way

---

[21] Aristotle, *IV Topic.*, c. 1.
[22] *Lib. de Causis*, prop. 17.

it includes immensity. In the first sense, the objection is true, but not in the second; for the infinite — in as far as it is the infinite divine being — is infinite in the fullest sense, and can turn itself simultaneously and without limit to all things however many and of whatever sort, since it admits of no limitation.

14. To the final objection that whatever is totally simple is not multiple in its idea nor in the cognitive assimilation thereof, it must be said that multiformity can be understood in terms of formal cause or in terms of expressive cause. In the first way, multiformity is found in that being which contains the natures of diverse forms within itself. Such multiformity is incompatible with highest simplicity. In the second way, multiformity is found in that being which contains the ideas of a multiplicity of forms in itself; and in this way, it is compatible with highest simplicity. Just as the most simple being, in its highest actuality, has the highest power by which it can effect all things distinctly and fully, so it possesses the highest truth by which it can represent all things eternally, as was made clear above in the question concerning the eternal reasons.[23]

ARTICLE II

WHETHER THE TRINITY AND THE HIGHEST SIMPLICITY CAN EXIST SIMULTANEOUSLY

Next the question is raised whether trinity and highest simplicity can exist simultaneously. For many reasons, they seem to be incompatible.

OBJECTIONS

1. Abstract being is simpler than concrete being. Therefore a nature that has no supposite is simpler than a nature existing in several hypostases. But the trinity demands the existence of a nature in several hypostases; therefore the trinity entails a diminishment of the highest simplicity.

2. Again, that which is identical with itself is simpler than that which is diverse.[1] Therefore any being in which there is identity in every respect is more simple than a being in which some sort of diversity is found. But the trinity is impossible without some sort

---

[23] Cf. *Q. de Sci. Christi*, q. 2 ff. (V, 6 ff.).
[1] Aristotle, *V Metaph.*, text. 16 (IV, c. 9).

of diversity. Therefore it cannot exist together with the highest simplicity.

3. Again, that which is common is simpler than that which is proper, as is clear because that which is proper contains within itself a common quality as well as some reality beyond this. But there can be no true trinity unless the distinct and incommunicable properties of the three persons are found there. Therefore, it is impossible to affirm the trinity without affirming some departure from the highest simplicity.

4. Again, whatever is absolute is simpler than that which is relative; since, as Augustine says, "Every relative being is a real entity even if the relationship is excluded."[2]

Hence, the relative includes the absolute; but there cannot be a trinity of persons without a plurality of relations; therefore, etc.

5. Again, the elements of a definition are simpler than the object defined, but the concept of nature is included in the concept of persons. Therefore nature is always simpler than person. Therefore, the concept of person cannot exist together with the highest simplicity. But the trinity cannot exist except in the persons; therefore the trinity is repugnant to the highest simplicity.

6. Again, the part is always simpler than the whole. But unity is part of the trinity, and one person is part of three persons. Therefore, if trinity implies true plurality and true plurality implies true totality, and true totality excludes the highest simplicity, it follows that the trinity cannot exist together with the highest simplicity.

7. Again, a point is always simpler than the continuum; therefore, unity is simpler than number; therefore a unity of persons is simpler than a trinity of persons. But any being which is excelled in simplicity by another is not the supremely simple being. Therefore, it is impossible that the trinity exist together with the highest simplicity.

8. Again, person is either just as simple as the essence, or it is not. If it is not, then either person does not exist in the divine, or the divine being is not the most simple. However, if person is just as simple as the essence then just as the essence — because of the highest simplicity — is not compatible with a plurality of divine essences, it follows for the same reason, that person is incompatible with a plurality of persons.

9. Again, person adds something over and above nature either in the real order as well as in the logical order, or in the logical order alone, or in neither way. If it is taken in the first way, then it

---

[2] *De Trin.*, VII, c. 1, n. 2.

lacks the highest simplicity; if it is taken in the second way, any concept which does not correspond to a reality is both empty and false; if it is taken in the third way, then as the nature is not multiplied, neither is the person.

10. Again, either everything that corresponds to person corresponds to nature and *vice versa*, or not. If such a correspondence is found, then when person is distinguished, nature also is distinguished; and this would not be the most simple being. If such a correspondence is not found, then as the affirmation and the negation of the same thing cannot be true under the same formality, therefore they can be true only under distinct formalities.[3] But any being that includes distinct formalities is composed. Therefore, etc.

11. Again, either one person differs totally from the other, or it corresponds totally with the other; or it differs partly and corresponds partly. If it corresponds totally, then it has nothing proper to itself, and therefore it is not distinguished from the other. If it differs totally and if one is God, then the other is not God. If it corresponds partly and differs partly, since this is not in the same respect, there is a composite being.

12. Again, when one person communicates with the other, it either communicates whatever it has or it does not. If it does not, then it gives something of itself and retains something. Therefore it is both composed and selfish. If it communicates itself totally, then it communicates its quiddity and thus its personality. If you say that personality is not communicable, it may be argued to the contrary that personality is as simple as nature, as you say. Therefore, just as nature is communicable, so, it seems, is person.

13. Again, that which is proper to a person is either something real or it is not. If it is not something real, then it adds nothing; and therefore it does not distinguish that in which it exists. If it is something real, it is either located in the essence or it is not. If it is located in the essence, since the property distinguishes that in which it is located, then the nature and essence are multiple, which is contrary to the trinity. If it is not located in the essence but in the person, then there is something real in the person that is not in the essence. Therefore a property necessarily introduces composition into the person.

14. Again, relation is a property of the person; either it falls under the concept of substance, as do the other predicaments, or it does not. If it does fall under the concept of substance, then just as substance neither distinguishes nor is distinguished, neither is the property. Therefore there is no trinity. If it does not fall under

---

[3] Aristotle, *III Elench.*, c. 5 (c. 25).

substance, then it implies something more than substance; therefore it is lacking in simplicity. Consequently, if it is impossible for a person to exist without a property, then it is impossible for it to exist together with the highest simplicity.

15. Again, as a point is not composed of its relations, so it is not really multiple. Therefore if God is more simple than a point, then in no way is there any real distinction in Him.

16. Again, absolute being is prior to relative being. Therefore, a distinction based on an absolute property is prior to one based on a relative property. But the more prior a being is, the greater is its simplicity. Therefore if a distinction based on absolute properties is not compatible with the highest simplicity, then neither is a distinction based on relative properties.

ARGUMENTS IN AGREEMENT

1. It is possible to ascertain that one being is simple because it is united in one, and that another being is simpler because it is one being that is multiplied in many. This being is simpler, because — like a universal — it is one in many, yet it is not absolutely simple, because it is numbered. Therefore, if something were to be one in many but not multiplied, that would be most simple. But the highest simplicity must be attributed to the divine being. Therefore the trinity does not destroy the simplicity of the divine essence.

2. Again, a plurality of natures is not repugnant to simplicity of person, as is clear in Christ. Therefore, if a diversity of natures contributes more to composition than does a plurality of person, it seems that, even more so, the plurality of person in no way diminishes the simplicity of nature. Therefore it stands, etc.

3. Again, God can create without any diminution of His simplicity. Therefore, if to generate and to spirate is an intrinsic act, all the more does He generate and spirate while doing no violence to His highest simplicity. But the trinity exists because He generates and spirates. Therefore, etc.

4. Again, to know is an act that in no way is opposed to simplicity, but rather is consonant with it and attests to it. But any mind in knowing itself generates a likeness of itself, which is said to be a word distinct from the mind that generates it.[4] Therefore, as the act of knowledge can exist together with the highest simplicity, so also can generation, and for the same reason, the production of

---

[4] Augustine, *De Trin.*, IX, c. 11, n. 16.

the Holy Spirit. Therefore, it seems that the entire trinity exists simultaneously with the highest simplicity.

5. Again, as Augustine, says in the sixth book *On the Trinity*, "In spiritual matters, to be greater is the same as to be better."[5] But in the blessed trinity, each person is supremely good. Therefore, three persons are neither better nor greater than one. But in every composition, some reality is added which in some way is an increase. Therefore, the highest trinity does not involve composition in any way. Therefore in no way is it repugnant to simplicity.

6. Again, the highest simplicity does not exclude but rather includes the highest perfection. The highest perfection does not exclude but includes plurality. Therefore, the highest simplicity does not exclude but includes a plurality of persons. Therefore, it is not repugnant, but supremely fitting.

7. Again, the highest simplicity does not exclude, but rather includes the highest power and virtue, because as was proved above,[6] a power is infinite to the degree that it is united in itself. But the highest and most actual power implies the highest and most perfect communication and production; and this implies the trinity. Therefore, the trinity necessarily exists together with highest simplicity.

8. Again, light is predicated of spiritual substance both created and uncreated, and of corporal substance, in terms of a certain proportion and analogy. But the fact that material brightness is produced does not decrease the simplicity of material light. Neither does spiritual light, such as a thought or a word produced by the mind, decrease the simplicity of the intellectual substance by the mere fact that such light is produced. Therefore the production of the eternal brightness from the Father in no way diminishes the simplicity of the eternal light.

9. Again, the simplicity of a point or of a unity or of any created principle whatsoever does not exclude but includes a plurality of relations and respects; and this is not an imperfection but a perfection. But every perfection ought to be attributed to God. Therefore, the highest simplicity together with a plurality of relations are not contradictory in reference to God. But "relation unfolds trinity," as Boethius says; therefore, etc.[7]

10. Again, where there is neither matter nor position in space, there can be no separation. Therefore, a production that prescinds from matter and place does not imply any separation. Therefore it

---

[5] C. 8, n. 9.
[6] A. 1, fund. 6 of this question. Also, *Q. de Sci. Christi*, q. 6, resp. (V, 34-35); *Lib. de Causis*, prop. 17.
[7] *De Trin.*, c. 6.

can exist together with total lack of division, and therefore with total simplicity. Therefore, if it is by such a production, that the persons of the trinity are produced, then the trinity can exist together with the highest simplicity.

CONCLUSION

The trinity of persons does not destroy the highest simplicity, nor does the highest simplicity exclude the trinity.

Response. The first principle is simultaneously a trinity and most simple in such a way that the trinity does not destroy the highest simplicity, nor does the highest simplicity exclude the trinity. This indeed we hold most certainly by faith.

But so that we might understand this to some degree, two things should be noted from the start; first, the different kinds of personal distinction, and second the different types of divine attributes.

Concerning the first, as Richard writes in his book *On the Trinity*,[8] one person is distinguished from another person in three ways; namely, by origin alone, by quality alone, or by origin and quality together. The first mode is found in God, the second in the angelic spirits, and the third in man. Men are qualitatively distinct from each other because of the different accidents and properties by which one individual is distinguished from another.[9] And they are distinguished from each other in origin because one human being is born from another. Angels, however, are qualitatively different because they differ in substance and in formal properties. But they are not distinguished by reason of origin because no angel proceeds from another angel. But the divine persons, being entirely one in substance and in form and having no accidents, are not distinguished by reason of quality but only by reason of origin. And that origin, moreover, emerges not from something distinct from the person, but rather from the person itself; as God knows through Himself and is identical with His understanding, so the Father generates through Himself and is identical with generation. Likewise, the Son is identical with filiation. Therefore, if in God there is the truest sort of origin, then there is the truest personal distinction.

Furthermore, if the person is its own origin, then there is no composition whatever in the person; it is thus as simple as is the essence. There is, therefore, total lack of real distinction between

---

[8] IV, c. 13 ff.
[9] Porphyr., *De praedicab.*, c. de specie.

person and essence as well as between person and property and essence. Therefore person truly is the essence and property, and the essence is the property and person, and the property is the person and the essence. But how can any composition be conceived where there is such lack of distinction ? Therefore, it is necessary to understand that supreme simplicity is found in such a distinction of persons. Consequently, since it is impossible to conceive of any composition here, the trinity of persons and the highest simplicity are not repugnant. It is very helpful for the sake of clarity to study the kinds of personal distinction, the ignorance of which has led heretics into error.

Also, we should consider the different kinds of divine attributes; for difference can be seen in terms of the essential modes of being, in terms of the modes of relation, and in terms of modalities of the intellect. Relative to being or essence, no diversity or difference can be found in God; because His being is one and most simple. The same is true with respect to His absolute mode of being, because just as in God essence is not distinct from existence, so in God being is not a reality distinct from mode of being. The reason for this is that in God essence and power are identical, and we cannot say that He could exist in various ways. And therefore, since the modes of being are identical with His essence, all predicates which signify the absolute mode of being fall under the concept of substance with the exception of relation, which refers to a relative mode of being; and this mode of speech passes into substance in relation to the subject so that the hypostasis is identical with its own property, and no composition is involved;[10] but it continues to exist in relation to its term, so that a true distinction is preserved. For a distinction between the relation and the subject would involve composition; but the difference between the relation and its term involves only distinction. Therefore in God no distinction is to be found relative to essence, existence, or the absolute modes of being; it is found, however, in the three modes described above. But the difference found in the modes of being is based on the persons as they relate to each other; because even though they all have the same being, they have it in different ways, since one has it from itself and the other has it from another. This is enough diversity to forbid the identification of one person with another. Those modes, as was shown above, while they do not involve composition, do create a true distinction.

---

[10] In analyzing relation, Bonaventure distinguishes the *esse in* and the *esse ad*. In the trinity, the *esse in* passes over into substance, while the *esse ad* remains in the persons.

But the difference in the relative modes resides in the persons as they relate to the essence. Since "to proceed from" pertains to the person and not to the essence, it follows that the person refers to and is related to the other persons, but the essence does not. For this reason, person is distinguished while the essence is not. Now, from this difference it does not follow that one person is separated from the other, but it does mean that something can be predicated of the person which cannot be predicated of the essence, and *vice versa*. It is from this difference that the three modes of speaking about God arise: namely, what, who, and which one;[11] namely, notion, person, and essence. And from this it follows that, if we suppose person, notion is not supposed, and *vice versa*. The same can be said of essence. From the differences in the modes, a figure of speech emerges in speaking of God, as is clear to one who reflects on the matter.[12]

The difference which arises from the modalities of the intellect resides in the essential properties which are fully identical with each other, as are truth and goodness, but our mind understands them by means of diverse causes and under different concepts, and therefore it gives them different names. This is the smallest differentiation that can be found in reference to God because it exists in us rather than in God. Hence, the highest simplicity exists not only with personal distinction but also with multiple forms of attribution. Therefore the arguments for this position are to be conceded; it is easy enough to respond to the opposite arguments.

REPLIES TO THE OBJECTIONS

1. Concerning the first argument to the contrary, that abstract being is simpler than concrete being, it should be said that this is true only in that being in which form and supposite are different and in which, therefore, the abstract and the concrete are real. But in regard to God, the concrete in the proper sense is not found in Him, but is attributed to Him by us. Similarly when it is argued that a nature which is not one in many supposites is simpler than one which is one in many supposites, it should be said that this is true relative to a reality that is more perfect when it is distributed

---

[11] In quid; in quis; in quae.
[12] Aristotle, *I Elench.*, c. 3 (c. 4). This is a technical term used by Aristotle to designate a sophistical argument based on forms of expression. Such an argument is found when, because of a verbal similarity, a reality which is not the same as another is interpreted as though it were; e.g. when masculine is interpreted as feminine, or quantity as quality.

in many than it is in only one, as is the case in number. But this is not so in the position proposed here, because the divine essence and nature is as completely and perfectly in one of its hypostases as it is in the three.

2. To the objection that a being which is identical with itself is simpler than one which is diverse, etc., it should be said that there is a diversity or distinction that comes from addition, such as that which exists between different species which are distinct by reason of various differences added beyond the genus. And there is a distinction which comes not from addition but from origin such as the distinction which exists in the divine persons which are distinguished by the fact that one emanates from the other. And this involves no composition, as was explained in the principal argument.

3. To the objection that that which is common is simpler than that which is proper, it must be said that this is true when the common is limited and restricted by the proper, for such a case admits of both composition and distinction by reason of that which limits and restricts, as is clear in the case of the universal and the particular. But this is not the way in which the common is found in God, since the essence — even though it is common in God — is not restricted nor limited nor distinguished in the persons.

4. To the objection that the absolute is simpler than the relative, it must be said that there are two sorts of relative being. In one sense, it implies a relation to something that is essentially different. In another sense, it implies a relation only to something which is consubstantial. In the first sense, relation includes a certain dependence, and for this reason it implies a lack of highest simplicity. In the second sense, it involves no dependence and no lack of supreme simplicity, above all when the supposite itself is its own property, which serves as the basis of the relation. It is in this manner and not in the first manner that relation is affirmed in the properties of the divine persons; and thus no composition is introduced.

And if it is objected that "Every relative being is a real entity even if the relationship is excluded," it must be said that if this is understood with reference to the first sort of relative being, it is true not only with respect to the cause of our knowledge, but also with respect to the object. If it is understood in the second way, it is true with respect to the cause of our knowledge, because in addition to the reality of the relation, the Father includes an hypostasis, which — however — is not something distinct from His personal property.

5. To the objection that the elements of a definition are simpler than the object defined, it must be said that this is true in the case of a formal direct definition, in which the defining elements are

essential parts constituting the very thing defined. But such is not the case here, because — properly speaking — the divine persons are not defined; and because the nature does not directly fall under the definition of person; and because, furthermore, that definition is concerned with the meaning of the words *person* and *nature* with respect to the way they arise in our mind more than with respect to their own being, which can neither be comprehended nor defined because of the highest simplicity and immensity of the divine being.[13]

6. Again, to the objection that the part is always simpler than the whole, it must be said that this is true. But in assuming that one of the persons is a part of the trinity, it is false, because every whole involves something more than a part thereof. And as we have said often, no property is greater in the three persons than in one; for each of the persons is the supreme being, and supremely true and good. Therefore, though the trinity in God includes the reality of plurality, it does not for that reason include the reality of a true totality.

7. Again, to the objection that a point is always simpler than a continuum, and unity simpler than number, it must be said that this is true in the case of number in the strict sense, which is an aggregation of diverse unities. But number in this sense is not found in the trinity of divine persons, for this reason that there is here no aggregation of any unities, nor of entities nor of truths. But it is the repetition of the same unity in different subjects. And the very word implies this, for we say *trinity*, that is the unity of three.[14]

8. Again, to the objection that person is as simple as the essence, or it is not; it should be said that it is equally simple in reality. And when it is objected further that, because of its highest simplicity, the essence does not allow of other essences, it must be said that there is no similarity, because if there were a plurality of divine essences, there would then be harmony and essential difference. I say there would be harmony because each of these would be God; I say there would be differentiation because there would be a plurality of beings, and this would not be possible without addition and composition.[15] But such is not the case with a plurality of persons, since — as has been shown — they are not distinguished from each other by the addition of something real, but only by natural origin. Therefore, simplicity of essence excludes a plurality of essence, and

---

[13] Avicenna, *Metaph.*, tr. 8, c. 4.
[14] Cf. above, Q. 2, a. 2, ad 16; *Q. de Sci. Christi*, q. 3, ad 8 (V, 15); Isidore, *VII Etymolog.*, c. 4, n. 1.
[15] Cf. above, Q. 2, a. 1, fund. 7.

a plurality of person does not exclude the unity of the divine essence, nor does it exclude simplicity of person.

9. Again, to the objection that person adds something beyond the essence either in the real order as well as in the logical order, etc., it should be said that it does add something in the logical order, because the concept of nature and property and hypostasis is included in the concept of person. Hence, the concept of person is a composite concept, but in such a way that just as there is no real composition, so there is no real addition there.

And if it is objected that such a concept is false, it must be said in reply that the objection is false, for there is something real that corresponds to the concept since these three realities are truly found in God; namely, nature, property, and hypostasis, each distinct by reason of its property. But in themselves they are entirely one by reason of the highest simplicity. Since our understanding cannot arrive at such simplicity, it understands these realities by means of distinct concepts and names them with different terms thereby introducing a certain type of composition which it does not attribute to the object known, but to itself, as was shown in the preceding problem.

10. To the objection that the affirmation and the negation of the same thing cannot be true under the same formality, it must be said that not only does it not imply a contradiction when several things are predicated of the same object though not in the same formal sense, but also when they are not referred to the same subject. And since person includes a relation to and a comparison with something else while the nature does not, it follows that something can be attributed to one and not to the other; yet it does not follow from this that there is any composition in these things nor any essential distinction. It is sufficient that this distinction be based on relation.[16]

11. To the objection that either one person agrees totally with the other, or that it agrees partly and differs partly, it must be said that one person coincides with the other in essence but differs in property. But in relation to the essence, that property is only a mode of being which is really identical with the essence, for the essence is the property itself and differs from it only in a relative aspect.

Now since composition arises in terms of the essence, and distinction arises in terms of relation, it follows that the difference between property and essence is such that it suffices for distinction but introduces no composition.

---

[16] Cf. above, Q. 2, a. 2, ad 5.

12. To the objection that a person either communicates whatever it has to the other or it does not, it must be said that it communicates whatever it has that is communicable, and this is the essence or nature. But the personality, or that relation which constitutes the person, refers to that reality which distinguishes it rather than to a reality which can be communicated. Therefore, even though the person does not communicate this, there is nonetheless a perfect communication here because with the communication the distinction remains preserved.

13. To the objection that the property of a person is either something real or it is not, it must be said that, formally and properly speaking, the property of a person is a relation, which includes a relation to the divine essence and to the person which it distinguishes as well as to the person from which it is distinguished. In terms of the relation to the person from which it is distinguished, it is a true reality because it really differs from the other person, as the Father is really distinguished from the Son by reason of paternity. In terms of the relation to the person in which it is found, or also in terms of the relation to the essence itself, it is only a mode of being which involves no composition in God, because — as was shown earlier — there is no difference in God between His being and being-in-this-way, or the modes of being, just as there is no difference between "living and living in blessedness."[17]

14. To the argument that the property of the person either falls under the concept of the substance or it does not, it must be said that a relation has two aspects, namely, the subject in which it is found and the term to which it relates the subject. In the first way, like the other categories, it falls under substance; but not in the second way. And since that property, more than the other categories, implies a comparison to another it follows that it does not pass into the category of substance even though all other things are said to do so, not because in some way it signifies a reality that is not the essence, but because it is fitting that relation be predicated of some reality to which essence is neither referred nor predicated. Whence, without doubt, the essence is the subject which is related but not the term to which it is related. Therefore, while distinction is preserved, there is no composition.

15. To the objection that a point, because of its simplicity, is neither composed of its relations nor numbered, it must be said that there is no comparison, because the relations of a point are extrinsic while the personal relations are intrinsic. Therefore, however much a point can be said to be principle and end with respect to diverse

---

[17] Augustine, *Confess.*, XIII, c. 3, n. 4.

lines, yet no one hypostasis can be called simultaneously Father and Son, because no person can be the principle of its own origin.

16. To the objection that absolute being is more prior than relative being, therefore a distinction based on an absolute property is prior to one based on a relative property, it should be said that this does not hold, since every distinction includes some relation. And furthermore, that distinction which is closer to the first and highest unity is certainly prior. And that is the sort of distinction in which unity is not multiplied, and such a distinction cannot be essential, but relative. Whence, it can be said either that the argument is not conclusive, or that the proposition is true only of that sort of relation which implies some dependence. But this type of relation is not admitted in reference to the distinction of the eternal persons. Therefore this involves no contradiction with the fact that the divine being is most simple just as it is first and most absolute, as appears from the foregoing.

QUESTION IV

WHETHER THE TRINITY EXISTS TOGETHER WITH THE HIGHEST INFINITY

Next the question is raised whether the trinity exists together with the highest infinity. Two questions are asked about this. The first is, whether the divine being is infinite in the highest degree. The second is, whether the trinity and the highest degree of infinity can exist together.

ARTICLE I

WHETHER THE DIVINE BEING IS INFINITE IN THE HIGHEST DEGREE

As to the first question, we can proceed to show that the divine being is infinite in the highest degree in the following way.

ARGUMENTS IN AGREEMENT

1. First, it is shown in the confession of faith contained in the *Symbol*: "Immense is the Father; immense the Son, immense the Holy Spirit, and yet there are not three immensities but one immense being."[1] Therefore, there is one immensity in them. Therefore it is fitting for them by reason of their essence.

2. Again, Damascene writes: "We must believe that the one God is immortal, eternal, and uncircumscribed."[2] Therefore, if these attributes are fitting only for one who is absolutely infinite, it is clear, etc.

3. Again, III *Kings* 8 writes: "If heaven and the highest of heavens cannot contain you, how much less this house which I have built?"[3] Therefore, if the being of God can be contained and

---

[1] Athanasian Creed.
[2] *De Fide Orthod.*, I, c. 8.
[3] Verse 27.

circumscribed by nothing, it must be admitted that it contains the nature of the infinite in an unlimited degree.

4. Again, in the fourth chapter of the first book Damascene writes: "God is infinite and incomprehensible. And this alone is comprehensible about Him; namely, His infinity and incomprehensibility."[4]

5. Again, Augustine writes in the *City of God*, 11: "Every infinity terminates in God in a certain ineffable manner."[5] But any being for whom the infinite is finite is absolutely infinite. If, therefore, the divine being is of this sort, then it is infinite in every way.

6. Again, in terms of reason, it is the common conception of the mind[6] that God is that being than which nothing greater can be thought, neither because of itself nor because of another. But one can think of something greater than any finite being. Therefore in a true and proper sense, the divine being has the quality of the infinite.

7. Again, it is possible to think of something as being equal to any finite being through duplication. But nothing can be equal to the divine being however much it is understood to be multiplied. Therefore, it is necessary that the divine being be infinite with absolute infinity.

8. Again, every finite good can be multiplied by the addition of some other finite good. But the highest good cannot be multiplied by the addition of anything, neither in reality nor in the order of knowledge.[7] Therefore, it is not a finite good. And it must be either finite or infinite; therefore, etc.

9. Again, God's essence is identical with His eternity. But His eternity is infinite since it has neither beginning nor end.[8] Therefore His essence is infinite. But, if His essence is infinite, so is His being. Therefore, in view of the first statement, the divine being is entirely infinite, even in itself.

10. Again, in God being and power are identical because of His supreme simplicity. But the divine power is infinite since He is omnipotent and has power over extremes that are infinitely distant, as is clear in production from nothing. Therefore, the divine being is absolutely infinite.

11. Again, the power and wisdom of God are infinite, since there would not be so many things possible and knowable unless a plurality of beings could exist. In a similar way, since God would never

---

[4] *De Fide Orthod.*
[5] C. 18.
[6] Boethius, in lib. *Quomodo Substantiae in eo, Quod Sint, Bonae Sint*, etc.
[7] Cf. Q. 3, a. 1, ad 4 above.
[8] Rich. of St. Victor, *De Trin.* II, c. 4.

actually be in so many creatures unless He were first able to be in a plurality, it is necessary that the divine being be infinite precisely as being.

12. Again, God is the most perfect cause of things in the order of efficiency, exemplarity, and finality. But because of His supreme perfection, He is efficient cause in such a way that He Himself is not an effect; and exemplary cause in such a way that He Himself is not a copy; therefore, He is final cause in such a way as to be infinite. Therefore, as the divine being is not an effect, so also it is infinite.

13. Again, the principle of all limitation is matter or something material. But since the divine being is pure act, it is devoid of all material qualities; therefore it lacks limitation and finiteness. Therefore, it is absolutely infinite.

OBJECTIONS

1. Infinite is predicated by reason of a deficiency in the finite, as injust is predicated because of a deficiency in the just. But a habit, if it is truly a habit, is always more noble than its privation. Therefore, the condition of the finite is more noble than the infinite. But that which is more noble ought always to be attributed to God. Therefore, etc.

2. Again, in created beings, infinity arises from matter, and finity arises from form. But, as Boethius says, "God is form without matter."[9] Therefore, it seems that He has no trace of infinity, but that He is most finite in Himself.

3. Again, nothing that essentially pertains to a particular being can be truly separated from that being. But God is the end which satisfies and completes the desire of our mind. Therefore, in no way can the divine being be infinite, neither by the denial of the end, since He is the terminal point, nor in as far as He is our completion.

4. Again, "finite and infinite are properties of quantity."[10] But true quantity is not predicated of God; therefore, neither is true infinity. But if any quantity is affirmed, it is that of virtue, which corresponds to power and not to essence. Therefore, nothing leads us to say that the essence is infinite.

5. Again, the infinite is identical with the immense. But the immense is predicated through the denial of measure and mode. Therefore the infinite lacks mode; it is without measure. But that which lacks mode also lacks form and beauty. Therefore, since this is not fitting for the divine being, it is clear, etc.

---

[9] *De Trin.*, c. 2.
[10] Averroes, *I Phys. Aristot.*, text. 15 (c. 2).

6. Again, whatever is infinite is said to be so through opposition to and distance from that which is the least. But the least being is the simplest being in any genus.[11] Therefore the infinite involves the negation of simplicity. But the divine being is most simple; therefore it is not infinite.

7. Again, no infinite being can be an end, because nothing is the cause of its opposite, and "nothing gives to another what it does not possess."[12] But God is the end of all beings as their most perfect end. Therefore, God is not infinite; neither in His being nor in any of His attributes.

8. Again, whatever is limited by the supreme truth which judges all things in their reality is not absolutely infinite. But God is limited with respect to Himself, otherwise He would exceed Himself. Therefore, the divine being is not infinite in reality; therefore, etc.

9. Again, if God could produce only one being and no more, the divine power would be said to be finite. Therefore, since power and being are one in essence, and since the divine being is only one, it follows that the divine being is finite.

10. Again, unity in itself is finite in the highest degree, since it is the principle of all measure according to number. Therefore, if the divine being is one, therefore it is measured, and therefore it is finite.

11. Again, every being which can be said to be this determined thing is more finite than a being which is not specific but common and undetermined. But common being, in as far as it is universal being, is finite. Therefore, since the divine being is proper and determined, it is itself finite to the greatest degree.

12. Again, every being that is spatially separated from another is finite in terms of its existence in space. Similarly, whatever exists separately in being is finite according to its natural existence. But the divine being is separated in being from all others in the highest degree, since this is proper to the first and most perfect mover.[13] Therefore, in terms of its natural existence, the divine being is finite.

13. Again, in matters pertaining to God it is true that, because of His supreme simplicity, those things which are predicated abstractly are also predicated concretely, and *vice versa*. If, then, a being is said to be finite by reason of an end, and if it is true and proper that God is the end, then it is also true that God is finite. Therefore, it is false that He is infinite.

---

[11] Aristotle, *V Metaph.*, text. 12 and X, text. 3 ff.
[12] Aristotle, *II Elench.*, c. 3 (C. 22).
[13] Aristotle, *XII Metaph.*, text. 41 (XI, c. 7), and *Lib. de Causis*, prop. 20.

14. Again, any being that is comprehensible is finite. But whatever is simple is comprehensible. Therefore whatever is simple is finite. But the divine being is simple; therefore it is finite. The minor premise is proved since whatever is known in its totality is comprehended. But when the simple is known, it is known in its totality, since it has no parts, and it is necessarily finite not only in itself but also in relation to us.

15. Again, either there is something finite in God, or there is not. If nothing in God is finite, then since a finite being knows nothing except in a finite way it follows that we know nothing of God; therefore we will never find beatitude. But this is a most unfortunate inconsistency. Therefore, something in God is finite. Therefore, either we must attribute parts to God, or we must say that there is nothing finite in God. Therefore, in no way should God be said to be infinite.

CONCLUSION

Because God is supremely simple, the divine being and power are infinite in as far as the infinite denies any limit with respect to quantity of power.

Response. In order to understand the above, we must note that in this question, which includes a multiplicity of terms, before anything is affirmed or denied, it is necessary to distinguish how a word is used.[14] It must be understood, therefore, that *infinite* is used in two ways: namely, privatively and negatively. When it is used privatively, it negates the act while an aptitude for the act remains. In this sense, infinite refers to that which has a natural aptitude to reach a limit yet does not do so in actuality, and thus it designates incompletion.

When it is used negatively, however, it simply negates all limit and finitude. But this can be understood in two ways in accordance with the two meanings of end (= *finis*); for end designates both end-as-limit and end-as-completion. Consequently, infinite is predicated in two ways, either by negating end-as-completion, and thus an evil can be described as infinite; or by negating end-as-limit, and this can have two meanings according to the two meanings of limit. Limit can be understood with reference to material quantity and with reference to spiritual quantity. The first refers to the quantity of weight, the second to the quantity of power. Therefore, when infinite is understood as the negation of a limit in the quantity of weight it always implies some degree of incompleteness — either

---

[14] Aristotle, *II Elench.*, c. 2 (c. 17).

in act or in potency — because it indicates a lack of simplicity. This type of quantity cannot exist together with simplicity in the same being and in the same respect. Such a being is never infinite in act but only in potency; in act it is always finite.[15] But when infinite is understood as the negation of a limit in quantity of power, it implies not imperfection but rather the highest perfection since it is not contrary to simplicity. Indeed, it cannot exist except in a being which is supremely simple. And it is in this way that the authority of Scripture and the confession of faith attribute infinity or immensity to the most simple God Himself.

Therefore, the divine being — in as far as it is infinite — is supremely simple and absolutely highest. Since it is supremely simple, it is supremely unified in itself and in its power. And since it is supremely unified in itself, it has nothing that contracts, limits, or determines it, or includes it in any category; and therefore it is beyond and above all other beings.[16] Furthermore, because it is supremely unified in its power, therefore, being and power are identical in it in every way; and therefore wherever God's being is, there also is His power. And where His being is, there is the center and origin and fount of His power. And where the fount and origin and center of His power is, He can always produce a great number of effects. Therefore, wherever He is capable of acting, He is always able to do even more; and hence His power as well as His being necessarily possesses infinity. This conclusion agrees with what is said in the *Liber de causis:* "Every power is more infinite to the degree that it is more unified";[17] etc. Therefore, this sort of infinity is not repugnant to simplicity; indeed it is in harmony with it in a marvelous and inseparable concord.

Furthermore, since it is absolutely highest, it must be entirely immense. For this reason, nothing can equal it; neither in intensity nor by multiplication, as Augustine writes in the eighth book *On the Trinity;*[18] and it is necessary that He possess in Himself infinite nobility and goodness, for it befalls the finite good, however excellent it may be, at times to be exceeded or to be equaled through the multiplication of other finite goods, as Augustine says.

Also, since it is absolutely highest, nothing can be or be thought of as greater or better. But thought can exceed any finite thing; for if a thing is thought to have a limit, it is understood that something can be superior to it at least in thought. Therefore, if the

---

[15] Aristotle, *III Phys.*, text. 56 ff. (c. 6).
[16] Gregory, *II Moral.*, c. 12, n. 20.
[17] Propos. 17.
[18] Ch. 2, n. 3.

divine being, since it is supremely simple, is at the same time absolutely highest, it follows that it is necessary to say that it is absolutely infinite, as the arguments show. It is not granted, as some affirm, that it is finite in essence and infinite in power; for in God these are fully identical, and infinity in one necessarily implies and includes infinity in the other, since one can extend itself to nothing without the other. And, furthermore, since in spiritual realities, the greater is identical with the better, and since essence and power are of equal goodness, they will necessarily be equal with the infinite.

This may aid us in understanding how simplicity is not repugnant to immensity. For if, as Augustine says, "there the greater and the better are identical,"[19] just as it is possible to understand that whatever is supremely simple is the best, so also it is possible to understand that it is the greatest; just as it is possible to understand that the supremely simple is supremely powerful, so it is possible to understand that what is most simple is most infinite. Just as it is possible to understand that it is present to all by its power, so also it is possible to understand that it is present by reason of its essence. And just as all beings are impotent, as it were, in comparison with the divine power, so also all beings are very small in comparison with the divine essence. Whence, compared to the divine being, the entire world is like a very small thing. This is what is said in *Wisdom* 11:[20]

> "In your sight the whole world is like a grain of dust that tips the scales, like a drop of morning dew falling on the ground;"

and in *Isaiah* 40:[21]

> "See, the nations are like a drop on the rim of the pail, they count as a grain of dust on the scales;"

and later:

> "All the nations are as nothing in his presence, for him they count as nothingness and emptiness."

Therefore, it must be conceded that not only is the divine power infinite, but so also is the divine being as the arguments given for this position show.

---

[19] *De Trin.* VI, c. 8, n. 9.
[20] Verse 23.
[21] Verse 15 and 17.

REPLIES TO THE OBJECTIONS

1. To the objection that the infinite is defined by a negation, it must be said, as has already been stated, that even though in the creature infinity implies a privation in the finite both in reality and in the verbal expression, yet in as far as it is posited in God, it implies a most true affirmation in reality and a greater completion than that which is found in the finite. It is not predicated because of the lack of some element which pertains to the completion of His being, as is already clear, but because of the lack of any limit and abridgement which would imply a deficiency with respect to the state of most perfect completion. Therefore, that argument does not hold.

2. To the objection that infinity arises from matter, it must be said that this is true according as infinity is based on the quantity of weight which, indeed, takes its origin from the material principle. But the case is quite different when infinity is based on the quantity of strength because active power takes its origin from the form. It is in this way and not in the former mode that infinity is affirmed of God. Therefore that objection does not hold.

3. To the objection that God is the end, therefore He is not infinite, it must be said that God is the end with respect to created beings but is Himself not limited, since He is end not as though He were the intrinsic end of a being, but in as far as He is that end to which is directed the entire desire of any being which is capable of being beatified. Therefore infinity is not opposed to end understood as the goal of creatures, but only to end in the sense of an intrinsic limit. Therefore, that objection does not hold.

4. To the objection that finite and infinite are properties of quantity, it must be said that while in God there is no quantity of weight, yet there is quantity of power. And this quantity of power refers not only to that power operating without, but the quantity of power also refers to the excellence of strength, both with respect to the absolute and with respect to the relative. Therefore, it can be attributed to any being of which grades of excellence can be affirmed in comparison with other beings. Such is the case, however, not only with respect to the divine power, but also with respect to the divine being. Therefore, the concept of infinity is fitting in relation to both.

5. To the objection that the infinite and the immense lack measure and mode, it must be said that in a limited nature, the lack of measure and mode is a defect; but in a nature that is superior to every confining limit, it involves no defect; because according to Augustine, "God is mode without mode;"[22] which means that His immensity

---

[22] *Lib. de Natura Boni*, c. 3.

is His proper mode, which is not constrained by the limits of any measure. And in this sense, the lack of mode does not include lack of form or beauty, but rather it includes the excellence of both.

6. To the objection that the infinite is defined by opposition to that which is least, it must be said that this is true where infinity is based on a quantity that is repugnant to simplicity, as is the quantity of weight; but it is not true where infinity is based on the quantity of power, because this is harmonious in the highest degree, as has been said.

7. To the objection that no infinite being can be an end, it must be said that when infinite is understood as the negation of completion, it is not an end as something which brings to completion; and when infinite is understood as the negation of a terminus, it is not an end in the sense of being an intrinsic terminus; but it can be an end in the sense of that which fulfills and beatifies, since the desire of a being which is capable of beatitude is never satisfied except in a being that possesses immense goodness, where it can desire nothing further.

8. To the objection that whatever is limited by the supreme truth cannot be infinite, it must be said that the statement "Something is limited by the supreme truth" can be understood in two ways. In the first way it means that the highest truth judges that this being is limited by the highest truth; and in this sense, the proposition is true. In the second way it means that it does not exceed the judgment of the highest truth, being immense in itself, to be capable of comprehending all immensity in itself. In this way, it does not follow that that which is finite in relation to it is finite in an absolute sense. Indeed, there is a sophism in the transition from the relative to the absolute.

9. To the objection that if God could produce only one being and no more, the divine power would be said to be finite, it must be said that there is no parallel; since His power is directed *ad extra* to created effects which are finite. Hence, if He could produce only one being, it would follow that His power extended only to the finite and therefore would itself be finite. But the case is different with the divine being in that it is absolute and, as it were, *ad intra*. And though it be only one, yet that one is immense, both because that being has no limitations within itself, and because it is the fount of all being, and because nothing can exist without the divine being. Therefore, since the divine essence exists in all beings, so does the divine power; even on the impossible supposition that a plurality of infinite beings existed, God would exist in all of them. From this it follows that just as the divine being is infinite, so is the divine power.

10. To the objection that unity is finite in the highest degree, etc., it must be said that this is true of that sort of unity which enters into the constitution of a being or a number as a part, a term, or a completion. And this is a unity through addition; when it is united with another being, it produces a greater number. Such a unity takes its origin from the limitation which form introduces to matter. Therefore, it is the principle of measure in discrete quantity.[23] But the divine unity is not of this sort, since it does not enter into the constitution of another part, for it is most perfect; nor does it take its origin from elsewhere, since it is first. Therefore it is neither limited nor measured, but rather, it is immense since it is neither limiting nor limited, neither by another nor by itself.

11. To the objection that every being which can be said to be *this being* is more finite, it must be said that *this being* is said properly because of a distinction from a mere quality;[24] and that being exists *here and now* because of determinations of space and time. In general, for the individuation of an existing being there must be a combination of accidental properties which are not found in this way in another being. But such is not the case with the divine being. Even though the divine being is said to be *this being* because it is being in the fullest sense and is distinguished from every other being, yet it is not contained in any category. Therefore it cannot be said to be individualized through any contraction or through any addition, whether of matter or of any essential or accidental property. Therefore, it is *this being* in such a way that it is not limited by space or time, but exists always and everywhere in a more excellent manner than any universal, which depends on a particular being and for that reason admits of some contraction. Therefore, while a universal being is finite, yet nothing stands in the way of the divine being infinite.

12. To the objection that every being that is spatially separated from another is finite, it must be said that there is no parallel, since a being which is spatially separated from another is separated in such a way that it is not in the other; and for this reason, it is contracted, limited and finite. But that which is separated from another through an essential difference can nevertheless be in the other; as God is essentially distinguished from the creature and yet is nonetheless in every creature by power, presence and essence. Therefore, from this mode of formal separation, finitude and limitation cannot be inferred as it can be from the mode of local separation.

13. To the objection that abstract qualities are predicated con-

---

[23] Aristotle, *De Praedicam.*, c. De quanto.
[24] Aristotle, *De Praedicam.*, c. De substantia.

cretely in God and *vice versa*, it must be said that the abstract term which corresponds to a concrete finite being and which is predicated in the concrete is *finitude* and not *end*. For, the concrete term derived from *end* is not *finite* but *that which limits*, just as the term *finite* is taken from *finitude*. Therefore the argument is not valid.

14. To the objection that any being that can be comprehended is finite, it must be said that the divine being cannot be comprehended by a finite power though it is simple, because its simplicity and immensity are rooted in the same property; namely, in that it possesses infinite power, as was shown earlier. And therefore, as it cannot be known in parts because it is supremely simple, neither can it be comprehended totally because of its supreme immensity.

15. To the final objection that either there is something finite in God or there is not, it must be said that whatever is proper to God, as something existing in Him, since it is identical with God and is not a part of God, necessarily partakes in the nature of the infinite; but because "everything that is received in another is received not after the manner of what is received but after the manner of the receiver,"[25] and since the power of the created intellect is finite, for this reason, it knows Him in a finite way, and therefore it is capable of finding its beatitude in Him. This knowledge is not false since it attributes the finitude to the knower himself and to his knowledge but not to the God who is known, since it knows the infinite itself even though it cannot comprehend its infinity, as was fully shown in the question concerning the knowledge of the soul of Christ.[26]

ARTICLE II

WHETHER THE TRINITY AND INFINITY CAN COEXIST

Next it is asked whether the trinity can exist together with infinity or immensity. That they are incompatible appears in the following way.

OBJECTIONS

1. Since the creature is finite, whatever is contained in the creature is finite. Therefore, since the divine being is immense, whatever exists in it is infinite in act. But in God there is number or

---

[25] *Lib. de Causis,* prop. 10, 20, 24.
[26] *Q. de Sci. Christi,* q. 6 (V, 32-37).

plurality of persons. Therefore, it is necessary that this be extended infinitely. Therefore, there is not a trinity of persons.

2. Again, since there is a two-fold infinity — namely, in power and in number — it is impossible that the divine being should lack infinity of power. If we affirm a true plurality in God for the same reason that we affirm true power in Him, it is necessary that this plurality be infinite.

3. Again, a power that is infinite in every way emanates infinitely when it emanates to the full extent of its infinite power. But the divine power is infinite in this way, and in the production of persons it emanates to the full extent of its infinity. Therefore the conclusion is the same as above.

4. Again, the person that produces the other two either can produce more persons or it cannot produce more. If it cannot, then it loses its power when it produces them; if it can, then either it is not of the supreme liberality, or it must necessarily produce without limit.

5. Again, if the light of the sun were immense, it would generate an infinity of rays from itself. Therefore, since the eternal light is immense, and the brightness proceeding from it is a true person,[1] it is necessary that an infinity of persons exist. Therefore the trinity and infinity do not exist together.

6. Again, either the production of the persons corresponds to the power, or not. If it does not, then it ought not be affirmed in that being which is supremely powerful. If it does, then a greater multiplicity corresponds to a greater power; and the greatest multiplicity corresponds to the greatest power; and an infinite multiplicity corresponds to an infinite power. Therefore, the trinity does not exist with infinity.

7. Again, if the divine power were engaged in its total actuality in the production of creatures, it would necessarily produce infinite creatures. Therefore, since it is thus engaged in the production of the persons, it is necessary — if the power is infinite — that it produce infinite persons.

8. Again, since the divine intellect is infinite, it must necessarily know infinite objects. Therefore, since the divine expression is infinite, it is necessary that it express infinite objects. But there are as many expressions as there are words; and there are as many persons as there are words. Therefore, there exists an infinity of persons.

9. Again, for an intellect to be perfect it is not sufficient that it know itself, but also that it knows that it knows. Therefore, if

---

[1] *Hebr.* 1, 3.

an intellect is to be of infinite perfection, it must necessarily reflect upon itself with infinite reflections. But in knowing itself, it generates a word; therefore, by the second reflection it generates a second word; and so on into infinity. Therefore, if infinity is to be attributed to God, trinity must be excluded.

10. Again, either God can know more than three persons, or He cannot. If He cannot, then His intellect is finite and limited. If He can know more, since nothing can be known which is not in some way present either in itself or in its principle, whether proximate or remote, therefore it is necessary either to conclude that the divine knowledge is limited, or to affirm more than three persons in the divine being, either actually or potentially.

ARGUMENTS IN AGREEMENT

1. Supreme immensity does not stand in the way of the highest perfection of a productive power, neither for one producing by way of nature nor for one producing by reason of will or liberality; therefore it does not stand in the way of the highest perfection in the productive act. But a perfect productive act necessarily requires a point of repose both on the part of the principle and on the part of the term; but there would be no such point if one were to proceed to infinity. Therefore the supreme infinity of the divine being does not imply an infinity of persons.

2. Again, infinity in God does not exclude the perfection of order — for it does not follow from the fact that God is infinite that therefore He is lacking in order — but perfect order necessarily posits a first, a middle, and a last.[2] Where these are present, there is found not number without limit, but only a trinity. Therefore, etc.

3. Again, infinity in God does not exclude the perfection of union, for this is necessary for supreme delight. But a perfect union cannot exist unless one person proceeds immediately from the other; otherwise there would not be the highest form of relationship. But this relationship does not extend beyond the number three.[3] Therefore, etc.

4. Again, immensity in God does not exclude perfect beatitude; but knowledge of the person pertains to the essence of beatitude. Therefore, if a creature cannot know an infinity of persons at one and the same time, it is impossible that any soul should ever find its beatitude in God. Therefore, if immensity exists together with perfect beatitude, it exists with a plurality of persons. But no plu-

---

[2] *Q. de Sci. Christi*, q. 1, ad 6 (V, 6).
[3] Rich. of St. Victor, *De Trin.* IV, c. 2 ff.

rality is so fitting to the soul capable of beatitude as a trinity; therefore, etc.

5. Again, the infinity of the divine being does not exclude unity of essence, for God is both one and immense. Therefore, if unity is more distant from immensity than plurality is, however small; and if immensity can exist together with unity, even more so can it exist together with the trinity.

6. Again, the immensity of the divine being does not exclude simplicity of nature. Therefore, if absolute simplicity is more repugnant to immensity than is plurality of whatever degree, then if infinity can exist together with simplicity, all the more so can it exist together with the trinity.

7. Again, the infinity of the divine being does not exclude personal property, therefore it does not exclude true distinction of the persons; therefore it does not include confusion. But where number is infinite, there is confusion; and where there is confusion, there is lack of distinction. But if we are not to affirm this in the divine being, then the plurality of persons is finite in number. Therefore, infinity is not repugnant to the trinity in God.

8. Again, the infinity of the divine being does not exclude causality in accordance with the three types of causes: namely, efficient, formal, and final; nor does the infinity in God affirm other modes of causality. Therefore, if it is possible for the three types of causes to coexist, it is likewise possible for a trinity of persons to coexist, especially since there is a mutual correspondence between these in the appropriation of power, wisdom, and goodness, which correspond to the three persons and to the three types of causality.

9. Again, the infinity of the divine being does not exclude the conformity between the Creator and the creature according to a double representation; namely, that of vestige and that of image. Therefore, if in the image there is a representation of the distinction and origin of the divine persons corresponding to the persons; if there were an infinite number of persons in the trinity, there ought to be an infinite number in the image. But if this is impossible, it follows that the trinity of persons is not repugnant to the divine immensity.

10. Again, the immensity of the divine being does not exclude the indwelling of God in the mind through the gift of the Holy Spirit. But if there were an infinite number of persons producing and produced, since each of the productive persons sends and gives the person produced, then in the sanctification of each soul it would necessarily happen that an infinity of persons would stand between the sanctified soul and the person who first sends or sanctifies. Therefore, if it is impossible to traverse the infinite, it would be impossible

for the soul to return to the first principle through sanctification if there were an infinite number of persons. But since the immensity of God exists together with the indwelling by grace, in which the Son, who is the image of the Father, leads us back to the Father through the gift and bond of the Holy Spirit, the immensity of the divine being is compatible with the trinity of persons.

CONCLUSION

In God the supreme infinity exists together with the trinity of persons.

Response. Without doubt, supreme infinity exists together with a plurality of persons in God. This is clear from the following.

Infinity is affirmed in God not because of defect but because of excess. And, I say, it is an excess not of superfluity but of perfection and nobility.[4] Because infinity in God does not include superfluity or diminution but highest perfection, therefore in the emanation of the divine persons we must affirm immensity in the one producing, as well as in the one produced and in the mode of production; but not an infinity in number. For if there were a numerical infinity of persons in God, this infinity would necessarily result either in a defect or in a superfluity. Since there are two perfect modes of emanating, one by nature and one by liberality, either the two persons emanating in these modes do not perfectly possess the full immensity of the producing power and thus they would be imperfect; or they do possess it, and others would be superfluous. But if it is impossible that there be anything superfluous or defective in the divine being because of its immensity, it is necessary to affirm that God is triune and immense.

Furthermore, since the infinity of the divine being includes immensity in the one producing, as well as in the one produced and in the mode of production, and since the divine being in its immensity cannot be duplicated but is only one, it follows necessarily that in God there is only one paternity, only one filiation, and only one procession; and thus there is only one Father only one Son, and only one Holy Spirit. And therefore it is necessary to say that God is immense and a trinity. Just as if there were several gods, none would possess in himself the immensity of the whole divinity, but only part of omnipotence and perfection, so if there were several Fathers, none would possess the immensity of paternity; if there were several Sons, none would possess the immensity of filiation, but only a part thereof. For if any one of them were to possess the

---

[4] Cf. preceding question.

entire fullness and immensity of paternity, there could be only one paternity among them, just as there can be only one deity in several persons. It remains, therefore, that if there is true infinity and true plurality in the divine being, the plurality cannot be extended beyond the trinity to an infinity, in accordance with the statement of pious faith.

Finally, because infinity includes every form of completion, it does not exclude the perfection of power, order, union, beatitude, representation, and inhabitation. And since all of these necessarily lead to the understanding of the trinity in three persons, as is clear from the previous objections, it is evident that the supreme immensity is in no way repugnant to but rather in harmony with the eternal trinity. Therefore the arguments for this position are to be conceded.

REPLIES TO THE OBJECTIONS

1. To the contrary objection that just as whatever is contained in the finite creature is finite, so it is necessary in the case of God that whatever exists in Him is infinite, it must be said that — as has already been indicated — an infinity of power and dignity befits the divine being, but not an infinity of weight or number. And such an infinity is found both in the essence and in the persons, both in the ones producing and in the ones produced, both in the persons as such and in their emanations. And this is found totally and integrally in three persons. Therefore it is not necessary to extend the persons to numerical infinity because of the infinity of the divine being.

2. To the objection that God cannot lack infinity of power, etc., it must be said that there is no parallel between these two modes of infinity, for while the greatness of power includes a proximity to simplicity rather than distance from it, a numerical multitude includes distance from unity and simplicity. And God, the divine being, is immense in such a way that at the same time He is supremely simple and one; from this it follows that an infinity of power is proper to the divine being while an infinite number of persons is not.

3. To the objection that a completely infinite power emanates infinitely when it emanates to the full extent of its power, it must be said that since in God perfection and infinity are inseparable, the objection is true concerning each mode of emanation and diffusion which corresponds to supreme perfection. This is the case with the two perfect modes of production; namely, that of nature and that

of liberality; and each of these is necessarily unique in itself, and is neither doubled nor tripled; nor do they extend to infinity because this would imply superfluity and defect, as was shown above.

4. To the objection that the person who produces the other two either can produce more or He cannot, it must be said that to be unable to produce more than two persons does not imply a lack of power but rather the fullness of power; for in those two productions the productive power manifests itself most perfectly and infinitely, both as to the immensity of the persons produced and as to the actuality of the productions; for the generative and spirative power in the Father has its actuality in generating and spirating in the same way in which it exists eternally and in no other way. Thus, as splendor emanates continually from the sun, so the Son, who is the "splendor of the Father" emanates continually from the Father in an even more excellent way.

5 & 6. To the objection that if the light of the sun were immense, it would generate an infinite number of rays from itself, it must be said that there is no parallel. For the light emanating from the sun is not absolutely perfect nor is it equal to its origin. Therefore, from one production alone it does not contain within itself the full power and clarity of the light from which it radiates. Indeed, it receives and shares in the fullness of the fontal light to a greater or lesser degree according as it is nearer to or more distant from its source. But it is very different in the case of the Son, who is the Word of the Father and the most perfect splendor, in all things equal to the Father, receiving from the Father everything that the Father Himself has; and therefore as the infinity of the eternal light does not exclude equality with the eternal ray emanating from it, neither does it include an infinite multiplication of rays since one ray alone contains within itself that total immensity.

7. To the objection that if the divine power were engaged in its total actuality in the production of creatures, then it would produce infinite creatures, etc., it must be said that there is no parallel for two reasons; first, because the creature is finite and therefore does not correspond fully to the productive power, and second, because the creature is distinguished essentially from the being that produces it as well as from other creatures because of the distinction in their intrinsic principles and in the accompanying accidents. But such is not the case in God, both because the person produced is as infinite as the person that produces it, and because the distinction is not one of essence but one of origin.[5] Therefore, since there are only two distinct and distinctive origins, only two emanating persons

---

[5] Rich. of St. Victor, *De Trin.* IV, c. 13 ff.

can exist and can be conceived of, in whom the immensity of the fontal productive power shines forth most perfectly.

8. To the objection that since the divine intellect is infinite it knows infinite objects, it must be said that even though God knows infinite objects, He comprehends all things in Himself alone because in knowing Himself, He knows all things; so also, though He expresses many things, yet He expresses all things in one Word. For in the very same Word in which the Father expresses Himself, He expresses all other things.[6] For in knowing Himself in one, most perfect act of knowledge in which there is perfect correspondence between the act of understanding and the subject of the act, and *vice versa*, the Father generates a Word which is the similitude of the Father and equal to Him in all things. Whence, as the Father, in knowing Himself, knows whatever can be known, so in speaking the Word, He expresses everything that He can express and everything that can be expressed in the deity. Whence, neither He nor any other person in the trinity can speak another word, since whatever can be said is said in Him.

But if you object that just as God has infinite ideas with respect to intelligible beings, so also He ought to have an infinity of words; it must be said that there is no parallel, because the reason and the idea include a relation to and a similitude of intelligible beings to be created and produced, or capable of being produced, and such possible beings can be multiplied in innumerable and diverse ways. On the other hand, the Word includes a relation to the speaker and to the first intellect and highest principle of which the Word is the hypostatic similitude. Therefore, in no way can multiplicity be attributed to it, neither in reality nor in our understanding, just as multiplicity can not be attributed to the first principle that knows itself first of all and principally through itself.[7]

9. To the objection that an intellect of infinite fullness must reflect upon itself with infinite reflections, etc., it must be said that in the case of the divine intellect *to know* and *to know that one knows* are identical even if the act of knowledge is repeated a thousand times or an infinite number of times, since in God, the subject, the object, and the act of knowing are one and the same. Therefore, the very first act in which God the Father knows Himself is the most actual and most perfect act, just as is the Word that corresponds to it. Therefore, it is not necessary to introduce a plurality of words in God. But the case is different with the created intellect whose act and operation is distinct from the subject and the object of know-

---

[6] Augustine, *Confessions* XI, c. 7, n. 9.
[7] *Q. de Sci. Christi*, q. 3, ad 19 (V, 16).

ledge; for which reason it can be multiplied and repeated and numbered many times as often as the mind reflects upon itself as subject, or upon the act of knowing or upon other objects distinct from itself.

10. To the final objection that either God can know more than three persons or He cannot, it must be said that to be unable to know more persons can be understood in two ways; either because of a limitation of the mind in the act of knowing, or because of the correctness of judgment and the impossibility of departing from the way of truth. In the first way, it is not fitting for the divine intellect since it is immense, but in the second way, it is fitting. Therefore, it follows that He cannot know more persons, because such knowledge — even though it would appear to be perfect — in reality would be a departure from truth and a falling into error. Whence, as the immensity of truth is in no way mixed with falsehood, so the immensity of intellectual light renders the divine intellect totally free of any error. For this reason, the divine intellect does not know any being greater than itself, nor another God, nor a plurality of persons beyond the number three, not because it is limited, but because it is most perfectly infinite.

And from these arguments the solution to the whole question is clear.

QUESTION V

WHETHER THE TRINITY OF PERSONS CAN EXIST TOGETHER WITH HIGHEST ETERNITY

Next it is asked whether the trinity of persons can exist together with the highest eternity. Two questions are raised about this. The first is whether the divine being is eternal. The second is whether trinity and eternity can exist together.

ARTICLE I

WHETHER THE DIVINE BEING IS ETERNAL

Concerning the first question, we can proceed as follows. That the divine being is eternal.

ARGUMENTS IN AGREEMENT

1. The authority of Scripture shows this in *Exodus* 15: "The Lord will reign forever and ever,"[1] and in *Romans* 1: "His everlasting power and divinity."[2]
2. Truth of faith shows this also: "The Father is eternal; the Son is eternal; the Holy Spirit is eternal" it says in the Athanasian Creed.
3. Again, the same conclusion may be derived from arguments of necessity. For Richard (of St. Victor) argues as follows: Whatever exists of itself is eternal.[3] But the divine being exists of itself since it is first; therefore, etc. The major is clear; for if it were not eternal, then at some time it would not have existed, and it would not have given being to itself nor to others; and hence it would never have been. The minor is self-evident.

---

[1] Verse 18.
[2] Verse 20.
[3] *De Trin.* I, c. 6, 8 and 11.

4. Again, whatever is its own being is eternal, for being cannot not be; therefore it cannot begin or cease to be; therefore it has neither a beginning nor an end. Therefore if God, being supremely simple, is His own being, He is being in an absolute sense.[4] Therefore He is fully eternal.

5. Again, that which is truth itself is eternal. But the divine being is truth itself, therefore, etc. The minor is clear. Augustine proves the major in the *Soliloquies:* Truth can neither be thought nor said not to exist.[5] Indeed, it follows that if there is no truth then some truth exists, because if no truth exists then it is true that no truth exists, or there is no truth. Therefore, being cannot be dissociated from truth in any way; therefore it always was, is, and will be.

6. Again, that being which is supremely infinite is eternal, for if it were to have a beginning, its duration would be finite. But the divine being is infinite.[6] Therefore, it is necessarily eternal; otherwise, if it were not eternal, neither would it be immense.

7. Again, that being in which there is supreme immortality is eternal; "that which comes into being through change tends toward change."[7] But supreme immortality resides in the divine being which is, of its very essence, life itself, or the very act of living. Therefore, the divine being necessarily possesses eternity.

8. Again, every being in which there resides supreme happiness is eternal. But since the divine being is most perfect, it is of this sort; therefore, etc. The major is proved since that happiness which has neither beginning nor end is greater than that which begins at a particular moment of time. Therefore, if the divine being is supremely happy, it necessarily follows that it is eternal.

And again, all happiness includes the lack of an end.[8] Therefore, the most perfect happiness includes the lack of a beginning.

9. Again, every being in which supreme simplicity exists is eternal. And the divine being is of this sort; therefore, etc. The minor is evident. The major is proved because in any being which possesses supreme simplicity, there is no difference between beginning, middle, and end; and no such being has a past and future,

---

[4] Boethius, *Quomodo Substantiae in eo, Quod Sint, Bonae Sint.*
[5] I, c. 15, n. 27 ff., & II, c. 2, n. 2; c. 15, n. 28; and Rich. of St. Victor, *De Trin.* II, c. 2.
[6] Cf. Q. 4, a. 1 above.
[7] Damasc., *De Fide Orthod.* I, c. 3 & II, c. 7; Aristotle, *XII Metaph.* text. 39 (XI, c. 7).
[8] Augustine, *De Beata Vita*, c. 2, n. 11; *De Civ. Dei*, XI, c. 11; XIV, c. 25.

but dwells only as present. But any being of this sort is eternal.[9] Therefore, etc.

10. Again, being is divided into eternal, aeviternal, and temporal; and the aeviternal is more perfect than the temporal, and the eternal is more perfect than both of the others. But that which is more perfect is always to be attributed to the most perfect being. Therefore the supreme eternity is to be attributed to God.

11. Again, every being in flux must be reduced to something permanent. Therefore fluid duration most be reduced to permanent duration, therefore the present that passes into the past is reduced to a present that abides always. But such a present is not found in a defective being. Therefore it is necessary that it be found in the creative essence. It is, therefore, necessary that the divine being be eternal.[10]

12. Again, what is true of the future does not begin to be true at that future time, but is true always; what is true of the past remains true forever. But the future and the past are necessarily reduced to the present. Therefore it is necessary to affirm a truth which is always present without end and without beginning. But this is the eternal truth, and it cannot be affirmed of any other being than the first principle. Therefore, it is necessary that the divine being be eternal.[11]

OBJECTIONS

1. Eternity is a measure; but nothing that is immense has measure; for any being that has measure is not immense. Therefore, etc.

2. Again, measure is proportionate to that which is measured; but nothing can be proportionate to the divine being. Therefore, in God there is no eternal duration.

3. Again, eternity is the lack of beginning and end.[12] But nothing lacks that which it is. Therefore, if God is the beginning and end of all things, then the divine being does not lack these attributes. Therefore, it cannot be eternal.

4. Again, lack of completion implies defect; principle and end indicate completion. Therefore, God cannot be deprived of these. But eternity implies the privation of these qualities. Therefore, it should not be attributed to the divine being.

---

[9] Augustine, *Lib. 83 Qq.*, q. 19.
[10] *Lib. de Causis*, prop. ult.
[11] Anselm, *Monolog.*, c. 18.
[12] Rich. of St. Victor, *De Trin.* II, n. 4.

5. Again, eternity is the lack of past and future. But God truly was and is and will be. Therefore, the divine being does not possess eternity.

6. Again, if A is past time and B is future, it is true to say that God existed in A and will exist in B; and the contrary is false. Therefore, A is truly past for God and B is truly future. Therefore, the divine being has a past and a future; therefore it is not eternal.

7. Again, that which is eternal is interminable, since according to Boethius, "eternity is the possession of interminable of life."[13] That which is interminable is circular; but that which is circular is posterior to that which is straight. But only that which is absolutely first should be attributed to the divine being; therefore eternal duration should not be attributed to Him.

8. Again, in accordance with our manner of knowing as well as with the natural order, the circumference is posterior to the center. But, what the circumference is to the center, eternity is to time. Therefore, time should be attributed to God rather than eternity. Therefore, if it is unfitting to attribute temporality to God, the same is true of eternity.

9. Again, where eternity is, there also is totality, which is clear from the argument of Boethius: "Eternity is the simultaneous and total possession of interminable life."[14] But where there is totality, there is the possibility of being divided and of being reduced to parts. But this cannot be attributed to God since He is supremely simple. Therefore, etc.

10. Again, continuous extension is never found without the possibility of division, therefore continuous duration is never found without true totality, and hence divisibility. Therefore, a being that is incapable of having parts does not possess real duration and is not said to be "simultaneously total;" therefore, etc.

11. Again, where there is eternity, there — by definition — is simultaneity.[15] But where there is simultaneity, there is distinction, because simultaneity involves relation and relation involves distinction. But the divine being is totally without distinction. Therefore it is not eternal.

12. Again, if the fullness of simultaneity resides in the divine being, then present, past, and future are simultaneous. But in the case of those beings which exist simultaneously, that which ac-

---

[13] *Lib. V de Consol.*, prosa 6; Aristotle, *VIII Phys.*, text. 64 ff. (c. 8) *I De Caelo et Mundo*, text. 5 ff. (c. 2).
[14] *Lib. V de Consol.*, prosa 6.
[15] From the definition of Boethius cited in n. 9 above.

companies one accompanies the others. Therefore, if aeviternity always accompanies the divine future, it likewise accompanies the divine past. Therefore, just as it lacks an end, so it lacks a beginning. But this is impossible. Therefore, it is impossible to attribute perfect, eternal duration to God. Therefore, eternity should not be attributed to the divine being.

13. Again, either eternity adds something beyond the *now* of eternity, or it does not. If it adds nothing, then that which coexists with the *now* of eternity is eternal. But the *now* of time coexists with the *now* of eternity. Therefore, it coexists with the whole of eternity, and therefore it is eternal. If it adds something, then eternity is composed, and therefore it is not fitting for God.

14. Again, even though the point is the beginning, middle, and end of extension, it is impossible to conceive of extension within a point. Likewise, it is impossible to conceive of duration within the *now*.[16] Therefore, if eternity involves duration, it involves something beyond the *now* of eternity. Therefore, it is repugnant to the highest simplicity. Therefore, it is impossible that it exist in the most simple being of God.

15. Again, the divine being, power, knowledge, and will or foreknowledge are measured by the same measure. But the divine foreknowledge is not measured by eternity since God ceases to foresee some beings. Therefore, neither is the divine being measurable by eternity.

16. Again, the divine being and operation are measured by the same measure, because in God, substance, power, and operation are one and the same. But if the divine being is measured by eternity, so also is the divine act of creation. Therefore, God creates eternally and from eternity; for this reason an eternal creature is produced. But this is false; therefore that from which it follows is false.

17. Again, all truth is measured by time, by aeviternity, or by eternity. But the fact that the world was to be created was true in God before the creation of the world. Therefore, it was measured either by eternity or by time. But it was not measured by time, for time did not exist then. Therefore, it was measured by eternity. But this truth ceased to be true. Therefore, it is evident that eternity has an end. But the divine being has no end. Therefore, it is not possible to attribute eternity to the divine being.

---

[16] Aristotle, *IV Phys.*, text. 103 ff. (C. 11), and VI, text. 24 ff. (c. 3).

CONCLUSION

The divine being is eternal, because it is both simple and infinite.

Response. The divine being is eternal in that it is both simple and infinite. Because it is infinite, it lacks beginning and end; for, if it had either of these, in that respect it would have termination and limitation; and thus it would not have supreme immensity. Because it is simple, it lacks both prior and posterior which necessarily include diversity and some composition. Therefore, supreme simplicity involves total simultaneity; supreme immensity involves total interminability; and when both of these attributes are joined together, they constitute eternity. For eternity is nothing other than the "simultaneous and total possession of interminable life." And since these two qualities — namely, immensity and simplicity — are found together in no other being but God, therefore the quality of eternity cannot be communicated to any being other than God.

Furthermore, since these two qualities are beyond our ability to imagine or to appreciate, therefore eternal duration cannot be understood correctly by anyone who does not first lay aside his imagination.

These two attributes must be joined together if we are to understand the most infinite and simple duration of the divine being, and thus also its true permanence which lacks beginning, and interpolation or expansion, and division or termination; indeed, it has no succession whatsoever. And this sort of argument arrives at a necessary conclusion because of the union of these two attributes, however much it may seem to our imagination that they are contrary to one another.

Something similar to this can be found in God. Just as God, being both simple and immense, is totally present in distant places and even though these places are distinct from one another, still He who is present in them does not for that reason lack supreme unity and simplicity; so also because of its immensity, the divine being, which is eternal is present to different moments of time; even though these moments are distant from each other and are spread apart, yet, because of His supreme simplicity, He is not distant from Himself. And as the divine incircumscribability is present to all places and yet is not extended in them, even though they themselves are truly extended, so the divine eternity is present to all moments of time, yet it does not undergo succession in them even though they truly have succession.

Now, in creatures — even though a complete likeness cannot be found because of their deficiency — yet a certain limited likeness can be found which can lead us to understand the eternity of the divine being if we abstract from the defect by means of our intellect. In a certain way, this likeness can be noticed both in the image and in the vestige. For in the soul — which is the image of God — there exists the recall of past things, the knowledge of present things, and the foreknowledge of future things.[17] These exist in the soul simultaneously in such a way that those things which occur in succession in distinct moments of time are united and bound together in the soul, which is a spiritual substance; yet because the soul is limited and receives from some being outside itself, it lacks that perfect simultaneity. But God receives nothing and is in no way limited; and therefore it is necessary to understand all things as present to Him without beginning or end. And this is to understand eternity.

In time, which is the vestige of eternity, present, past, and future truly exist in such a way that what was future later becomes present and then past, because it is rooted in mutable and fluid being, or in movement itself. Therefore, if the present is understood to be rooted in immutable and stable being which has neither beginning nor end, that would be understood to be eternal.

So, if one proceeds by correct reflection from creatures to the creator by removing all imperfection and retaining every perfection, it is possible to achieve a certain understanding of the eternity of the divine being. However, as long as we are in the flesh, this will not be a perfect understanding; since, while we live here "we have no knowledge without succession and time";[18] and therefore it is very different from eternity unless by chance it is elevated to a higher level by a special gift; as Augustine says, "when we comprehend something eternal in our mind, we are not in this world."[19] Therefore, it is clear that the divine being is indeed eternal; and it is clear what the necessary reason for this is, and how our thought can arrive at this. The arguments that prove that the divine being is eternal must be conceded.

REPLIES TO THE OBJECTIONS

1.2. To the opposing objection that eternity is a measure, it must be said that, even though in terms of our manner of knowing, eternity is predicated as a measure, yet in reality and truth, it indicates nothing other than the being of the divine substance; and as that being is immense, so also is eternity immense. Therefore, it is

---

[17] These are integral parts of prudence according to Cicero, *II Rhet.*, c. 54.
[18] Aristotle, *De Memoria et Reminisc.*, c. 1.
[19] *De Trin.* IV, c. 20, n. 28.

said to be equal to itself not because of a common term — since that which is immense has no term — but because of the lack of mutual excess. And thus our response to the first and second objection concerning the nature of measure becomes clear, since those arguments proceed from that sort of measure which is distinct from the thing measured, which both terminates and is terminated, and hence can have meaning only in reference to a finite being. All these things are excluded from the divine eternity. Yet it is not false to speak of measure in terms of our mode of knowing in as far as our knowledge represents the divine being in the mode of duration; and that duration — even though infinitely exceeding every creature — neither exceeds nor is exceeded with respect to the divine being itself.

3. To the objection that eternity includes the lack of beginning and end, it must be said that in as far as beginning and end are taken in the definition of eternity, they are identical with the initial and final term in the duration of a being. But such terms do not exist except in a being that begins and ceases to exist. Therefore, when I say that God is beginning and end, the notions of beginning and end are used equivocally. Hence, there are two weaknesses in the argument; first, because God is beginning and end with respect to things outside Himself, and second, because He is beginning and end in the order of causality. Therefore, when it is said that eternity is the lack of beginning and end, beginning and end are understood as internal to God and in accordance with the reason of duration.

4. To the objection that the lack of beginning and end implies a defect because each of these has the nature of a completing part, etc., it must be said that beginning and end, in as far as they indicate a terminus, involve limitation and defect, even though they seem to signify completion. Therefore, on the contrary, even though their absence seems to be a privation for our manner of knowing, yet it is a positive reality on the part of the thing; for a duration which lacks beginning and end is true in such a way that it contains nothing of non-being within itself.

5. To the objection that eternity is the lack of past and future, it must be said that past and future are attributed to something in two ways; either as a disposition in the thing known or in the knower himself. Likewise, when it is said that something has happened in the past or that it will happen in the future, this can be understood in two ways; either in the mode of when-ness and inherence, or in the mode of simultaneity and coexistence. Therefore, when it is said that eternity is the lack of past and future, it must be said that this is true in as far as past and future include the disposition of a being which is said to have existed in the past in such a way that

when the being is measured, there remains in it an affection or a certain disposition which is called *when*, according to what is said elsewhere, namely, that "when is contained in every being that begins to exist."[20] Moreover, when it is said of God that He was and will be, the past is not a disposition in the thing known, but in the knower. And this is not predicated by reason of commensuration, when-ness, and inherence, but by reason of duration, a certain simultaneity, and coexistence. Hence, all those statements are improper in a certain sense. We speak of eternity hesitantly in terms of various moments of time because our mind does not rise up to an understanding of eternal things unless it is led through time as long as we are wayfarers.

6. To the objection that it is not said of God that He did exist in the future, nor that He will exist in the past, it must be said that this is not because there is any succession or variation in the divine being, but because of the connotation of coexistence in the past or future; in which there is variation to the extent that the past cannot be said to be future and future cannot be said to be past. Hence, while the future is not predicated of the past nor the past of the future, this is not because past and future refer to another being or another mode of being in God, but only in the created being.

7.8. To the objection that eternity is identical with interminability, it must be said that this does not do justice to the full reality of eternity, since eternity involves not only interminability, but also simultaneity. And just as in the mode of interminability, it includes a certain intelligible circumference lacking beginning and end, so in the mode of simultaneity, it includes the simplicity and indivision of the center-point.[21] Both of these are affirmed together with respect to the divine being because it is simultaneously simple and infinite. Therefore, eternity is understood as a circle, and it includes no posteriority, neither with respect to the circumference nor with respect to the center. Thus we can clarify our response to the objection from time which assumes the function of a center-point with respect to interminable eternity. This argument, like the previous one, proceeds from an insufficient base, since it considers eternity only in as far as it is the measure of immense being, while it ought to be considered simultaneously that it is the measure of the simple and indivisible, and these are properties which can in no way be found in the measure of time.

9. To the objection that where eternity is found, there also is totality, it must be said that the totality which is affirmed in eternity

---

[20] Gilbert Porret. in lib. *Sex Principiorum*, c. De quando.
[21] Alan of Lille, *Theolog. Regul.*, regula 7.

does not refer to the quantity of weight, but to the quantity of power in which the reality of greatness and immensity stands together with perfect simplicity. Therefore, it does not follow that where there is totality, there is divisibility. This is not true except of that sort of whole which is truly quantitative and in which necessarily there are distinct parts since such a totality involves true quantity. Or, it can be said that the phrase *total and simultaneous* is used with respect to perfection rather than with respect to the distribution of some integral whole into parts.[22]

10. To the objection that continuous extension is never found without the possibility of division, it must be said that there is no parallel because extension always involves parts outside of parts, and hence corporality, quantity, and the possibility of division,[23] while duration refers to undivided being which is found not only in composite beings but in simple beings as well.

11. To the objection that eternity involves simultaneity, it must be said that simultaneity is included in eternity not because of the condition of con-duration and co-existence of diverse beings capable of duration, but rather because of the lack of succession in the continuity of a being which endures. Hence, eternity is defined as *total and simultaneous* because in it there are no elements which succeed one another, and not because there are various and diverse realities existing simultaneously in it. Hence, simultaneity refers to nothing other than the supreme, simple, and undivided presence, and this involves no intrinsic diversity.[24]

12. To the objection that if in God past, present and future are identical, then the creature which, in its own way is measured by the divine future ought also to be measured by the divine past, it must be said that there is no parallel; and one cannot be inferred from the other. The reason for this is that, while in God to have no beginning and to have no end are identical, there is a great difference between these in the creature. For since the creature is produced from nothing, it is essential to it that it have a principle and a beginning. But it is not repugnant to the created nature that it have no end or termination; nor is the opposite of this essential to the creature, because the tendency of the creature is to the contrary. But it does not follow from this that if the creature can be compared to God with respect to the future, it can also be compared to Him with respect to the past. Just as it does not follow that since justice

---

[22] Aristotle, *V Metaph.*, text. 30 ff. (IV, c. 25 ff.). Cf. above, Q. 4, a. 1, resp. and ad 2.
[23] Aristotle, *De Praedicam.*, c. De quanto.
[24] Boethius, *V De Consol.*, prosa 6.

and immensity in God are identical; and since the creature can be assimilated to God's justice, it can also be assimilated to His immensity; so also the kind of argumentation given above makes neither proper inferences nor correct conclusions.

13. To the objection that eternity either does or does not add something beyond the *now* of eternity, it must be said that as in eternity there are both simultaneity and interminability, or simplicity and immensity so the *now* of eternity signifies that duration in terms of simple simultaneity, while eternity does so in terms of interminable immensity. Just as interminable immensity adds nothing in reality beyond the indivisibility of the divine simplicity and simultaneity, but only in terms of our knowledge, so also eternity adds nothing beyond the *now* of eternity. Just as it does not follow that the creature comprehends the most simple God, and therefore that it comprehends God as immense, so also it does not follow that if something coexists with the *now* of eternity, then there is something that coexists with interminable eternity. Those qualities which are identical in God correspond to distinct and varied qualities in the creature, as is clear in the case of goodness and wisdom; and of justice and mercy, according to the treatment given above.[25]

14. To the objection that even though the point is the beginning, the middle, and the end of extension, it is impossible to conceive of extension within the point itself, it must be said that there is no parallel, for while the point is the beginning of extension, yet it does not possess the entire essence of extension nor is it a constitutive part thereof. But the *now* is the entire essence of duration, not only in things eternal and aeviternal, but also in temporal duration as well. The reason for this is: extension possesses all its parts simultaneously; and "a point is a substance in place,"[26] hence, it necessarily involves position in matter. And therefore, since it is indivisible, it cannot be the essence of a divisible whole nor a constitutive part thereof, since any part of a continuum is continuous. But it is different in the case of duration, for here there never is anything but that which is present and indivisible, even in the case of successive duration. Therefore, it is not surprising that the essence of duration can be included in the *now* especially in the case of a being in which there is no difference between being and essence, as is the case in eternity.

15.16. To the objection that the divine being and power, knowledge and foreknowledge are measured by the same measure it

---

[25] Q. 3, a. 1, resp. and 6 ff.
[26] Aristotle, *I Poster.*, c. 23 (c. 27); *I De Anima*, text. 68 (c. 4), and *V Metaph.*, text. 12 (IV, c. 6).

must be said that this is true with reference to the principle significate but not with reference to the connoted significate. From this the response to the following objection from creation is clear. For the intrinsic act is eternal as is the substance; but the effect is temporal since it is a creature.

17. To the objection that before the creation of the world it was true that the world would be created in the future, it must be said that this proposition, though it is but one, nonetheless implies a double truth. For if, before the world came to be, it is said that the world is to be created in the future, this is not true except in the sense that, in some way, the world has some reality in its cause; and in this sense, the proposition is true with eternal truth. Further, it is not sufficient that the world have being only in its cause; indeed, for the proposition to be true, it is necessary that at some time the world have existence outside of its cause. And since, before the world came to be, its being was not yet created but was to be created, therefore it is not true with created truth, but with the truth of that which is yet to be created. And since when a thing begins to exist as a created thing, it ceases to be something to be created in the future, therefore that proposition which signifies a thought that is true from eternity ceases to be true not because of a termination in eternity, but because of a beginning in time, since something temporal should be understood together with the eternal. And with this the response to the present question is clear.

ARTICLE II

WHETHER THE TRINITY CAN EXIST TOGETHER WITH ETERNITY

Next it is asked whether the trinity can exist together with eternity. It seems that they are incompatible.

OBJECTIONS

1. Wherever eternity exists, there is total simultaneity;[1] but where there is total simultaneity, there is no order; where there is no order, there is no emanation; where there is no emanation, there can be no plurality of persons. Therefore, if there is supreme and true eternity in the divine being, it is impossible that there be a true trinity or plurality of persons.

---

[1] From the definition of Boethius.

2. Again, "a cause is anything from whose being another follows";[2] namely, the effect. But it is certain that the effect does not follow from the cause because of diversity, since they can exist simultaneously; therefore the effect follows the cause because of production. Therefore, where there is production, there is something antecedent and something consequent. But where these exist, there is not true eternity. Therefore, etc.

3. Again, if there are three persons in the trinity, either they are equally first, or they are not equally first. If they are equally first, then one cannot proceed from the other, and hence they cannot coexist in the same nature. But if they are not equally first, then they are not simply and equally coeternal. Therefore, the same conclusion follows as above.

4. Again, every corruption necessarily supposes a final term;[3] therefore, every production or emanation posits an initial term. But the trinity cannot exist without emanation or production, and therefore it cannot exist without some sort of beginning. But this is incompatible with eternity. Therefore, etc.

5. Again, eternity is interminable duration.[4] Therefore, if there is an eternal trinity in God, there must be an interminable production or emanation of persons. But production or emanation without a term is never perfect because it never terminates in a being that is produced. Therefore, either the trinity is not perfect or it is not eternal.

6. Again, in God existence and perdurance are absolutely identical. Therefore it is the same thing to have a principle of being and a principle of duration. But there can be no true trinity unless one person possesses the principle of existence by production. Therefore, this cannot be unless it possesses a principle of duration. But this is incompatible with eternity.[5] Therefore, etc.

7. Again, person is not greater in power or actuality than essence. But the divine essence cannot produce another essence coeternal with itself; therefore neither can a person produce another person coeternal with itself. Therefore either there is not a trinity of persons in the divine essence, or the supreme eternity is not found there.

8. Again, every being is either created or uncreated. Likewise, every being is either of itself or of another. But every created being

---

[2] Aristotle, *II Phys.*, text. 37 (c. 3); *II Metaph.*, text. 6 ff. (I, brevior, c. 2); *V Metaph.*, text. 2-4 (IV, c. 2); Avicenna, *Metaph.*, tr. 4, c. 1.
[3] Aristotle, *V Phys.*, text. 7 (c. 1).
[4] Implied in the definition of Boethius.
[5] Rich. of St. Victor, *De Trin.* II, c. 4.

is of another; therefore every uncreated being is of itself. But everything eternal is uncreated; therefore everything eternal is of itself. There is, therefore, nothing eternal that is of another. But there can be no trinity unless one person proceeds from another. Therefore, where there is trinity, there is not eternity.

9. Again, whenever any power, whether finite or infinite, projects itself into some act with the full totality of its power, it is impossible that it project in another act at one and the same time. But in the act of generating, the paternal power fully projects the immensity of its total power, since the Son is as great as the Father. Therefore, it cannot produce another person in the very same act. Therefore, if it produces a third person, this will be either before or after the generation of the Son. But this cannot be in the fullness of eternity. Therefore, either there is no trinity in God, or there is no true eternity.

10. Again, wherever there is production, there one being receives existence from another. But nothing receives what it already possesses. Therefore, if the Son is produced by the Father, He receives existence from the Father. Therefore, He did not possess that existence before He received it. But whatever receives an existence not previously possessed receives a beginning of duration; and no such being is eternal. Therefore, eternity cannot coexist with production, and hence neither can it coexist with the trinity.

11. Again, eternity expresses presence; whence the eternal is always present according to its own proper nature. But emanation in God, and above all generation in the proper sense, is more properly expressed in terms of the past than in terms of the present; since it is more proper to say that the Son was always generated and was always born than to say He is generated and born.[6] Therefore, it seems that these two things cannot exist together. Therefore, if the trinity cannot exist without true production, it cannot exist together with true eternity. But against this there are innumerable authorities both in the Old and in the New Law.[7] But it is shown from reason.

ARGUMENTS IN AGREEMENT

1. "Relative terms naturally exist simultaneously."[8] Father and Son are truly relative terms, as are Spirator and Spirit. Therefore, they are simultaneous by nature. Therefore, if any of the persons is

---

[6] Gregory, *XXIX Moral.*, c. 1, n. 1.
[7] Cf. Q. 1, a. 2 above.
[8] Aristotle, *De Praedicam.*, c. de his quae ad aliquid.

eternal, it is necessary that all the persons be eternal, since they are simultaneous by nature. What follows from this is evident; namely, that because of His supreme simplicity, relation in God cannot be an accident, nor something added from elsewhere. Therefore, it is necessary that the three persons be absolutely simultaneous.

2. Again, the mind of the Father has always existed and known simultaneously because His being is identical with His knowledge and does not precede His knowledge either by nature or by any duration. But to know in one's mind is to draw a word from oneself. Therefore, the Father simultaneously exists and generates the Word. But the Word cannot be except as a Word that is pleasing and loved;[9] and therefore it is united to the lover. Hence, if the divine knowledge exists together with eternity, so also eternity exists together with the trinity.

3. Again, it is proper to the perfection of a power to produce its acts readily. Hence some powers produce acts in an imperceptible time,[10] and others do so in an instant; and others do so simultaneously with their duration and with posteriority in accordance with their nature. And all this is found in creatures. Therefore, if the divine power is supremely powerful and absolutely exceeds any created powers, it is capable of producing and actually does produce in such a way that whatever is produced is simultaneous in nature with the one producing.

4. Again, the Father can communicate deity and omnipotence to the Son, otherwise, it would not be the Son. But deity is itself eternity, and God could not exist if He were not eternal. Therefore, the first person can communicate eternity to the others; therefore the trinity and eternity can exist together.

5. Again, the uncreated light has greater power to produce brightness than does the created light. But created light never exists without brightness therefore neither does the uncreated light. Therefore, if the brightness is the person that is produced, it is clear, etc.

6. Again, the trinity exists together with immensity, and immensity necessarily includes eternity.[11] Therefore, even more so, a true and perfect trinity exists together with true and perfect eternity. Therefore, there is no repugnance between them.

7. Again, the trinity exists together with supreme equality.[12] But equality exists not only in terms of power, but also in terms of

---

[9] Augustine, *De Trin.* IX, c. 10, 11, n. 15 ff. Cf. *Q. de Sci. Christi*, q. 6, resp. (V, 34-35).
[10] Aristotle, *IV Phys.*, text. 127 (c. 14).
[11] Cf. Q. 4, a. 2 above.
[12] Cf. Q. 2, a. 2, fund. 10 above.

duration, in which nothing can be equal to the eternal unless it is coeternal with it. Therefore, if the trinity exists together with supreme equality, it exists together with eternity as well.

8. Again, whenever a power and its act are identical, if the power can be eternal, the same is true of its act, especially when nothing extrinsic or created is connoted. But in the Father, the ability to generate is identical with the act of generation; and the same is true of the ability to spirate. Therefore, if it is necessary that the Father has the power to generate eternally, then it is necessary to admit that He has generated eternally.[13]

9. Again, where being and relation are absolutely identical it is necessary that they be measured by the same measure. But, indeed, the being of the Father is identical with His relation to the Son, and *vice versa;* since in God there is no composition.[14] Therefore, if being is eternal, so also is the mutual relation of the persons.

10. Again, in the created image, essence and power exist simultaneously; and each of the three powers exists at the same time with the others, as is manifestly clear in the human soul. Therefore, since the harmony among the divine persons is greater, all the more will each one be coeternal with the other; — as perpetuity is related to the image, so eternity is related to the creative trinity. Whence, "from the perpetuity of things, the eternal Creator is clearly shown." Therefore, the eternity of the trinity can be clearly inferred from the perpetuity of the image.

CONCLUSION

The trinity of persons necessarily exists together with eternity.

Response. The trinity and eternity necessarily exist together; and this conclusion is drawn from the essential properties, from the emanations of origin, and from the personal relations.

From the perspective of the essential properties, I say that the trinity exists together with the highest unity, simplicity, and immensity of essence, as has been shown above;[15] therefore, the being of the divine persons is one, most simple, and immense. But eternity refers to the essence, which in the trinity is not numbered, composed, or limited. It follows, therefore, that in the three persons, there is true eternity because of immensity; there is the highest eternity because of absolute simplicity; and there is one eternity because of

---

[13] Aristotle, *III Phys.*, text 32 (c. 4).
[14] Cf. Q. 3, a. 2 above.
[15] Cf. Q. 2, 3 and 4.

unity of essence. Therefore, eternity does not exclude the trinity, since the trinity necessarily includes eternity. The same conclusion can be drawn from the emanations of origin, in terms of the one producing, and the one produced, as well as in terms of the mode of production. Because of its supreme likeness, the one produced possesses full equality; because of the natural diffusion or communication, the production is fully necessary. Therefore, if the person producing is eternal, it is necessary that the act of producing be eternal, as well as the person produced and the mode of production. It is clear, therefore, that the trinity and eternity are not only not mutually repugnant, but are marvelously harmonious and necessarily exist together.

The same conclusion can be drawn from the personal relations. For the divine persons are distinguished by their relations; I say, not by extrinsic relations but by intrinsic relations; not by accidental relations but by permanent ones; not by relations that diminish, but by ones that are most fulfilling. Since an intrinsic relation, which is not accidental but perfect, coexists together with its supposite, and since a relation and its correlations are simultaneous in nature, relations of this sort include the highest simultaneity in the divine persons. They involve no limitation because they exist together with the highest infinity. And since nothing else is required for eternity other than simultaneity together with absolute interminability, and supreme interminability together with absolute simultaneity, the trinity necessarily coexists with eternity, and eternity with trinity, since the trinity does not exclude but includes eternity. Whence, Augustine writes in the eleventh book of *The City of God*, chapter 28: "God, in whose image we were created, is true eternity and eternal truth, and eternal and true love. And He is Himself the eternal, true, and beloved trinity."[16] As eternity is not repugnant to love and truth, so it is not repugnant to the trinity, and not *vice versa*. Therefore, the arguments which demonstrate this must be conceded.

REPLIES TO THE OBJECTIONS

1. To the first contrary objection that where there is eternity, there is total simultaneity, it must be said that the simultaneity of eternity excludes the order of prior and posterior, but it does not

---

[16] XI, 28. The original text would read in translation: "It is, therefore, because we are men, created to the image of a Creator, whose eternity is true, His truth eternal, His love both eternal and true, a Creator who is the eternal, true, and lovable trinity, in whom there is neither confusion nor division..."

exclude the order of origin. But when it is said that the trinity includes order, this is understood not of the order of priority and posteriority, but of the order of origin and natural emanation, according to what Augustine says, that "there is an order not by which one is prior to another, or one is posterior to another, but by which one proceeds from the other."[17]

2. To the objection that the effect follows the cause not by reason of diversity but by reason of production, it must be said that neither of these by itself is a total, sufficient, and perfect cause; but both must be taken together. Therefore, the effect follows the cause because it emanates from it in such a way that it differs essentially from the cause. And because of this, it is not as perfect as the cause, nor is it equal to the cause in duration and in full equality of power. But the case is different in the divine production where the one producing and the one produced possess one and the same essence and therefore total equality in duration as well as in power.

3. To the objection that the persons are either equally first or they are not, it must be said that, in terms of the negation of prior and posterior, they are equally first, but in terms of the order of origin, they are not equally first. But it does not follow from this that they are not equally coeternal because — as was shown above — the excellence of these emanations, which are supremely perfect by reason of simplicity and immensity, includes the coeternity of the persons producing and the persons produced.

4. To the objection that corruption implies a final term, it must be said that there is no parallel, because corruption always involves a defect and a movement from the complete to the incomplete; but generation does not; for one sort of generation takes place by the eduction of something from potency to act, and because of its imperfection, this sort necessarily involves an initial term; but there is another sort of generation which takes place through the most actual communication in accordance with the total perfection of the producer and of that which is produced, and of that from which it is produced, and of the mode according to which it was produced. It is this sort of generation which is attributed to God; and since it involves no imperfection, it includes no initial term.

5. To the objection that eternity is interminable duration, it must be said that the term of a production can be understood in two ways: in the one principal sense, namely, as the actual reality produced; or in another related sense, namely, as that which is not produced anew. And this related meaning is found in those beings in which there is a distinction between the process of being produced

---

[17] *Lib. II Contra Maximinum Arian.*, c. 14, n. 8.

and the product of the process. Therefore, when it is asked whether or not generation in God has a term, it must be said that if *term* is understood in the first sense, it has a term because the Father generates the Son in such a way that the Son is begotten. But it is not true if *term* is understood in the second sense, since the Son is always begotten and is always generated, because in Him the process of being produced and the product of the process are identical because of the perfection of the supreme simplicity and actuality.

6. To the objection that in God existence and perdurance are identical, it must be said that the principle of duration can be understood in two ways; in one way, relative to the production and communication of duration; in another way, relative to the beginning of duration. If *principle* is accepted in the first sense, the Father is not only the principle of being for the Son but the principle of duration as well; for just as He gives Him being, so He gives Him eternal being. But if it is taken in the second sense, it is not true and the argument is not conclusive because of the different meaning of principle.

7. To the objection that person is not greater in power and actuality than the essence, it must be said that there is no parallel since the divine essence cannot produce another essence either from its own self or from another being that would be coeternal and equally first with itself. Therefore, it must produce from nothing. Hence, it is necessary that the essence produced in this way should have being after non-being, and that it should begin to exist when it moves from non-being to being. But the case is different in the production of one person from another person, because the person producing and the one produced possess one essence and one nature. Therefore, because of the one and undivided essence it is not necessary that the production of one person from another should involve a beginning.

8. To the objection that every being is either created or uncreated, and likewise every being is either of itself or from another, it must be said that *to be from another* can be taken in two ways; either to be essentially from another, or to be personally from another. Taking it in the first sense, as essential difference, it corresponds to the division of being into created and uncreated which form two essentially different extremes. In the second sense, it does not correspond to this division. If we pass from one meaning to the other, a figure of speech emerges because of the change in the mode of predication as we move from essence to person.[18] And such a mode of predication does not apply to God.

---

[18] Aristotle, *I Elench.*, c. 3 (c. 4); cf. Q. 2, a. 2, ad 7 above.

9. To the objection that when an infinite power projects itself into act with the totality of its power, it cannot project itself into another act at one and the same time, it must be said that this is true when such a power acts totally in terms of the productive power and the mode of production. But the minor is false, because, even though the Father produces the Son in accordance with His immense power, yet He generates Him and He does not spirate Him. Therefore, in accordance with the other mode of production which takes place by spiration together with the Son, there is a production of another person since those two productions are not mutually exclusive but are naturally united. As is clear in the case of the mind, the actual consideration of the intellect does not impede but rather contributes to the fact that the affections are turned to the good that is known and seen, so also the generation of the Word proceeding from the mind does not stand in the way of the breath of love which embraces both.

10. To the objection that wherever there is production, there one being receives existence from another, it must be said that there is a type of production in which there is a distinction between the process of being produced and the product of the process; and there is a type of production in which these are completely identical. Likewise, reception can be taken in two senses. In one sense, *to receive* and *to have received* are different; in the other sense, they are fully identical. The first meaning corresponds to the first type of production; the second meaning corresponds to the second type of production. The objection is true relative to the first, but not relative to the second; and it is in this way that the Son receives being from the Father. For He always has received and always receives, because the Father always generates and has always generated, as may be clearly concluded from the foregoing.

11. To the objection that eternity expresses the present while generation is explained better in terms of the past, it must be said that the eternal generation is always most actual and most complete. While the actuality of any act is better expressed in terms of the present, completion and perfection is best expressed in terms of the past. Hence, the eternal generation cannot be adequately expressed in any temporal terms, though it is necessary to use temporal terms to express it since it is beyond all time and possesses whatever perfection can be expressed by temporal language. Hence, because of its perfection, it is fittingly spoken of in terms of the past; and because of its actuality, it is fittingly spoken of in terms of the present; because of its continuation and indefectibility, it is fittingly spoken of in terms of the future. Since all these are one in that generation, it cannot be sufficiently explicated through any word. It

is not surprising that the sound of temporal words is inadequate to express the most quiet silence of that eternity and of that eternal generation, which is better understood than it is expressed; which, in the present, is believed rather than understood; and which will be better seen in the future than it is believed now, for as our Savior says: "This is eternal life; that they know You who alone are true God, and Him whom you have sent, Jesus Christ."[19] In no way can we arrive at this unless our intellect be more fully elevated beyond the changes of time, and beyond the fog of our phantasms to the freedom of that supercelestial quiet.

---

[19] *Jn.* 17, 3.

QUESTION VI

WHETHER THE TRINITY CAN EXIST TOGETHER WITH SUPREME IMMUTABILITY

Next the question is asked, whether the trinity can exist together with supreme immutability. And two questions are asked in reference to this. The first is, whether the divine being is immutable; the second is, whether the trinity and supreme immutability can exist together.

ARTICLE I

WHETHER THE DIVINE BEING IS IMMUTABLE

Concerning the first question, we proceed as follows. That the divine being is immutable is shown in the following ways.

ARGUMENTS IN AGREEMENT

1. First, by authority, *Malachy* 3 writes: "I the Lord do not change."[1] The *Glossa* writes: "He says this lest it be thought that there is any element of changeability in God."[2] The *Psalm* says: "You will change them, and they will be changed; but you yourself remain the same." The *Glossa* says, *immutable*.

2. Again, the same thing can be shown by reason as follows. The divine being is simply and universally first. But immutable being is prior to the mutable, because the mutable must be reduced to the immutable.[3] Therefore, if it is universally and principally first, then it is universally immutable.

---

[1] Verse 6.

[2] *Glossa ordinaria*, found in Strabo and Lyranum, according to Jerome. The following citation is *Psalm* 101, 27.28. The Gloss is found in Peter Lombard and Lyranum (interlinear).

[3] Aristotle, *VIII Phys.*, text. 33 ff. (c. 5); and *XII Metaph.*, text. 35 ff. (XI, c. 7).

3. Again, the divine being is the ultimate, to which all other beings tend as to their supreme end.[4] But other beings find their rest in the highest and final end; they can find rest in no being which is not entirely immutable in itself. Therefore, the same conclusion follows as above.

4. Again, as the philosophers say and as reason convinces us, the divine being is absolutely and in every way necessary.[5] But anything that undergoes any change in some way lacks necessity with respect to that in which it is changed. Therefore, if the divine being is necessary it is immutable.

5. Again, the divine being is most perfect. But whatever is most perfect cannot be improved nor can it be defective. But anything that changes either acquires something or loses something.[6] Therefore, the divine being cannot be changed in any way.

6. Again, the divine being is most simple. Therefore, it has nothing of an accidental nature.[7] But, in everything that undergoes change, either something is added, or something is removed. Therefore, mutability cannot exist with simplicity. Therefore, it is necessary that the opposite be true. Therefore, the divine being is immutable.

7. Again, the divine being is immense. But whatever is changed is changed either into a better state, or into a worse state, or into an equal state. But that which is immense cannot be greater or less, nor can it have an equal. Therefore, it is absolutely immutable.[8]

8. Again, the divine being is eternal, as is clear from the foregoing.[9] But, in some way, there is a prior and a posterior in every change. But in no way can this be found in eternity. Therefore, no change can be found in eternity. It remains, therefore, that the divine being is entirely immutable.

9. Again, every change is either a movement to being, or a movement away from being, or a movement within being, because everything that undergoes change either receives being, or loses being, or moves from one state of being to another, or moves from one mode of being to another.[10] But God is pure being itself, since He exists of Himself as pure act. Therefore, He can be changed in

---

[4] Boethius, *De Hebdomadibus, sive Quomodo Substantiae*, etc. Aristotle. *XII Metaph.*, text. 52 (XI, c. 10).
[5] Avicenna, *Metaph.*, tr. 1, c. 8 & tr. 8, c. 4 ff.; Algazel, *I Philos.*, tr. 2, c. De esse possibili.
[6] Aristotle, *VI Phys.*, text. 40 (c. 5).
[7] As shown in Q. 3, a. 1 above.
[8] Rich. of St. Victor, *De Trin.* II, c. 3.
[9] Cf. Q. 5, a. 1; q. 4, a. 1 above.
[10] Aristotle, *V Phys.*, text. 7 (c. 1).

none of these ways; and no other types of change are possible. Therefore, He is immutable.

10. Again, every change is either substantial or accidental. But God is not changed substantially, since He is incorruptible; nor is He changed accidentally, since there are no accidents in Him.[11] Therefore, He admits of no changeability whatsoever.

OBJECTIONS

1. *Wisdom* 7 writes: "Wisdom is mobile beyond all motion."[12] It is certain that this speaks about uncreated wisdom. Therefore, if she is the most mobile of all, it seems that the divine being is the most changeable among all changeable beings. If you say that this refers to wisdom as a cause, then the objection can be raised that a being which is mobile both causally and formally is more mobile than one which is mobile in only one of these ways.

2. Again, there is a hierarchy among creatures according to their degree of mobility, because the highest element is more mobile than the lowest;[13] and the first heaven is more mobile than the other spheres; and the glorified body is more mobile than the heavens; and spirit is more mobile than the glorified body. But every perfection should be attributed to God. Therefore, etc.

The same conclusion is shown by reason in seven ways.

3. First, on the basis of relation. Every being to which something accrues from time is mutable. But the divine being is of such a sort, since in relation to time it is called Lord, Refuge, and King. Therefore, it is changeable. If you say that "there is no change in relation"[14] Ambrose argues to the contrary in the following way: If the Father became Father from a state in which He was not the Father, He would be changed. Yet, to be Father includes a relation. Therefore, this does not hold.

4. Again, names of this sort either designate something that is identical with God, and in this case they do not begin; or they designate something created, and in this sense they are not predicated of God; or they say nothing, and in this sense it is no more proper to predicate them of God than of any other being; or they signify something added to God, but this necessarily supposes movement. Therefore, etc.

---

[11] Aristotle, *V Phys.*, text. 1 ff. & *XI Metaph.*, c. 10 (X, c. 11).
[12] Verse 24.
[13] For example, fire is more mobile than earth.
[14] Aristotle, *V Phys.*, text. 10 (c. 2); Ambrose, *I De Fide*, c. 9, n. 59.

5. Again, this can be shown also in terms of action. Everything that becomes an agent after being a non-agent, moves "from rest into act."[15] But anything of this sort is changed and altered in some way. But God is of this sort. Therefore, etc.

If you say that this change is on the part of the creature, the objection can be raised to the contrary that the fact that the creature is produced does not cause God to produce; but rather the contrary. Therefore, the cause of this change is to be affirmed first of all in God.

6. Again, any agent that performs a multiplicity of actions in such a way that distinct acts are performed at distinct moments of time necessarily undergoes change. But God is such an agent because at one time He produces, and at another He conserves; at another He spares and at another He punishes. And no one of these actions is identical with the others. Therefore there is some change in God.

7. Again, the same thing can be shown on the basis of mission. Every true mission and descent is a true change. But, according to the Scriptures, the Son of God was sent into the flesh and descended from heaven.[16] And this cannot be attributed to His human nature. Therefore, He is changed and changeable in His divine nature.

8. Again, in as far as He is man, the Son of God is something. But it is impossible that He should acquire a quality that He did not previously possess without undergoing change in Himself, just as something acquires a whiteness which it did not previously possess. This is all the more true relative to the acquisition of a substance. Therefore, if the Son of God was made man, it is necessary that that hypostasis was changed.

9. Again, the same thing can be shown on the basis of indwelling. Whatever begins to exist and ceases to exist in another is changed at least accidentally. But by grace, God begins to exist in the penitent person and ceases to exist in the sinner; and by His essence, He begins to exist in a nature that is generated and He ceases to exist in a nature that is corrupted. Therefore, etc.

10. Again, if one thing exists inseparably in another, when the latter is moved so is the former necessarily moved because, as the Philosopher says, "when we are moved, etc."[17] But by reason of His essence, God is present in every creature, and in no way is He separated from them. Therefore, He is moved necessarily when the creature is moved.

---

[15] Aristotle, *II De Anima*, text. 45 (c. 4).
[16] *Rm.* 8, 3; *Gal.* 4, 4; *Jn.* 3, 13; *Eph.* 4, 9.
[17] *II Topic.* c. 3 (c. 7).

11. Again, the same thing can be shown on the basis of power as follows. Whoever is capable of doing something at one moment but is not capable of doing it later possesses a power that undergoes change. But before He created the world, God could create it; but now He cannot. Therefore, etc. If you say the ability to create is not an absolute power; on the contrary; it follows that whatever the Father can do, the Son can do. But the Father can create; therefore the Son also can create. Furthermore, this is no explanation since the same thing follows from any other sign of the divine will, however great or of whatever sort. If you say that the inference should be: "He could have created," the same thing is truly said of a blind man; namely, "he could have seen."

12. Again, whatever God can do is possible. But, if He can do now whatever He could have done, then whatever was once possible for God is possible now. But this is false in regard to anything that is accidentally impossible; and, according to the Saints and Doctors, such things are impossible for God. Therefore, the same conclusion follows as above; consequently the divine power is changed.

13. Again, the same thing can be shown on the basis of knowledge, since a person who ceases to know something undergoes some change in his knowledge. But God knew that the world was to be created; but now He does not actually know this, for it is completely false. Therefore, etc.

14. Again, it follows necessarily that if God knows something, then it is true.[18] Therefore if He now knows actually whatever He did know, then everything that was true is now actually true. But this is false; so also is that premise false from which the conclusion is drawn. It remains, therefore, that the divine knowledge is changeable.

15. Again, the same thing can be shown on the basis of the will. As Augustine says, "The will is the proximate and immediate cause of things."[19] But when the cause is posited, the effect is posited also. Therefore, the divine willing does not precede its act of production in duration. Therefore when He begins to produce, He begins also to will. Therefore, etc.

16. Again, any person who wills something which he is capable of not willing is necessarily changed. But God wishes to save a certain wayfarer. Either it is possible or it is impossible for Him not to will this. If it is impossible, then that man cannot be damned, or the will of God would be frustrated. If He is capable of not

---

[18] Augustine, *De Civ. Dei*, XI, c. 10, 3.
[19] *De Trin.* III, c. 4, n. 9; *De Gen. contra Manich.* I, c. 2, n. 4.

willing this; but anyone who is capable of not willing something after willing it can undergo change. Therefore, etc.

17. Again, it is impossible that any voluntary agent whose operation is in conformity with its will should will one of a pair of contraries and effect the other; and *vice versa*. But at one time God puts to death, and at another He gives life.[20] And He does many other incompatible actions. Therefore, it is necessary that His will desires one thing at one time, and the contrary at another time. But any will that operates in this way undergoes change. Therefore, the divine will is changeable. But the divine will is identical with God's being. Therefore, etc. If you say that the reason for this lies in the effect; this is of no significance since God does not will something because it happens, but rather the reverse. It remains, therefore, that mutability arises in principle from the divine will.

CONCLUSION

The divine being is utterly unchangeable.

Response. Without doubt, the divine being is completely unchangeable. And it is necessary to affirm this, even though we cannot understand it perfectly; wherefore, all agree in affirming it. Indeed, all men who think correctly — not only the Saints but the philosophers as well — affirm that the divine being is immutable in as far as it is most simple, immense, and eternal.

In as far as it is most simple, it is immutable in its form; in as far as it is immense, it is immutable with reference to place; in as far as it is eternal, it is immutable with reference to time. But all movement and change can be reduced to one of the above-mentioned differences, according to Augustine and Hugh.[21] Therefore the divine being can in no way be compatible with movement or change.

Again, in as far as it is simple, it is immutable in itself, for it possesses nothing which is not of its own essential being, because "there is nothing accidental, but only subsistent truth," as Hilary says.[22] In as far as the divine being is immense, it is not changeable from one place to another; for it cannot be transferred in place because it is present everywhere in its totality. In as far as it is eternal, it cannot be changed together with another, because it remains stable while other things come and go.

Finally, in as far as it is most simple, it can be changed neither

---

[20] 1 *Sm.* 2, 6.
[21] I *Sent.* d. 37, p. 2, dub. 2; Hugh of St. Victor, *I De Sacramentis*, p. 3, c. 15; *Lib. VII Erudit. Didasc.*, c. 19.
[22] *De Trin.* VII, n. 11.

in relation nor in operation because neither of these includes anything diverse or accidental in itself; therefore the divine being is not changed nor is it composed by the addition or loss of such things. Since it is immense, it is changed neither because of mission nor because of indwelling, because its mission and indwelling is not realized by becoming circumscribed nor by undergoing a local change; rather, it is realized through presence and manifestation. Since it is eternal, it is changed neither in will nor in power, nor in knowledge, since whatever God knows, wills, and can do He knows, wills and can do eternally. Since there is no changeability in eternity, neither is there changeability in God's knowledge, will and power. As is apparent to anyone who has studied the matter, the divine being is unchangeable in every way. And everyone admits this.

As the understanding of eternity requires that one understand God to be both simple and immense, so the understanding of immutability requires that one understand simultaneously the supreme simplicity of God together with His eternity and immensity. Because He is simple, nothing is accidental to Him; because He is eternal, nothing is added to Him and nothing is lost; because He is immense, everything that is proper to perfection is fitting for Him. Therefore, without undergoing any change in Himself, He is capable of producing and not producing; willing and not willing; foreseeing and not foreseeing; listening and not listening, as befits His supreme perfection. And as He can produce many things, though He Himself is one; and temporal things, though He is eternal; and finite things, though He is infinite; and beings that are composed, though He is simple, so He can produce things capable of variation and change, though He Himself remains unchangeable.

And this is what Hugh says in the first part of *On the Sacraments*: "That which is naturally innate to every rational soul should be held firmly; namely, that God is immutable. He cannot be increased since He is immense; nor decreased since He is one; nor changed in place, since He is everywhere; nor changed in time, since He is eternal; nor changed in knowledge, since He is most wise; nor changed in affection, because He is the most good."[23] From this it appears how and why we understand that God is unchangeable in His being.

To understand the objections, it must be noted that whatever is said of God with respect to creation signifies the divine essence primarily while it connotes something in the creature. This can happen in two ways; either actually or habitually. In terms of the principal significate, it is God Himself, who is neither changed nor multiplied; and who neither begins nor ceases. That which is connoted or co-

---

[23] *Lib. I*, p. 3, c. 13.

known is some reality that is or can be created. From this perspective, there is beginning and end, and variation, but in different ways in accordance with the diverse modes of connotation. Since that which is predicated of God connotes the creature in act, it can begin and end, and it can inhere or not inhere without change in God but not without change in the creature. This is evident when we say that God conserves something. Since this connotes something which is capable of being created and connotes it in habit or in terms of aptitude, then there cannot be a beginning, but there can be an end; and it can inhere or not inhere without change in God or in the creature. The reason for this is the connotation of the future. But the future never begins to be future, as Anselm says; but it does cease to be future when it becomes the present.[24] And indeed it is possible that a future contingent would not come into existence, and this would involve no change since such a contingent designates nothing actual in reality.

If one grasps this, it is clear that two opposite predicates can be attributed to God without any change in Him. But there are certain predicates which demand a change in the creature, as in the case of temporal qualifications; and there are other predicates which do not demand change. Therefore, it can be understood in what sense it is necessary to affirm that the divine being is absolutely immutable. Hence the arguments that prove this should be conceded.

REPLIES TO THE OBJECTIONS

1. To the contrary objection that wisdom is more mobile than all other mobile things, it must be said that a thing can be said to be mobile in three ways; either by reason of efficient causality, or by reason of representative exemplarity; or by reason of an inherent variation. Wisdom is said to be supremely mobile in the first and second ways, because these are perfections; but not in the third way, since this involves imperfection. Or it can be said that since anything which is mobile in terms of place is made present in many places by its movement; and the more quickly it is moved, the more quickly it is made present at many places. So it is that since the divine wisdom is most present to all, it is said to be the most mobile of all mobile things not because it passes from one place to another, but because it is present to all. This is what Dionysius says in chapter 9 *On the divine names:* "In a religious sense, God is considered to be moved, not according to transfer, or change, or alteration, or change of mode or place; not in reference to straight or circular movement,

---

[24] *Monolog.*, c. 18.

nor in reference to movement combining both; nor in reference to intelligible, or animal, or natural movement. But God acts by means of His substance; and He contains all things and is completely provident in reference to all things; and He is present to all in their movement; guiding the movement and operations of all existing things."[25]

2. To the objection that there is a hierarchy among creatures according to their degree of mobility, etc. it must be said that there are some qualities that befit creatures in greater or lesser degrees in such a way that no imperfection is implied; such as unity, goodness, and truth. And with such qualities, the highest degree is to be attributed to God to whom every perfection is fitting. There are other qualities that involve some perfection together with imperfection, such as mobility which involves a certain actuality together with possibility.[26] And because of the imperfection inherent in such qualities, they cannot and ought not be attributed to God in the proper sense, neither in the superlative degree nor in any lesser degree.

3.4. To the objection from relation, that God receives something from time, it must be said that in predicates of this sort, as was touched on in the solution, one must distinguish the principle significate from that which is connoted. The principal significate, indeed, refers to God and is therefore eternal and immutable; but that which is connoted refers to the creature, and is therefore temporal and mutable. The fact that those predicates are said to begin or to cease is not to be referred to God, but is to be referred to the created effect. And the point of the objection is clarified, since words of this sort indicate something that is God and something that proceeds from God. It is by reason of the former that they are predicated, not by reason of the latter. It is by reason of the latter that they begin and end, not by reason of the former; since in order that a composite whole be temporal or contingent, it is sufficient that it possess temporality or contingence in any of its parts.[27]

5.6. To the objection from action, that a being which is not an agent becomes an agent, it must be said that there is one sort of agent that acts of itself and another sort that acts through something other than itself. The first sort of agent cannot be changed in acting since it neither receives nor loses anything in its action because its action is identical with itself. But the above proposition is true

---

[25] Paragr. 9.
[26] Cf. a. 2, arg. 2 of this question. Concerning this solution, see also Anselm, *Monolog.*, c. 15.
[27] Cf. Q. 7, ad 3 below.

VI. IMMUTABILITY AND TRINITY 233

with respect to the second sort of agent which is not identical with its action. However, God is an agent in the first way and not in the second since, by reason of His simplicity, He is identical with His action.

And if you should object that if He is identical with His action, then just as He does not begin to exist, so He does not begin to act; it must be said in response that He does not begin to act by reason of His own intrinsic act which is identical with Himself, but by reason of the extrinsic effect which is the creature, which has a beginning and is diversified according to the variety of creatures. From this the response to what follows concerning the plurality of actions is clear. A plurality of incompatible acts are attributed to God not because of a plurality of intrinsic acts but because of the plurality of connoted effects. For since the intrinsic act is God Himself, it is one and immutable, and eternal; but since the extrinsic effect is created, it is multiple, changeable, and temporal — taking time in the broad sense.[28] And this involves no change in the divine being.

7.8. To the objection based on mission, that every mission and descent is change; it must be said that in reference to God, mission is not taken in the proper sense but in a metaphorical sense; and in God it refers to nothing other than the emanation of one person from the other and the manifestation of this in a created effect. Therefore, as God — Father, Son, and Holy Spirit — is present to all times and places according to essence, power, and presence, even though He dwells in heaven in glory and there manifests Himself in clear light, when He begins to manifest Himself in the lower creatures, it is as though He begins to be present where He had not been present; and for this reason He is said to be sent and to descend, not because of any change or new condition on His part, but only because of the revelation and manifestation made to us and realized in us.

If one objects that the Son of God began to be man, and that *man* refers to some reality that exists in Him; it must be said in response that *man* is predicated of the Son by reason of the union of the two natures in one hypostasis. Therefore, since the union is spoken of in terms of relation and can be attributed to someone in a new sense without any change in him but solely because of a change in the other term of the relation, as is clear in the relation of right to left;[29] it follows that the Son of God, without change in

---

[28] Time is understood as it is the measure of the duration of any creature, not only the corporal but the spiritual as well.
[29] Boethius, *De Trin.*, c. 5.

His eternal person, began to be man solely by reason of a change in the nature He assumed, which was simultaneously formed and united to the Word. And as the Word is not changed in the formation of that nature so He is not changed in the assumption of the nature that has been formed.

9.10. To the objection based on indwelling, namely, that God begins to exist in the penitent by grace; it must be said that one being is said to exist in another in two ways; either in such a way that it somehow depends on the other and is limited and defined by the other; and since in this way it begins to exist in the other, it is changed with that beginning, and it is moved in the movement of the being in which it exists, as is clear with the existence of the universal in the particular, and of form in matter, and of that which is localized in place, and of an accident in its subject. But God exists in the creature by essence and influence in such a way that He does not depend on the creature, nor is He limited and defined by the creature. Therefore, when He begins to dwell in another, this is not because of a change in Himself, but only because of a change in the creature or in the intermediate influences by reason of which God is said to begin to dwell in the creature; namely, by influencing the creature through a new grace.

Likewise, while He is present in the creature, yet He is not moved with the movement of the creature, as is the case with those things of which the Philosopher says, "When we are moved, those things which are in us are moved," since He does not depend on the creature and is neither limited nor defined by it. Hence, as a ray of light is in the air and yet is not moved with the movement of the air, and as the soul is present totally in each part of the body and yet is not moved with the movement of the individual parts because it is not limited by any part, so also we should understand the matter at hand. Thus, the response to the present objection becomes clear.

If one objects that it does not seem intelligible that one being should exist inseparably in another and yet not be moved with the change of the other, it should be said that we can understand this if we understand God to be simultaneously most simple and immense. Since He is immense, He is within as He is without.[30] Since He is most simple, He is in no way distant from Himself however great may be the local distance and separation among the beings in which He is present. Therefore, however much those beings in which God is present are thought to be changed, in no way can God be said to be mutable, neither in reality nor in thought. For in every movement and change we must understand that something

---

[30] Gregory, *II Moral.*, c. 12, n. 20.

is acquired and something is lost; and therefore, there must be some distance between the extremes. Since God is simultaneously infinite and simple, in no way can this be said of the divine being, neither of itself nor accidently. Therefore, the images of our phantasy are deceptive in this case.

11.12. To the objection from power, namely, that He cannot now do what He could do in the past, it must be said that to be unable to do now what one could do in the past can be taken in two ways; either because of some defect introduced in the productive power itself, or because of a change in the condition of that which is possible. For that which is possible and true can be made impossible by a change in reality; just as before I read something, it is true that I have not read it; but after I have read it, this is no longer possible. It is said to be *impossible by accident*. As Augustine says in *Against Faustus*, this is impossible for God since such a possibility corresponds not to power but to impotence, because it is against the highest truth to bring it about that something which has existed should not have existed.[31] Therefore, since the divine power remains always uniform, everything of whatever sort and whatever quantity that He could do, He can do now in as far as He exists of Himself. However, because many true things become false and many possible things become impossible, in as far as this arises on the part of the effects, it follows that He cannot now do everything that He could have done because not everything that was possible still remains possible; this comes about not because of a change in the efficient power, but because of a change with respect to the possible effects. From this the response becomes clear to what follows concerning that which is impossible by accident.

And if you object that the divine power does not in any way depend on the possible since it can produce all things from nothing, it must be said that this is true not because of dependence but because of connotation, since when it is said that God can produce some beings, at the same time it is insinuated that such a being is possible for Him and hence that there is nothing in it repugnant to the divine power, wisdom, and goodness that would stand in the way of its being produced in reality without doing violence to the full perfection of the divine power.

13.14. To the objection based on knowledge, it must be said that when God is said to know something, this can be understood in two ways: either that He has knowledge of some being, or that He judges that being to be true. In the first way, God's knowledge does not connote the existence of truth in the object known. And

---

[31] Lib. XXVI, c. 4 ff.

in this sense, whatever He knew, He still knows for He has knowledge of all those things which He has known from eternity. In the second way, God's knowledge connotes truth in the object known. And in this sense, He does not presently know everything that He has known just as He does not now do everything that He has done. And this is true not because of a change on the part of the knower, but only on the part of the object known.[32]

From this, the response becomes clear to the next objection concerning the truth of that which is known; since the divine knowledge posits truth in the object known when it is taken in one sense but not in the other, as is clear from the foregoing distinction.

15. To the objection based on the divine will, it must be said that a proximate and immediate cause can be taken in three ways: in terms of substance, or of disposition, or of act; by reason of substance when no other causing substance comes between the cause and its effect; by reason of disposition, when no new disposition is added to it in the production of the effect; by reason of act, when the cause is conjoined to the act itself. But the divine act can be taken in two ways; either as interior or as the efficient cause of an external effect. The divine will, therefore, is the proximate and immediate cause of beings that are to be produced by reason of substance, disposition, and intrinsic act, but not by reason of external efficiency except in reference to that time for which He wills it. And this is true of the divine will because it is supremely omnipotent and free. Therefore, even though from eternity He willed to produce the world, yet He did not will the production of the world to take place in eternity but only in time. Therefore, He produces in time while undergoing no change in His will; and the effect has a beginning while the cause does not. The objection concerning the proximate and immediate cause is understood of the proximate and immediate cause according to the three-fold distinction given above.

16. To the objection that God, who can will something, is capable also of not willing it, it must be said that the divine will connotes relation and order in reference to something in the future, and that future reality can either exist or not exist without change, as was said above in the principal solution. Therefore, with respect to future contingent things, God can be said either to will or not to will with no change in His will.

17. To the objection that God is a voluntary agent of such a sort that His operation is conformed to His will, etc., it must be said that there are two types of voluntary agents. There is one

---

[32] *Q. de Sci. Christi*, q. 1, ad 1 ff. (V, 5).

sort whose will is determined with reference to an object which is willed in such a way that the agent is not entirely sovereign with respect to all its effects, but at one moment it wills one thing, and at another moment, something else. And the objection is true with reference to a voluntary agent of this sort. There is another sort of voluntary agent whose will transcends all those beings which its providential wisdom disposes. As an agent of this sort at one and the same time disposes all those things which are produced successively in such a way that the disposition itself is not changed with the change in the object produced, so also the will, which is fully consonant with that disposition, remains unchanged. Hence, as the divine art and the divine counsel, by which a diversity of things are commanded and come to be, remain always unchanged in themselves, so also the divine will remains always unchanged even though those beings which proceed from it are changed, since at one and the same time, in an eternal and immutable act, it directs its glance as art, reason and exemplar, word and wisdom, and other similar things, to all those things which are eternally produced. No change is caused in these by the change in the external being, for God is in no way dependent on external beings, even though all things depend on His wisdom and will and power as on the cause that is most noble, stable, and sufficient; a cause that is primary and supreme.

ARTICLE II

WHETHER THE TRINITY AND SUPREME IMMUTABILITY CAN EXIST TOGETHER

Next the question is raised whether the trinity and supreme immutability can exist together. It seems that they are incompatible.

OBJECTIONS

1. It is impossible that there be species without genus.[1] But generation or production is a species of movement or change. Therefore, wherever there is generation, there is change. But the trinity does not exist except by reason of the fact that one person proceeds from another by way of generation. Therefore, etc.

---

[1] Porphyr., *De Praedicab.*, c. de communitatibus et differentiis generis et speciei.

2. Again, generation in creatures involves relation and change; indeed, it involves change in a more essential and fundamental way than relation. But there can be no generation in the supreme trinity without relation, otherwise there would be no true distinction. Therefore, for the same reason and for an even greater reason, generation cannot be admitted without change.

3. Again, it is impossible both in thought and in reality that anything should undergo corruption without change. But generation or production is directly opposed to corruption since, as the former is a movement to being so the latter is a movement to non-being.[2] Therefore there can be no generation without change; so also in the case of the divine persons.

4. Again, if one thing follows as a consequence from another, this is not changed when one and the same quality is added to each of these terms. Now, from the proposition: "there is generation in time," the consequence follows: "there is change in time." Therefore for the same reason, or for an even stronger reason, eternal generation implies eternal change. Therefore, it does not exist together with immutability.

5. Again, Augustine says the following: If the Holy Spirit could be generated, He could undergo change.[3] Therefore, generation in God implies change. But this cannot exist together with its opposite. But its opposite is supreme immutability. Therefore, etc.

6. Again, if there is production in God, it is either by necessity or by will. If it is by necessity, then supreme liberality and power does not exist in God. If it is by will, then the one who is produced could also not be produced; and therefore He could not exist; hence He could undergo change. Therefore, the same conclusion follows as above.

7. Again, that which is repugnant to any being because of its imperfect state is all the more repugnant to the state of perfection. But in the creature, there is only a certain degree of immutability. Yet in perpetual and incorporeal substances there can be no plurality such as would result from the production of like from like.[4] Therefore, neither is this found in God.

8. Again, whatever is repugnant to a cause is repugnant to its effect as well. But the reason why a generative power is given to creatures is "because they are greatly distant from the first cause and they are corruptible." Therefore, if the highest immutability

---

[2] Aristotle, *V Phys.*, text. 7 (c. 1).
[3] Alex. of Hales, *Summa*, p. I, q. 4, m. 1; Bonav., I *Sent.* d. 7, dub. 4.
[4] Rich. of St. Victor, *De Trin.* IV, c. 14.

is repugnant to corruption, it is also repugnant to production by generation. The minor is proved by the Philosopher.[5]

9. Again, it is impossible for God to produce a being from a substance distinct from Himself without a change in His substance. But God is capable of acting in reference to others only as He is capable of acting upon Himself or in reference to Himself. Therefore, He cannot produce from His own substance without a change in His own substance. Therefore, if the trinity exists by reason of production, etc.

10. Again, nothingness is more distant from the concept of changeability than is being. Therefore the production of a being from nothing is more distant from changeability than is the production of one being from another being; for nothingness is in no way capable of change.[6] But it is impossible for a being to be produced from nothing without mutability. Therefore, likewise when something is produced from another being.

11. Again, in terms of the cause of knowledge, form is more simple and prior to the supposite, just as nature is to person.[7] But it is impossible for a form to be produced from something without change in itself as well as in that from which it proceeds. For a similar reason, it is impossible that a supposite or person be produced without change.

12. Again, a whole is related to another whole in the same way as a part is related to a part. But if the Father produced the Son from part of His substance, then the substance would be changed necessarily in reference to that part. Therefore, when He produces totally, it is necessary that His substance be changed totally. Therefore, etc.

ARGUMENTS IN AGREEMENT

1. In the trinity, the production of one person from another person exists together with supreme simplicity as is clear from the above.[8] But where there is supreme simplicity, there is complete invariability and immutability. Therefore, the trinity and the sort of emanation that befits it is not repugnant to immutability.

2. The emanation of one person from another person exists together with supreme actuality. But where there is supreme actuality, there is total immutability, since "movement is the actuality

---
[5] *Lib. II De Generat. et Corrupt.*, text. 59 (c. 10).
[6] Aristotle, *IV Phys.*, text. 67 (c. 8).
[7] Cf. Q. 2, a. 2, conc. above.
[8] Q. 3, a. 2.

of a being in potency,"⁹ and whatever is changeable is in some way in potency. But whatever accompanies the antecedent, necessarily accompanies the consequent. Therefore, etc.

3. Again, there can be no variability in the highest eternity, since every movement involves something that is prior and something that is posterior, either in time or in nature.¹⁰ But the trinity of persons and their production exist together with eternity; and therefore with the highest immutability.

4. Again, "there is no movement in a relation."¹¹ But relation constitutes the trinity and the plurality of persons, as Boethius says: "Relation unfolds the trinity."¹² Therefore, for this reason it is impossible to affirm change or movement there. Hence, it exists together with the highest immutability.

5. Again, in that being for whom to be produced is simultaneous with having been produced, there is no prior or posterior, neither in duration nor in nature nor in reality. But this is found in every change. Therefore, etc.

6. Again, it is possible for God to produce creatures without change in Himself, because He produces of Himself.¹³ Therefore, in like manner, the Father can produce a person without change in His person or nature. For the same reason, the Son can be produced without change. Therefore, production does not demand that there be change in this case.

7. Again, God knows Himself without any change in Himself. But, in knowing Himself, He speaks; and in speaking, He generates the Word. Therefore He must generate the Word without any change; and for the same reason He must breathe the Holy Spirit. Therefore, etc.

CONCLUSION

The trinity of persons exists together with supreme immutability.

Response. The trinity of persons which exists in God by way of emanation of one from the other exists together with the highest immutability. There are two reasons for this; namely, supreme eternity and supreme simplicity. The supreme eternity is incompatible with any change; while supreme simplicity is incompatible with any possibility of change. Therefore, if the trinity exists together with simplicity and eternity; and if there is no change where there

---

⁹ Aristotle, *III Phys.*, text. 6 (c. 1).
¹⁰ Aristotle, *IV Phys.*, text. 99 & 131 (c. 11 & 14).
¹¹ Aristotle, *V Phys.*, text 10 (c. 2) & *XI Metaph.*, c. 11 (X, c. 12).
¹² *De Trin.*, c. 6.
¹³ Cf. a. 1, ad 5 & 6 above.

is eternity and nothing capable of change where there is simplicity; and if every sort of mutability is excluded where these are excluded, then the trinity and supreme immutability necessarily exist together.

And this becomes clear in the following way. Where there is eternity, there is nothing that begins and nothing that follows; therefore, there is no beginning, no succession, and no defection. Moreover, all change can be reduced either to the movement from non-being to being, or to the movement from being to non-being, or to a movement from one being to another being.[14] But a change to being does not take place without a beginning; a change from being does not take place without a defection; and a change in being cannot be realized without some sort of succession since it does not take place without variation. Therefore, eternity excludes every change; hence, it exists together with the trinity. Therefore in the excellence of the trinity, eternity excludes any change.

Because of its simplicity it contains nothing capable of change. For there exists in the trinity the highest simplicity of nature and person, and of each of these in relation to the other. By reason of this simplicity of nature, there can be no division in that from which the production arises. Because of the simplicity of person, there can be no composition in the being produced. Because of the simplicity in both, there can be no separation from the productive principle. From this it follows that there is nothing mutable in God, neither that which is produced, nor that which produces, nor that from which the production arises. In view of the fact that nothing is lost from the principle, and nothing new is introduced by that which is produced, and there is no division in the indivisible fundament from which the production is understood to arise, neither materially nor causally, but substantially; there is nothing there that could undergo change.

Therefore, if the supreme trinity is understood to exist in highest simplicity and eternity, it must also necessarily be understood to coexist with total immutability.[15]

Furthermore, since actual immutability united with highest simplicity and eternity demands the highest actuality, and the highest actuality is realized in the full conversion of being upon itself in knowledge and love; and since understanding includes a word, and love includes a union; just as it is not repugnant to but actually consonant with the immutability of the first principle that it know

---

[14] Aristotle, *V Phys.*, text. 7 (c. 1).
[15] At this point, all the manuscripts except one (i.e. Florence, bibl. Nation., cod. D. IV. 27) break off. The Florence Manuscript continues the text in a different but apparently contemporaneous hand.

and love itself, so also it is not repugnant to but consonant with His immutability that He generate a Word and breathe forth Love. Both of these befit Him immutably and actually at all times. Therefore, if immutability is correctly understood, it not only does not exclude but it includes the most blessed trinity because that which is supremely immutable is necessarily simple, eternal, and actual in accordance with the fullness of unlimited and perfect actuality. Therefore, the arguments in favor of this are to be conceded.

REPLIES TO THE OBJECTIONS

1. To the first contrary argument, that where there is generation there is change, it must be said that this is true with respect to creatures where generation consists in the passage from being in potency to being in act and where, as a consequence, there is change because that which is generated is now in a different state than it was in before. But in God the case is different since the divine generation is one of absolute actuality on the part of the principle and of the term, and of the production itself, and of that from which the production emerges. Hence, while in this case there is no acquisition of new being, yet there is the reception of true and actual and eternal being; therefore, even though there is a true production, yet there is no true change.

2. To the objection that generation involves change and relation, it must be said that if those qualities found in creatures are to be attributed to the Creator, they ought to be attributed in as far as they contain something of perfection but not in as far as they involve any imperfection. But movement and change always imply imperfection while relation frequently implies perfection, especially that relation which implies origin without any dependence in the most noble beings. And thus it is found in that eternal production.

3. To the objection that corruption cannot be understood without change, it must be said that there is no parallel, since corruption involves the loss of being, which indeed cannot be understood except in reference to being which was possessed previously. Hence, it necessarily includes change, and change cannot take place except in a being that is mutable and variable by reason of the imperfection which change implies. But generation is the communication or acceptance of being through consubstantiality. And this is possible with reference to the most perfect and most actual being because it involves no imperfection, as corruption does. For corruption is not the contrary of this sort of generation, but only of that sort of generation found in the creature which in a certain

way is both followed by and preceded by corruption. "For the generation of one being is the corruption of another," as the Philosopher says.[16]

4. To the objection that, since generation in time implies change in time, therefore generation in eternity implies change in eternity, it must be said that that mode of inference holds where there is no particular determination of being standing in the way; but such is not the case here, since eternal generation is of a different sort than temporal generation, as has been said; for it does not arise from a being in potency as does a temporal generation.[17] Therefore, it does not follow that if movement accompanies the one, it must also accompany the other; rather, the opposite is true.

5. To the objection that if the Holy Spirit were generated He would be changed, it must be said that the argument follows not because generation is identical with change, but because the consequence that follows from an inconsistent principle will itself be inconsistent.[18] If one supposes that the Holy Spirit receives being by way of spiration, which is really distinct from generation, then one necessarily assumes that He passes from one mode of emanation to another mode that is really distinct. Thus one necessarily implies change not because these modes of origin or emanation include movement or change, but because the passage from one to the other cannot be conceived of without movement. And since change is not admitted in the divine being, it is impossible that the person who is produced by spiration should be generated. And therefore, even though the Father generates and spirates, yet He is not changed, because both generation and spiration exist together in the person of the Father, and there is no movement from one to the other.

But these two modes cannot simultaneously befit one and the same person produced, and therefore if — even though it is impossible — this is thought to be realized in one of those persons, for the same impossible reason, movement is affirmed because a change in the mode of production is affirmed.

6. To the objection that production in God is either necessary or voluntary, it must be said that in God production is necessary in a certain sense and voluntary in a certain sense, as appears more clearly in the question dealing with necessity.[19] For the production does not take place by necessity of coaction but of immutability; and not by reason of a will that chooses, but by reason of a will

---

[16] *Lib. I De Generat. et Corrupt.*, text. 20 (c. 3); *II Metaph.*, text. 7 (I brevior, c. 2).
[17] Aristotle, *IV Phys.*, text. 114 ff. (c. 12).
[18] Aristotle, *VIII Phys.*, text. 36 (c. 5).
[19] Cf. the following question, a. 2.

of eternal acceptance through which the producer finds pleasure and delight in the most perfect production. Therefore, it does not follow that in God there can be variation of mutability or limitation of power, because He who is produced is produced necessarily, freely, and with power at the same time.

7. To the objection that immutability in a creature excludes generation, as is clear in the case of the angel, therefore, also in God; it must be said that this does not follow because, in generating, the creature cannot give its entire substance since it lacks the highest simplicity, actuality, and communicability; therefore it is impossible that something be generated of its substance without undergoing change. But the case under discussion is different, as has been said,[20] because in God the person who generates does not give a part of His essence but the whole of His essence which is supremely simple and perfect. It can be said, however, that a spiritual creature possesses an intrinsic generation which is the generation of a word by the mind; among all created things, this bears the greatest likeness to the eternal generation.

8. To the objection that the cause of generation and corruption is greatly distant from the first cause, it must be said that this is not the entire reason. For, if man had remained in the state of innocence, he would not have undergone corruption, but he would have generated. Hence, that generation arises more from the supreme perfection, fecundity, and actuality of the first principle than from the need to fill up any lack arising from corruption in the productive principle itself. Therefore, the Philosopher is speaking of the cause of generation in terms of the state of fallen nature but not in general terms and in accordance with that most perfect generation which is the origin of every production. For the Author of beauty has established all these things,[21] and He who grants the power of generation to others cannot Himself be sterile; according to what is said in the final chapter of *Isaiah*.[22]

9. To the objection that God cannot produce a being from a substance distinct from Himself without change in His substance, it must be said that there is no parallel. Since the creature is mutable and not completely simple, when it is affirmed that some being is produced from it, it is also affirmed that the creature itself undergoes change; since in this case there cannot be total identity between that which is given and that which is received and the intermediate

---

[20] Q. 2, a. 2, resp. & ad 3.
[21] *Wisdom*, 13, 3.
[22] *Is.* 66, 9.

act. But in God, it is entirely the reverse as has become clear in the previous reflections.

10. To the objection that there can be no production out of nothing without some change, it must be said that there is no parallel, for no being can be produced from nothing without receiving being after non-being from a principle that is essentially distinct from itself. Whence, while nothingness of itself is not mutable, yet the eduction by virtue of which something which previously did not exist becomes a being necessarily involves a beginning and a change. But such is not the case in that production by which one person is produced from the eternal substance of another person who produces eternally, since in that case there is no new being received, nor does anything begin to be. Hence there is no change.

11. To the objection that form cannot be produced without change, therefore neither can the supposite, it must be said that there is no parallel for the production of a form involves a substantial difference between the one producing and the one produced; for nothing produces itself.[23] And therefore, since the form is produced, it is necessary that it be produced by another form which, while it is other, is yet truly the productive cause and is naturally prior to the form that is produced. Therefore, in such a production, change is necessarily included. But such is not the case in the production of a supposite or of a person in as far as there is one nature and essence in both, and therefore they are simultaneous realities. In such a case, there is neither change nor movement, because there is neither prior nor posterior, nor anything new.

12. To the objection that a whole is related to the whole as a part is related to a part, it must be said that in God, properly speaking, there is neither part nor whole, in the sense that a whole is understood to contain a plurality of parts.[24] And it does not follow that if a being produced in part involves a change in part, then similarly a thing produced from the entire substance would posit a change in reference to the whole, since — as was previously touched upon — a production in part involves a division, and it affirms the loss and the acquisition of something, which necessarily includes change. But a production from the whole substance involves nothing of this sort, but rather excludes all elements which would include movement as was shown in the main argument. For there is neither division in the principle producing, nor composition in the being produced, nor anything new in the production, nor any variation with respect to any of the above.

---

[23] Aristotle, *II De Anima*, text. 47 (c. 4); *II Poster.*, c. 17 (c. 14).
[24] Aristotle, *V Metaph.*, text. 30 ff. (IV, c. 25 ff.).

QUESTION VII

WHETHER THE TRINITY CAN EXIST TOGETHER WITH NECESSITY

It is asked next whether the trinity can exist together with supreme necessity. Two questions are raised with regard to this. The first question is whether the divine being is supremely necessary. The second question is whether the trinity and supreme necessity can exist together.

ARTICLE I

WHETHER THE DIVINE BEING IS SUPREMELY NECESSARY

The question is asked, therefore, whether the divine being is supremely necessary. It seems that such is the case.

ARGUMENTS IN AGREEMENT

1. Whatever is immutable and eternal is supremely necessary.[1] But the divine being is of this sort. Therefore, etc.
2. Again, it is necessary that everything of nobility and perfection be attributed to God in the highest degree. But it is certain that necessity is more perfect than knowledge. Therefore, etc.
3. Again, whatever exists in such a way that it is impossible for it not to exist or to be conceived of as not existing is necessary in the highest sense. But the divine being is of such a sort.[2] Therefore, etc.
4. Again, whatever possesses being of itself and through itself and according to itself, is entirely necessary. But such is the divine being, since it is first. Therefore, etc.
5. Again, it is impossible that there be necessity in an effect

---
[1] Cf. Q. 5, a. 1 & q. 6, a. 1 above.
[2] As shown above, q. 1, a. 1.

except by reason of the cause. Therefore, if necessity is not in God, then there is no necessity in any being. Therefore, nothing is necessary. But if nothing is necessary, then nothing is impossible; therefore all things are possible. Therefore it is possible for one thing to both exist and not exist at the same time. But this is absurd.[3] Therefore, etc.

6. Again, it is impossible that there be necessity in a composite being except by reason of a necessity existing in a simple being. Therefore if the most simple being lacks necessity, it is impossible that necessity be affirmed in any complex or any composite being. But it is absurd that no argumentation should be necessary.[4] Therefore, etc.

OBJECTIONS

1. Every necessary being is determined to exist in one way and not in another; whatever is determined in some respect is finite. But the divine being is infinite, therefore, etc.[5]

2. Again, nothing that is indifferent to opposites is necessary; but the divine power, will and activity are indifferent to opposites; therefore they are not necessary. But the divine power, will, and activity are identical with the divine being. Therefore, the divine being is not necessary.

3. Again, no changeable quality can be attributed to a being that is immutable. Therefore no contingent quality can be attributed to a being that is supremely necessary. But something contingent is attributed to God. Therefore, etc.

4. Again, just as impossibility is repugnant to power, so necessity is repugnant to will. But the divine power is of such a sort that all things are possible to it, and in no way can impossibility be attributed to God.[6] Therefore, since the willing of God is most perfect, it seems that no necessity is allowed in the divine being.

5. Again, if a cause is necessary, so is its effect.[7] But God is the first and highest and immediate cause of all things. Therefore, if there is necessity in God, than all things are necessary.

6. Again, to the degree that a being is more contingent, to that degree it is more indifferent; and the more indifferent it is, the

---

[3] Aristotle, *IV Metaph.*, text. 9 ff. (III, c. 3) & IX text. 17 (VIII, c. 8).
[4] Aristotle, *I Poster.*, c. 3 ff.
[5] Aristotle, *V Metaph.*, text. 6 (IV, c. 5) & IX text. 3 & 10 (VIII, c. 2 & 5).
[6] *Lk.* 1, 37.
[7] Aristotle, *XI Metaph.*, c. 7 (X, c. 8). Concerning the minor, cf. Augustine, *De Trin.* III, c. 4, n. 9.

more it is common; and the more common it is, the more simple it is.[8] Therefore, the more contingent a being is, the more simple it is. Therefore that which is most simple is most contingent; therefore it is not necessary.

7. Again, whatever is necessary can be the object of knowledge just as whatever is probable can be the object of opinion.[9] But everything that can be known is either the principle of a demonstration or a conclusion that is demonstrated. But the divine being is neither of these. Therefore, etc.

8. Again, the more a being is necessary, the more certain it is; and the more certain something is, the more it is known.[10] But the divine being is hidden to the highest degree. Therefore, etc.

9. Again, just as a person is moved in vain if he desires the impossible, so also he is moved in vain if he fears the necessary.[11] Therefore, if the divine majesty is necessary, then in no way is it to be feared. But this is false and absurd. Therefore, etc.

CONCLUSION

The divine being is necessary with the most perfect necessity of immutability.

Response. In order to understand the preceding matters, it must be noted that there are three types of necessity; one which is entirely extrinsic, one which is partly intrinsic and partly extrinsic, and one that is entirely intrinsic. That necessity is entirely extrinsic which takes its origin from a principle that is exterior to it and allows of no cooperation.[12] And there are two types of this, one in relation to natural works and the other in relation to voluntary acts. So there are two types of necessity; namely, one of coaction and one of violence.

That necessity which is partly intrinsic and partly extrinsic is one that in some way arises from an intrinsic principle but is related to something outside either after the manner of a principal mover, or after the manner of a term that brings to rest. Thus, there are two types of necessity; namely, that of inevitability and that of indigence.[13]

---

[8] Aristotle, *XI Metaph.*, c. 1 (X, c. 1).
[9] Aristotle, *I Poster.*, c. 26 (c. 33); for the minor, ibid. c. 2 ff.
[10] Aristotle, *I Poster.*, c. 2; *I Phys.*, text. 2 ff. & *IV Metaph.*, text. 8 ff. (III, c. 3).
[11] Aristotle, *II Rhet.*, c. 3 (c. 2) & c. 23 (c. 19); *V Polit.*, c. 11 (c. 9).
[12] Aristotle, *III Ethic.*, c. 1; *V Metaph.*, text. 6 (IV, c. 5).
[13] For necessity of indigence, cf. Augustine, *Lib. 83 Qq.*, q. 22.

That necessity is entirely intrinsic which is in a being by reason of its proper nature. And this is the necessity of immutability and independence. Such necessity is found after a fashion in the creature, but it cannot be found in an absolute sense except in the creative essence. For it is that alone which does not admit any dependence. And all other beings necessarily depend on it since they are created.

This sort of necessity must be affirmed in the divine being because it exists in itself and of itself. Now, because it exists in itself, it lacks any principle of composition or any sustaining principle. Therefore, it can neither be changed nor cease to be. Since it exists of itself, it is not produced or created by another; therefore it can neither depend nor begin. Therefore, it possesses the highest and most perfect necessity, which excludes all change and dependence, all inevitability and indigence, all coaction and violence which express a defective necessity; on the other hand, it affirms the highest permanence and stability, the highest sufficiency and liberty. For, since it exists by itself, it is permanent and most stable; since it exists for its own sake, it is the alpha and omega.[14] Therefore, other beings, whether necessary or contingent, have their existence from it and because of it. Just as all mobile things emanate from one first immobile being and are reduced to it,[15] so all contingent things flow from one necessary being and are reduced to it. Therefore, necessity is found in the divine being, which is the origin and completion of all being, life, and understanding. And all things, whether they be necessary or contingent, cry out that the first principle is necessary. Therefore the arguments in favor of this should be conceded.

REPLIES TO THE OBJECTIONS

1. To the objection that whatever is determined in some respect is finite, it must be said that there are two types of determination. One is by way of limitation; this sort is realized by the addition of one thing to another, as disposition is added to the incomplete potency of matter. There is also a type of determination by way of perfection, as the highest good is ordered to do the good since it cannot be deficient and cannot do evil. In the first sense, determination is repugnant to infinity, but in the second sense it is not.[16] Indeed, this sort of determination is in harmony with the sort of necessity found in God, but the first sort is not.

---

[14] *Apoc.* 1, 8; Aristotle, *I Metaph.*, c. 3 (c. 2).
[15] Cf. Q. 1, a. 1, arg. 13 & 20 above. *Lib. de Causis,* prop. 18.
[16] Cf. Q. 3, a. 1, ad 4 & q. 4, a. 1.

2. To the objection that nothing that is indifferent to opposites is necessary, it must be said that the divine power, willing, and activity are said to be indifferent to opposites, not in and of themselves, but because of indifference in the effect to be produced. Hence, that indifference does not include any changeability in the divine power; but it affirms one power which is most simple and omnipotent in relation to all opposites so that it cannot be restricted to any particular one of them.[17] And this is more consonant with necessity than repugnant to it.

3. To the objection that contingent qualities cannot be attributed to a being that is supremely necessary, it must be said that when something is predicated contingently of God, there is included in that predicate both a principle significate and something that is connoted. The principle significate is nothing other than God; that which is connoted is an effect. By reason of the first, the predicate necessarily inheres in that being for which the predication is proper; by reason of the second, it is said to inhere contingently, and hence contingence is not affirmed in God, but rather it is produced by God. In predications of this sort, only those predicates which include the fullest degree of necessity are attributed to the divine being. But if it is said that an entire proposition is contingent, namely, that "God saves Peter," that is because the entire statement is of such a nature that the whole is named from its less perfect part, so that a proposition which contains one false part is called false, and a proposition which contains one contingent part is said to be contingent. The reason for this is that it is easier for a being to be destroyed than for it to be established.[18] A habit and its designation ought not be mixed with privation. But the designation of a privation proceeds in the opposite way, since some positive quality and habit is necessarily included in the concept of a privation.

4. To the objection that necessity is repugnant to will as impossibility is to power, it must be said that this is true of that necessity arising from outside such as the necessity of violence and coaction. But, as is clear from the foregoing considerations, it is not true with respect to intrinsic necessity such as the necessity of immutability.

5. To the objection that if a cause is necessary, so is its effect, it must be said together with Augustine, in the fifth book of the *City of God*, that some causes are made and nothing more; some

---

[17] Cf. Q. 6, a. 1, ad 11 ff. above.
[18] Aristotle, *VII Topic.*, c. 3 (c. 4); *II Ethic.*, c. 6; Ps.-Dionysius, *De Div. Nom.*, c. 4, § 31.

are made and make as well; and some only make.[19] Those causes he calls natural which are only made and are determined to one course. Those causes which are made and also make are free choice and will. Those causes which are only productive are identical with divine providence itself. He says that natural causes are produced but do not produce, not because they do nothing but because they act according to their innate nature, having no dominion over their acts as does a cause that possesses free choice. Such causes produce only one sort of effect which is like the cause itself. The objection is true concerning this sort of cause. But it is not true of a productive cause whose power is capable of either producing or not producing by reason of the dominion which it possesses over its action and the consequent effect. Just as such a cause is not changed because of the mutability and difference of the effects, so also it is not said to be contingent because of the contingence of its effects.

6. To the objection that the more indifferent a being is, the more common it is, it must be said that commonness is of two kinds; namely, one by reason of abstraction, and one by reason of indenomination. When it is said, therefore, that the more indifferent a quality is, the more common it is, this must be understood in terms of commonness by reason of indenomination; in this way we say that there is only one subject for the contrary qualities. This is true above all in those qualities of which one does not have a determinate cause in the subject.[20] But when the objection goes on to say that the more common a thing is, the more simple it is, this is understood of commonness by reason of abstraction. Hence, it does not follow from this that contingent beings include simplicity; rather it follows that those beings which exclude the highest simplicity include mutability. Hence, the highest simplicity can be found only in that being which is supremely necessary. Since the divine being is most simple, it is necessary that it be not contingent but necessary.

7. To the objection that whatever is necessary can be the object of knowledge; and that every object of knowledge is either a principle of demonstration or a demonstrated conclusion, it must be said that there is a necessity within the genus; and there is a necessity beyond the genus. And the latter is of two kinds; it is either beyond a determinate genus, or absolutely beyond every genus.[21] That necessity which is absolutely beyond every genus is found in God alone, who is above and beyond every class of being since He cannot

---

[19] Ch. 9, n. 4, Cf. above, Q. 2, a. 1, ad 8 & 9; q. 6, a. 1, ad 11 ff.
[20] Aristotle, *De Praedicam.*, c. De oppositis; *Lib. II Topic.*, c. 3 (c. 7).
[21] Aristotle, *V Metaph.*, text. 21 (IV, c. 16).

exist in a genus — neither of Himself, nor by reason of appropriation. Such necessity precedes and transcends all demonstrations, since it cannot be contained in any definition.[22] Therefore, when it is said that whatever is necessary is either a principle of demonstration or a demonstrated conclusion, it must be said that this must be understood in reference to necessity within a determinate genus, or in reference to necessity which can be appropriated to a determinate genus; as are the common axioms of the mind which enter into a demonstration in as far as they are appropriated. Hence, the argument is not correct in concluding that the necessity of the divine being is limited to a determinate genus.

8. To the objection that the more necessary a being is, the more certain it is, it must be said that something can be said to be more certain or more known than another in two ways; either absolutely, or in reference to us.[23] Therefore, the first proposition is true if it is understood in reference to a greater absolute certitude, but not in as far as it is understood of certitude in reference to us, since those things which are most certain and most clear in themselves seem to us to be obscure because of the weakness of the created intellect. Therefore, the Philosopher says that "as the eye of the bat is turned toward the light, so our eye is turned to the most obvious things of nature."[24] Nonetheless, even though the divine being in the fullness of its clarity is hidden to us as long as we are wayfarers, yet it is most certain and indubitable to us that God exists, as has become clearly apparent in the preceding questions.[25]

9. To the objection that the necessary is not to be feared, as the impossible is not to be desired, it must be said that that which is necessary in outcome or in effect should not be feared because fear is of no avail when something must happen in a determined way. But that being which is necessary because of its own intrinsic stability and which can assign us to eternal glory or to eternal punishment; this being, I say, is greatly to be feared both because of the grace that can be acquired, and because of punishment that can be avoided, since such a necessity does not exclude the liberality of the will and the justice of equity, as will become more clear in the following question.

---

[22] Avicenna, *Metaph.*, tr. 8, c. 4; Boethius, in lib. *Quomodo Substantiae in eo...*; Aristotle, *I Poster.*, c. 7.
[23] Aristotle, *I Poster.*, c. 2 & *I Phys.*, text. 2 ff.
[24] *II Metaph.*, text. 1 (I brevior, c. 1).
[25] Q. 1, a. 1 above. The Quaracchi editors argue from this reference that the present question is as genuine as the question cited, which Olivi expressly attributes to Bonaventure.

ARTICLE II

WHETHER THE TRINITY AND SUPREME NECESSITY EXIST TOGETHER

Next it is asked whether the trinity and supreme necessity exist together. It seems that they are incompatible.

OBJECTIONS

1. Augustine to Orosius: "The Father generated the Son neither by necessity nor by will."[1] But whatever is repugnant to generation is repugnant to the trinity. But necessity is of this sort. Therefore, etc.

2. Again, any agent which dominates over its actions is more perfect than one which does not.[2] But in the trinity, there cannot be a production except in the most perfect mode. But that which produces necessarily cannot dominate over its actions. Therefore, there can be no necessary production in God.

3. Again, any communication which arises from benignity is more perfect than one which arises from necessity. Therefore, in God either there is no communication of His nature at all, or there is no communication arising from necessity.[3] But there can be no trinity without communication. Therefore, etc.

4. Again, whatever is necessary is absolute. But anything that has a relation to something distinct from itself cannot be entirely necessary, as Avicenna would say.[4] But it is impossible for the trinity to exist unless it has reference and relation to some being. Therefore for the same reason it is impossible that the trinity exist together with necessity.

5. Again, no being that receives its existence from another can be necessary in the highest degree since it has its being and continued existence from outside itself so that it is not necessary in itself. But the trinity cannot exist unless there be some person there who is not from itself. Therefore, it is not compatible with the highest necessity.

6. Again, no being that can be thought not to exist is supremely true.[5] Similarly, no being that can be believed not to exist is supremely

---
[1] Or, *Quaest. 65 Dialog.* (among the works of Augustine) q. 7.
[2] Cf. preceding questions, sol. ad 5.
[3] Hilary, *De Trin.*, III, n. 3.
[4] *Metaph.*, tr. I, c. 7, & tr. 8, c. 4 ff. The minor in Boethius, *De Trin.*, c. 6.
[5] Cf. Q. 1, a. 1 above. That necessity presupposes truth is explained below in the response in as far as the true is identical with being.

necessary; for that which is necessary presupposes that which is true. But without doubt, the trinity can be thought not to exist. Therefore, etc.

7. Again, that which is repugnant to evidence is repugnant to certitude; and that which is repugnant to certitude is repugnant to necessity.[6] But a trinity in unity is repugnant to evidence since it seems in no way to be intelligible. Therefore, it is repugnant to supreme necessity.

8. Again, nothing that is entirely necessary is perfectly worthy of praise.[7] Therefore, if the person of the Father necessarily produces the person of the Son and that of the Holy Spirit, it is not worthy of praise in either of these. But nothing is more worthy of praise in God. Therefore, no praise of God is fitting. But this is to speak impiously. Therefore, etc.

9. Again, nothing that is simply voluntary is absolutely necessary. But the production of the persons in God is realized simply through the will; therefore, it is not through necessity. The major is proved because things that are necessary exist naturally, and nature must be distinguished from will. The minor is proved since that sort of production is delectable, acceptable, and pleasing in the highest degree. Therefore, it is supremely voluntary.

ARGUMENTS IN AGREEMENT

1. Whatever is necessary is immutable, and *vice versa*. But the trinity exists together with supreme immutability, as is clear in the previous question.[8] Therefore, etc.

2. Again, whatever is supremely one is absolutely necessary, and *vice versa*. But the trinity exists together with supreme unity.[9] Therefore, etc.

3. Again, there is a greater bond of unity in the production of one person from another than in the production of splendor and light. But these are necessary. Therefore, etc.

4. Again, it is impossible that the omnipotent should not possess supreme power; on the contrary it is absolutely necessary that such power be found in Him. But the supreme power is shown in the production of persons. Therefore, etc.

5. Again, any act which has God as principle and end is fully necessary. But the production of one person from another is such an act. Therefore, etc.

---

[6] Aristotle, *VI Topic.*, c. 3 (c. 6).
[7] Aristotle, *II Eudem.*, c. 7 (c. 6).
[8] Cf. above, Q. 6, a. 2.
[9] Cf. above, Q. 2, a. 2.

6. Again, that which is not distinct from the supremely necessary being is absolutely necessary. But the trinity is the entire divine essence. Therefore, etc.

CONCLUSION

The divine being as necessary and most liberal stands together with the trinity of persons.

Response. The divine being is necessary and nevertheless most liberal. And the holy trinity itself exists together with necessity and will if these are properly understood. As was said above concerning necessity,[10] not every type of necessity is fitting for the divine being nor for the blessed trinity, but the necessity of immutability and independence is; similarly, not every mode of willing is fitting for God. The will may be considered as adventitious, that is, as beginning to will after not willing; such a will is not found in God, neither with respect to Himself nor with respect to creatures, because of the immutability and necessity of God. There is also the antecedent will, and this is found in God, not with respect to Himself but with respect to the creature which it precedes by nature and by eternity. Thirdly, the will as concomitant and accepting is found in God both with respect to Himself and with respect to the creature; for the divine will approves and accepts every good, whether created or uncreated, whether contingent or necessary.

Therefore, while necessity and will are understood in three ways, it is the third form of each that befits the most high trinity; namely, the accepting will and the necessity of immutability; the accepting will, I say, because of the supreme charity in the producer and the supreme goodness in that which is produced, both of which necessarily include in themselves the will of complacency. And the necessity of immutability is found in God because of the indifference of essence and the independence of the person. Since in the three persons, the essence is entirely identical, there is one quiddity or entity, and one truth; and hence one necessity. Since the first person possesses its being of itself, it is absolutely necessary, hence, so are the second and the third persons. Again, since the essence is identical in the three persons, the distinctive relation of the trinity does not involve a relation to something outside itself. Therefore there is no dependence of one person on another; therefore they all exist equally and unchangeably. Therefore, if one is necessary, all

---

[10] Cf. previous question.

are necessary. Consequently, as was shown already, these three exist together; namely, trinity, necessity, and will. And there is no repugnance among them, but the highest harmony, just as the supreme unity, truth, and goodness exist in harmony.

That unity is highest which exists in many but is undivided, and this implies a trinity. That truth is highest which is infallible and most certain, and this implies necessity. That goodness is highest which is both lovable and loving; and this implies will. Therefore, the highest unity, truth, and goodness necessarily require that trinity, necessity, and will exist together. Therefore, since in the triune God, necessity is simultaneous with will, and will is simultaneous with necessity, it follows that He is the highest good by reason of His essence. Since in Him the supreme pleasure exists because of will, and the supreme security exists because of necessity, and the supreme happiness exists because of both of these, it follows that He is supremely beatifying through His influence, since our affection rests only in that good which is supremely lovable,[11] and our mind rests only in that which is supremely infallible and certain; and therefore we can be beatified only in a being that is both necessary and voluntary, which by nature is capable of being loved most fervently and known most certainly, and possessed most securely. Therefore, since the most blessed trinity is not only beatific but also beatifying, it follows that it is supremely consonant with that most perfect necessity, and in no way repugnant to it. And similarly with the most liberal will. Hence, the arguments in favor of this are to be granted.

REPLIES TO THE OBJECTIONS

1. To the first contrary objection from the authority of Augustine and Hilary,[12] it must be said that the teaching of both of these authorities is to be understood of necessity in the first and second sense, but not in the third, as is apparent from the above.

2. To the objection that any agent that dominates over its actions is more perfect, it must be said that this is true of an action that is distinct from the agent. But concerning that sort of action which, because of its supreme simplicity, is fully identical with the agent, the above proposition neither is nor can be true; for nothing

---

[11] Augustine, *De Civ. Dei*, XXII, c. 30, n. 5.
[12] In the objections above, the authority of Hilary is appealed to. This may be expanded by I *Sent.* d. 6, q. 1, arg. 2 ad oppos. where Bonaventure writes: "Item, Hilarius in libro *De synodis* (n. 58, XXV): non naturali necessitate ductus Pater genuit Filium: ergo non fuit ibi necessitas naturalis; nec necessitas alia, ut videtur: ergo, etc."

can be dominated over by itself. Therefore, the production in the divine persons is by way of supreme simplicity in which there can be no real distinction between the producer and the production; therefore the allegation of the above mentioned proposition cannot be maintained.

3. To the objection that any communication which arises from benignity is more perfect than one that arises from necessity, it must be said that this is true of that necessity which excludes benignity. But such is not the necessity which is affirmed in God; for this is understood as the necessity of communicating a gift essentially different from the giver; but this is not the sort of communication found in the emanation of the divine persons. Therefore, the argument is not valid since it is defective in two ways.

4. To the objection that whatever is necessary is absolute, it must be said that perfect absoluteness does not exclude an intrinsic relation, since such a relation, being indifferent by essence, implies no dependence; hence it is not repugnant to necessity. It is such a relation that exists in the divine persons. But if the absolute excludes relation, this is with respect to beings outside itself and essentially different from itself. Hence, while certain words used to speak of God express a relation between God and created things, that relation is not real on the part of God but only in terms of our manner of knowing for which there corresponds a real relation on the part of created beings.[13] The previous argument holds concerning this relation.

5. To the objection that no being that receives its existence from another can be necessary in the highest degree, it must be said that this is true with respect to a being that is essentially distinct from another, and when it has being that is distinct from the being of the giver. For it cannot be fully necessary since it depends on another being and on another nature that is essentially distinct. But such is not the case with the divine persons, since the person produced does not differ in essence from the person who produces, nor does it have another being. Since it has one and the same being and essence, and one essential truth, it follows that no dependence obtains here, but the producer and the produced together possess the same firm necessity and the same necessary firmness.

6. To the objection that no being that can be thought not to exist is supremely necessary, it must be said that this is true when that necessity is clearly evident, but not when it lies hidden. Hence, while the most blessed trinity can be both believed and thought not to exist now because it has not yet been revealed to us as it is,

---

[13] Cf. Q. 3, a. 1 & a. 2, ad 16 above.

yet when it will have become clear to us as it is, then in no way will it be possible to think of it as not existing.[14] The fact that now it can be believed or thought not to exist is not because of any lack of certitude or truth in itself, since it exists always and everywhere and supremely; but it is because of a lack of light on our part.

7. To the objection that whatever is repugnant to evidence is repugnant to certitude, it must be said that just as there is evidence that is real and evidence that is subjective, so also there is certitude that is real and certitude that is subjective. Therefore, when it is said that that which is repugnant to evidence is necessarily repugnant to certitude, this is true with respect to objective evidence and certitude, but it is not true of subjective evidence and certitude, since — as was already shown — something that is most certain in itself can be hidden for us. Furthermore, however much the trinity may seem to be repugnant to certitude, it is nonetheless very consonant with certitude since the Father declares Himself in His Word, and the Father and Son manifest themselves to us most certainly through the Holy Spirit.[15] Hence, while the imagination is incapable of understanding the trinity, nevertheless the illumined power of reason sees that only the trinity as trinity is the fullest reason for the knowledge of all truth; for it is by the illumined reason that whatever truth we know is retained in our memory; and being held by our memory, it is understood more clearly; and being understood, it pleases us and is loved by us.

8. To the objection that whatever is necessary is not fully worthy of praise, it must be said that there are two types of praise. There is one in which honor and dignity add some increase to the one praised; and such praise involves progress from an imperfect to a perfect state. This properly befits those wayfarers who could sin but do not do so, and who are fittingly praised and rewarded by God.[16]

There is another sort of praise by which the good itself is said to be commendable in as far as it is good. This is more fitting to something which is good by essence than to something which is good by participation; it is therefore more fitting for the unchangeable than for the changeable good; more fitting for the necessary than for the contingent. With this sort of praise God the Father is

---

[14] 1 *Jn.* 3, 2. Cf. Q. 1, a. 1 above.
[15] *Jn.* 16, 13 ff., & 17, 1 ff. For Augustine's view on Plato, cf. *De Civ. Dei*, VIII, c. 4.
[16] *Eccli.* 31, 9 ff., Augustine, *Enarrat. in Ps. 134*, n. 3.

praised in the production of the Son; and the Father and the Son in the production of the Holy Spirit, in their mutual love and in the diffusion of all good with respect to every creature.

9. To the objection that nothing that is simply voluntary is absolutely necessary, the response is clear from what has been said in the principal argument. Therefore, it is not necessary to delay over these things any further.

QUESTION VIII

WHETHER THE TRINITY CAN EXIST TOGETHER WITH SUPREME PRIMACY

Finally, it is asked whether the trinity can exist together with supreme primacy. It seems that it cannot.

OBJECTIONS

1. Because primacy in essence excludes every other essence. Therefore, it is impossible that there be two first essences since it would necessarily follow that neither of them would be first.[1] Therefore, if primacy in essence excludes a plurality of essences, for the same reason, primacy in person excludes a plurality of persons. Therefore, it is impossible that primacy should coexist with the trinity in God.

2. Again, primacy in causality excludes plurality, since it is necessary that there be only one first cause.[2]

3. Again, the final being relates to active production in the same way that the first being relates to passive production. But the last, in as far as it is last, does not admit of an active production that would produce a being from its substance; therefore neither does the first admit a passive production. Therefore, it is impossible that something should be supremely first and yet should have being that is produced. Therefore, it excludes perfect primacy.

4. Again, either those three persons are equally first or they are not equally first. If they are equally first, then one does not produce the other any more than the reverse. If they are not equally first, then the highest primacy does not exist in all the persons.

5. Again, either they are equally principle or they are not. If they are equally principle, then that which makes one to be principle of the other is true of the reverse. If they are not equally principle, then the nature of principle does not exist in them equally; hence neither does the nature of primacy.

---

[1] Cf. Q. 2, a. 1, arg. 6 above.
[2] Cf. I *Sent*. d. 2, q. 2, arg. 4 ad oppos.

6. Again, unity is prior to plurality both in reality and in thought.[3] Therefore supreme primacy is appropriate only to a being in whom there is unity without plurality. But the trinity includes true plurality. Therefore, it excludes perfect primacy.

7. Again, the more a being is prior, the more it is the fontal cause of production. Therefore, whatever is produced emanates necessarily from that being which is absolutely first. Therefore, if it is impossible for a person to emanate from itself, it is impossible for a person that is produced to exist together with perfect primacy.

ARGUMENTS IN AGREEMENT

1. To be first is the same as to be principle.[4] Therefore, that which is first from eternity is principle from eternity. But a being is principle in the fullest sense when it is active as principle and produces by way of a perfect production. Therefore, if the reality of perfect primacy exists in God from eternity, then the truth of intrinsic production is found there as well. But this is realized in the trinity. Therefore, etc.

2. Again, the more a being is prior, the more powerful and actual it is.[5] Therefore, the first principle is necessarily most actual and most powerful. But the act of the first principle, in as far as it is principle, is to be active as principle. Therefore, if it is necessary to affirm the highest actuality and power in the first principle because it is first, then it is necessary to affirm the truth of an eternal production, and hence the completion of a perfect trinity.

3. Again, that which is absolutely equal is prior to that which is unequal, both in reality and in our mind.[6] Therefore, it is impossible to understand the production of a being that is unequal unless one first understands the production of something that is equal. Therefore, if the production of the creature is a production of something unequal, the production of an equal cannot be realized except in the holy trinity. Therefore, the production of every creature necessarily presupposes the eternal trinity.

4. Again, that which can be understood to have existed from eternity is prior both in reality and in thought to that which can be understood to have existed from eternity neither in reality nor in thought. But the production of one being from another can be

---

[3] Aristotle, *II De Caelo et Mundo*, text. 22 (c. 4).
[4] Aristotle, *I Poster.*, c. 2.
[5] *Lib. de Causis*, prop. 1.
[6] Aristotle, *II De Caelo et Mundo*, text. 18 (c. 3); *VI Topic.*, c. 4 (c. 9).

understood to have been eternal while the production of something from nothing cannot have been eternal.[7] Therefore, the production of one being from another must necessarily be understood as prior to the production of creation in accordance with perfect primacy. But this cannot be conceived except in the uncreated trinity. Therefore, etc.

5. Again, the act of the first principle is above all to be active as principle or to produce. Therefore, since that which is principle is prior to that which is produced by the principle,[8] then the act of being principle or the production from the active principle is prior to the being that is produced by the principle. Therefore, if the production of the principle exists only in the divine trinity, it is necessary that if that principle be first, it be also a trinity.

6. Again, the first principle, in as far as it is first, is most simple and most spiritual. Therefore, it is necessary that it be intellect.[9] But every intellect that acts as principle does so through a word and a gift of love that is intrinsic to it. Whatever is a principle by way of word and love first conceives the word and breathes love before it produces an exterior effect. Therefore, it is necessary that if the first principle produces the being of something extrinsic to itself, it must first be productive within itself.[10] But this twofold production demands that God be a trinity. Therefore, it follows necessarily that if the first principle is first, it is also a trinity.

7. Again, being a principle in a natural and intrinsic manner is prior to being a principle in a voluntary and extrinsic manner. But a voluntary and extrinsic production corresponds to the first principle. Therefore, a natural and intrinsic production necessarily corresponds to it. But this is nothing else than to affirm the trinity. Therefore, etc.

8. Again, the perfect is prior to the imperfect both in reality and in our mind;[11] that which is complete is prior to that which is diminished; unity is prior to multiplicity; the simple is prior to the composite; the infinite to the finite; act to potency; the immutable to the mutable; the eternal to the temporal; the necessary to the possible. Therefore, if every creature that is produced is imperfect, lacking in the highest unity, composed, finite, and in potency, in some way it is temporal, variable, possible, lacking in actuality and supreme necessity. It is necessary, therefore, that before the pro-

---

[7] II *Sent.* d. 1, p. 1, a. 1, q. 2.
[8] Aristotle, *II Poster.*, c. 17 (c. 14).
[9] Aristotle, *XII Metaph.*, text. 39 (XI, c. 7); the major is shown in Q. 3, a. 1 above; cf. also, Augustine, *De Trin.*, IX, c. 7, n. 12 ff.
[10] Supply: Word and Love as that which is produced within.
[11] Aristotle, *VIII Phys.*, text. 75 (c. 9); also Q. 1, a. 1, arg. 12 ff. above.

duction of the creature there be a production of something most perfect, supreme, undivided, most simple, most infinite, eternal, immutable, and necessary. This cannot be through the production of something distinct in essence. It is necessary, therefore, that it be through the production of a person who is one in essence with the person producing, and equal in power, wisdom, and goodness. But this is to affirm the most blessed trinity.

CONCLUSION

Primacy not only does not exclude the trinity, but includes it.

Response. For a proper understanding of the foregoing, it must be noted that primacy not only does not exclude the trinity, but actually includes it in as far as the first principle is a trinity by the very fact that it is first. This is shown in the following way.

Supreme primacy in the supreme and highest principle demands the highest actuality, the highest fontality, and the highest fecundity. For the first principle, by virtue of the fact that it is first, is the most perfect in producing, the most fontal in emanating, and the most fecund in germinating. Therefore since the perfect production, emanation and germination is realized only through two intrinsic modes, namely, by way of nature and by way of will, that is, by way of the word and of love, therefore the highest perfection, fontality, and fecundity necessarily demands two kinds of emanation with respect to the two hypostases which are produced and emanate from the first person as from the first producing principle. Therefore, it is necessary to affirm three persons. And since the most perfect production is not realized except with respect to equals,[12] and the most fontal emanation is not realized except with respect to co-eternals, and the most fecund germination is not realized except with respect to consubstantial beings, it is necessary to admit that the first principle includes within itself three hypostases that are coequal, coeternal, and consubstantial. The primacy of the first principle, therefore, demands the most perfect trinity in order, origin, and distinction; of coequality, coeternity, and consubstantiality; it demands also the highest unity, simplicity, immensity, eternity, immutability, and actuality. Therefore, it requires a trinity in the first principle together with the above-mentioned essential qualities.

Therefore, since the first principle, by virtue of the fact that it is the first being, is supremely one; and for this reason it is supremely

---

[12] I *Sent.* d. 19, p. 1, q. 2, ad 3.

simple and immense; and for the same reason it is eternal, unchangeable, and necessary as may be gathered from the above;[13] and again, by the mere fact that it is the first being, it is most perfect in producing, most fontal in emanating, and most fecund in germinating, and this with respect to things that are equal, coeternal, consubstantial, distinct, original, and ordered, it follows that the first principle, because it is first, exists eternally with the fullness of all these perfect qualities. For this reason, it is in this principle, in as far as it is first, that all beings and all knowledge come to rest.

For this reason, Rachel, the symbol of the contemplative life, is interpreted to mean "the principle is seen,"[14] because he who contemplates this, in as far as it is the first principle that he contemplates, finds the rest and the final end of his desires, which are not brought to their end unless the first principle is clearly contemplated as both three and supremely one. Those arguments in favor of this conclusion are to be granted.

REPLIES TO THE OBJECTIONS

1.2. To the first contrary objection that primacy of essence excludes plurality, it must be said that there is no parallel; since a plurality of essences which are essentially different cannot be ordered to one another except in terms of prior and posterior. But a plurality of persons — since they have one essence and one being — can be ordered to one another in such a way that, even though the reality of origin is found among them, yet no posteriority is involved. This sort of plurality, therefore, does not destroy the supreme primacy since it includes no posteriority, which would be directly contrary to primacy.

From this, the answer to the following objections from causality becomes clear, since it is the order of essentially distinct causes that is seen in the relation of posterior being to that which is first; but this is not found in the origin of the persons.[15]

3. To the objection that an active production does not befit a final being, it must be said that there is no parallel, since the final being cannot be related to another that would be identical with itself, nor, because of its imperfection, could it produce another being equal to itself in all things. Therefore, in this case, it is necessarily

---

[13] Qq. 2-7.
[14] Augustine, *I De Consensu Evangelist.*, c. 5, n. 8; *Adversus Faustum XXII*, c. 52 ff.; Jerome, *De Nom. Hebraic.*, de Genesi.
[15] Cf. Q. 5, a. 2, ad 2 & 7 above.

contradictory that it be last and simultaneously productive, because it would then have some being posterior to itself.

But the case is different in terms of the principle, since active and passive production are not repugnant here since the highest perfection is found both in the one who produces and in the one produced; and no posteriority intervenes to diminish the perfection of absolute unity.

4. To the objection that they are either equally first or not, it must be said that first involves the lack of something prior; in another way, it means the lack of origin. Therefore, if a being is said to be first because there is nothing prior to it, then those beings which have nothing prior or posterior to themselves would be equally first.

But if a being is said to be first because of the lack of origin, that is, because it does not take its origin from another, in this sense, primacy resides principally in the person of the Father; and for this reason, the fontal-fullness for the production of all the persons is found in Him. Hence, because innascibility includes this property, the notion of the Father is said to be a property. But this would not be the case unless it simultaneously involved perfection and the cause of manifestation; also, it would be predicated in a relative sense.[16]

5. To the objection that they are either equally active as principle or they are not, it must be said that they are equally principle in the order of essence but not in the order of person; for the Father is principle of two persons; the Son is principle of one; and the Holy Spirit is principle of none. Therefore, since that primacy which is proper to the first principle in the order of essence is found equally in all three persons, the trinity exists together with supreme primacy; because, just as "not to be able to generate" involves no impotence in the Son, so "not to exist from oneself, but from the Father" involves no posteriority and therefore does not diminish the perfect primacy.[17]

6. To the objection that unity is prior to plurality both in reality and in thought, it must be said that this is true with respect to that plurality which results from the aggregation of unities. But it is not true of that plurality in which plurality is identical with the oneness of three, since in them there is one truth, one light, one cause of knowledge on the part of God Himself.[18] The fact that we come to know unity before trinity comes from the deficiency of our knowledge.

---

[16] Cf. Q. 5, a. 2, ad 3 & 6; and I *Sent.* d. 28, q. 1 ff.
[17] I *Sent.* d. 7, q. 2.
[18] Cf. Q. 2, a. 1, ad 2, & a. 2, ad 16 above.

7. To the objection that the more a being is fontal, the more it is prior in producing, it must be said that — as we have already seen — the first being may be understood in two ways; by way of the lack of essential anteriority, and by way of the lack of personal origin. Thus, it includes a two-fold fontality depending on whether it refers to the lack of essential anteriority or to the lack of personal origin. When it is taken to mean the lack of essential anteriority, it includes fontality with respect to the effects and essences to be produced. Thus, since this condition is equally fitting to all the persons, it is equally proper to all of them to possess the nature of fontality in the production of created beings, since they are not three but one principle of creation. But in as far as it involves the lack of personal origin, it befits only that person who is innascible; namely, the Father in whom resides the fullness of fontality for the production of the Son and of the Holy Spirit.

And, in a certain way, this sort of fontality is the origin of the other fontality. For, since the Father brings forth the Son, and through the Son, and together with the Son brings forth the Holy Spirit, God the Father through the Son and with the Holy Spirit is the principle of everything created; for if He did not produce them eternally, He could not produce through anything in time; and therefore He is rightly called the "Fount of Life"[19] by reason of this production within the trinity. "As He has life in Himself, so He grants to the Son to have life in Himself," etc.[20] Therefore it follows that eternal life consists in this alone, that the rational spirit, which emanates from the most blessed trinity and is a likeness of the trinity, should return after the manner of a certain intelligible circle — through memory, intelligence, and will — to the most blessed trinity by God-conforming glory.

---

[19] *Ps.* 35, 10.
[20] *Jn* 5, 26.

INDICES
of Biblical Citations
and of Authors and Works

INDEX OF BIBLICAL CITATIONS

(The references are first to chapter and verse in italics and then to the pages of this book in regular type. The order of the biblical books is that which corresponds to the order of appearance in a modern bible.)

Genesis *18:2*, 78, 130.
Exodus *3:14*, 13; *15:18*, 203; *20:2*, 138; *32:32*, 78.
Deuteronomy *6:4*, 136, 138; *6:13*, 136; *19:15*, 128; *32:39*, 138.
1 Samuel *2:6*, 229.
1 Kings (3 Kings) *8:27*, 184.
Psalms *4:7*, 118, 131; *13:1*, 113; *32:6*, 78, 130; *35:10*, 266; *80:10*, 138; *92:5*, 135; *101:27*, 224; *137:6*, 131.
Wisdom *7:24*, 226; *11:23*, 190; *13:3*, 244.
Ecclesiasticus (Wisdom of Sirach) *31:9*, 258.
Isaiah *4:3*, 78; *7:9*, 14; *40:15*, 190; *40:17*, 190; *66:9*, 244.
Daniel *12:1*, 78.
Malachy *3:6*, 224.
Matthew *18:16*, 128; *19:17*, 33; *28:19*, 74, 78, 122, 130.
Mark *16:16*, 74, 122.
Luke *1:37*, 247; *10:20*, 78; *18:19*, 32, 33.
John *1:4*, 130; *1:9*, 130; *3:13*, 227; *3:16*, 135; *5:23*, 57, 123; *5:26*, 266; *14:17*, 123; *15:16*, 57; *16:13*, 258; *16:14*, 57; *17:1*, 258; *17:3*, 30, 223.
Romans *1:19*, 20; *1:20*, 118, 203; *2:14*, 127; *8:3*, 227; *10:16*, 130.
1 Corinthians *13:12*, 75; *8:4*, 114; *13:9*, 121; *13:12*, 125.
2 Corinthians *3:18*, 130; *10:5*, 124, 132; *13:1*, 128.
Galatians *4:4*, 227; *4:6*, 57.
Ephesians *4:9*, 227.
Philippians *4:3*, 78.
1 Timothy *6:16*, 115.
Titus *1:1*, 139.
Hebrews *1:3*, 195; *2:3*, 132; *11:6*, 115.
1 Peter *1:19*, 137.
1 John *3:2*, 258; *4:8*, 33; *4:16*, 33; *5*, 78; *5:7*, 130, 150.
Apocalypse *1:8*, 161, 249; *3:5*, 78; *17:8*, 78; *20:12*, 78; *20:15*, 78.

INDEX OF AUTHORS AND WORKS

Alan of Lille, *De arte*, 111; *Theol. Reg.*, 211.
Albert the Great, 18.
Alexander of Hales, 18, 21-24, 33. *Summa*, 17, 18, 20-23, 32, 56, 78, 89, 238. *Disputed questions*, 21. *Glossa*, 21, 23.
Algazel, *Phil.* 160, 225.
Ambrose, 126. *De fide*, 226. *Expos. in Ps. 118*, 126.
Anselm, 18, 19, 22, 28, 69, 72, 73, 81, 112, 114, 118, 119. *Contra insip.*, 112, 119; *Monologion*, 112, 161, 162, 167, 205, 231, 232. *Proslogion*, 112, 114.
Aristotle, 24, 34, 44, 62, 69, 89, 108. *Analytica poster.*, 36, 108, 113, 115, 119, 126, 144, 148, 213, 245, 247, 248, 252, 261, 262. *Analytica prior.*, 148. *De anima*, 110, 150, 152, 162, 163, 213, 227, 245. *De caelo et mundo*, 206, 261. *De generat. et corrup.*, 142, 163, 239, 243. *De memoria et reminisc.*, 209. *De praedicam.*, 193, 212, 216, 251. *De soph. elench.*, 147, 173, 178, 187, 188, 221. *Ethics*, 110, 248, 250, 254. *Metaphysics*, 44, 89, 108, 110, 111, 126, 139, 140, 149, 150, 166, 171, 187, 204, 212, 213, 215, 224, 225, 226, 240, 243, 245, 247, 248, 249, 251, 252, 262. *Perihermeneias*, 113, 119, 153. *Physics*, 34, 89, 110, 111, 113, 147, 165, 168, 189, 206, 207, 215, 217, 218, 224, 225, 226, 238, 239, 240, 241, 243, 248, 252, 262. *Politics*, 248. *Rhetoric*, 248. *Topics*, 124, 139, 142, 148, 170, 227, 250, 251, 254, 261.
Athanasius, 74, 122, 184.
Auer, Iohann, 77.
Augustine, 13, 14, 15, 18, 19, 25, 41, 45, 47, 69, 70, 73, 74, 75, 95, 108, 109, 112, 114, 118, 122, 124, 126, 128, 143, 155, 165, 172, 189, 190, 204. *Confessions*, 109, 159, 182, 201. *Contra Faustum*, 126, 235, 264. *Contra Maximinum*, 220. *De beata vita*, 204. *De civitate Dei*, 109, 160, 185, 204, 219, 228, 250, 256, 258. *De consensu evangelist.*, 264. *De Gen. contra Manich.*, 228. *De moribus Manich.*, 143. *De natura boni*, 191. *De trinitate*, 108, 109, 122, 129, 155, 166, 172, 174, 175, 189, 190, 209, 217, 228, 247, 262. *De utilitate credendi*, 124. *Enarrat. in Ps. 68*, 155. *Enarrat. in Ps. 134*, 258. *Hypognosticon*, 122. *Lib. 83 Quaes.*, 124, 126, 128, 129, 163, 205, 248. *Quaest. 65 Dialog.*, 253. *Soliloquia*, 112, 204.
Averroes, 111. *De anima*, 111. *Physics*, 186.
Avicenna, 110. *Metaphysics*, 110, 160, 180, 215, 225, 252, 253.

Bernard of Clairvaux, 78. *De consideratione*, 150, 154.
Boethius, 19, 37, 69, 91, 108, 113, 143, 214. *De consolatione*, 108, 143, 150, 206, 212, 215. *De differentiis topic.*, 151, 161. *De hebdomadibus* (or *Quomodo substantiae*), 111, 185, 204, 225, 252. *De persona et duabus naturis*, 37, 150, 152. *De trinitate*, 149, 155, 157, 175, 186, 233, 240, 253.
Bonaventure, *passim*. *Brevil.*, 24, 28 *et passim*. *Comm. in Joan.*, 51. *Comm. in Lc.*, 78. *De reductione*, 27. *Epistola de tribus quaestionibus*, 23. *Hexemeron*, 23, 25, 27, 31, 35, 36, 43, 47, 52, 54, 71, 75, 80, 84. *Itinerarium*, 20, 25, 33, 35, 67, 68, 70, 71, 80. *Lignum vitae*, 78. *Quaestiones disputatae de scientia Christi*, 171, 175, 180, 194, 196, 201, 236. *Quaestiones disputatae de trinit.*, 24, 26 ff., 35, 36, 43, 45, 62, 68 ff. *Sentence Commentary*, 23, 24 *et passim*.. *Sermo de trinitate*, 26, 66. *Sermo I: De triplici testimonio*, 26.
Bougerol, J., 25.
Brady, I., 14.
Brosseder, J., 70.

Copleston, F., 14.
Cousins, E., 39, 42.

De Regnon, T., 17, 18, 22, 23, 24.
De Vinck, J., 25.
Doucet, V., 21.
Dumeige, G., 19, 20.

Forster, K., 77.
Francis of Assisi, 24, 32.

Gilbert Porretanus (de la Porrée), *Liber sex principiorum*, 211.
Gonzalez, O., 19, 20, 24, 75, 77.
Gössmann, E., 15, 22.
Gregory the Great, 16, 19. *Homiliae in evangelia*, 16, 125, 127, 141, 151. *Moralia*, 189, 216, 234.

Hayes, Z., 23, 27.
Hellmann, A. J. W., 53.
Hilary of Poitiers, 141. *De trinitate*, 141, 229, 253, 256.
Hirschberger, J., 14.
Hugh of St. Victor, 15, 69, 78, 95, 108, 121. *De sacramentis*, 108, 121, 229, 230. *Didascalion*, 229.

Imle, F., 18.
Isidore, *Etymolog.*, 180.

Jerome, 126. *De nom. Hebraic.*, 264.
Joachim of Fiore, 63.
John Damascene, 22, 69, 73, 108, 114, 117, 151. *De fide orthodoxa*, 108, 114, 151, 184, 185, 204.
John of Rupella, 21.
John Sarracenus, 23.

Kaup, J., 18.

Liber de causis, 36, 42, 111, 140, 160, 170, 175, 187, 189, 194, 205, 249, 261.

Macrosius, 134.
Mercker, H., 77.

Pannenberg, W., 70.
Pesch, O. H., 70.
Peter Lombard, 18.
Plato, 62.
Plotinus, 14.
Porphyry, *De praedic.*, 176, 237.
Prentice, R., 55.
Principe, W., 40.
Pseudo-Dionysius, 17, 18, 19, 21, 22, 23, 24, 25, 33, 45. *De caelest. hierarch.*, 142. *De div. nom.*, 142, 156, 231, 232, 250.

Quinn, J. F, 25, 79.

Ratzinger, J., 23, 63.
Rauch, W., 76.
Ribaillier, J., 19, 20, 29.
Richard of St. Victor, 13, 15-22, 24, 25, 28, 33, 35, 37, 73, 111, 114, 132. *De trinitate*, 15-17, 21, 37, 38, 111, 114, 133, 139, 140, 145, 152, 176, 185, 196, 200, 203, 204, 205, 215, 225, 238.
Rist, J. M., 14.

Salet, G., 19, 20, 29.
Schachten, W., 64.
Schindler, A., 14.
Schmaus, M., 14, 18, 70.
Seckerl, M., 70.
Stohr, 18, 38, 39, 56.
Sullivan, J. E., 14.
Szabo, T., 18.

Thomas of Aquinas, 17, 18, 37, 38, 41, 45.
Thomas of Vercelli, 23.
Tullius (Cicero), 126. *Rhetoric*, 126, 209.

Villalmonte, A. de, 18, 29.
Volk, H., 77.

Wiegels, M., 31.
William of Auvergne, 18.
William of Auxerre, 18.